T0246502

RUDY WIEBE
Essays on His Works

· ·

Essential Writers Series 56

Canada Council Conseil des Arts
for the Arts du Canada

ONTARIO ARTS COUNCIL
CONSEIL DES ARTS DE L'ONTARIO
an Ontario government agency
un organisme du gouvernement de l'Ontario

Canadä

Guernica Editions Inc. acknowledges the support of the Canada Council
for the Arts and the Ontario Arts Council. The Ontario Arts Council
is an agency of the Government of Ontario.
We acknowledge the financial support of the Government of Canada.

RUDY WIEBE
Essays on His Works

. . . .

edited by
Bianca Lakoseljac

GUERNICA
EDITIONS
TORONTO · CHICAGO · BUFFALO · LANCASTER (U.K.)
2023

Guernica Founder: Antonio D'Alfonso

Bianca Lakoseljac, editor
Michael Mirolla, general editor
Joseph Pivato, series editor
Rudy Wiebe front cover photo credit: John Ulan
David Moratto, cover and interior design

Guernica Editions Inc.
287 Templemead Drive, Hamilton (ON), Canada L8W 2W4
2250 Military Road, Tonawanda, N.Y. 14150-6000 U.S.A.
www.guernicaeditions.com

Distributors:
Independent Publishers Group (IPG)
600 North Pulaski Road, Chicago IL 60624
University of Toronto Press Distribution (UTP)
5201 Dufferin Street, Toronto (ON), Canada M3H 5T8

First edition.
Printed in Canada.

Legal Deposit—Third Quarter
Library of Congress Catalog Card Number: 2023934998
Library and Archives Canada Cataloguing in Publication
Title: Rudy Wiebe : essays on his works / edited by Bianca Lakoseljac.
Other titles: Rudy Wiebe (2023)
Names: Lakoseljac, Bianca, 1952- editor.
Series: Essential writers series ; 56.
Description: 1st edition. | Series statement: Essential writers series : 56
Identifiers: Canadiana (print) 20230200214 |
Canadiana (ebook) 20230200397 | ISBN 9781771838467 (softcover) |
ISBN 9781771838474 (EPUB)
Subjects: LCSH: Wiebe, Rudy, 1934-—Criticism and interpretation.
| CSH: Canadian literature (English)—20th century—History and
criticism. | LCGFT: Literary criticism.
Classification: LCC PS8545.I38 Z739 2023 | DDC C813/.54—dc23

Rudy Wiebe: Essays on His Works
is dedicated to author
Rudy Wiebe
with admiration and gratitude
for the power of his words,
splendour of his images,
and the innovative storytelling that helped
shape Canadian Literature in English
from the 1960s to the present
—and enticed me to pursue my calling

and as always
for Sierra, Austin, Michelle, and Adrian
who taught me what really matters

"Fact" is a thing witnessed as being done,
or experienced in the past and held as memory.

...

Fiction is the narratives, the stories we make
with words out of the facts of our lives.
—RUDY WIEBE, "WHERE THE TRUTH LIES: EXPLORING
THE NATURE OF FACT AND FICTION"

She remembered the book always being around;
it was very large and she'd never read it;
but sometimes, when she opened it and
looked at the pictures,
sometimes there were prairie flowers
drying between its leaves.

...

When you're approaching the fire, remember this:
Flowers are your best, your only protection.
—RUDY WIEBE, "FLOWERS FOR APPROACHING THE FIRE"

Contents

Bianca Lakoseljac

. . . .

Why This Book

Why the collection, *Rudy Wiebe: Essays on His Works*?

That is the question a number of my colleagues and friends have asked when I talked about compiling and editing the anthology which I have been working on for the past three years.

During my graduate studies at York University, I took a course, Special Topics: Frog Lake "Massacre"—1885. I read Wiebe's novel, *The Temptations of Big Bear,* and found it transformative. My perspective on history—from the Canadian colonial viewpoint; my inherited Eastern European history dominated by wars and continuous ethnic conflicts which culminated in the breakup of Yugoslavia—the country of my birth and idyllic childhood that will live in my memory; my family saga in Serbia which includes relations in Bosnia, Monte Negro, Croatia, among other regions; my personal life path which felt disconnected and discontented—all of that took on a different meaning. I began to look at life through a new lens—no longer seeing myself as a victim of circumstances, or wrong choices made, or unfortunate outcomes of providence. I turned to the "big picture," to how other societies in this expansive, magnificent, wondrous, yet often astonishingly brutal world fared.

Can a book do all that? Can it change one's outlook on life? *The Temptations of Big Bear* certainly altered my path. I also read William Cameron's (1862–1951) *The War Trail of Big Bear*. The two books compelled me to take a course in Native Canadian studies which introduced me to authors such as Tomson Highway, Basil H. Johnston, Thomas King, and more recently Tanya Talaga, to name just a few. Their works in turn, led me to many other outstanding Fist Nations authors: the wonderful Lee Maracle with whom I had been privileged to take part in writers' events such as at Another Story Bookshop in Toronto and chit-chat at Word-up in Barrie—and whose legacy will live on; poet, storyteller, and an Algonquin Traditional Teacher, Albert Dumont, Kitigan Zibi Anishinabeg— Ottawa's Poet Laureate, 2021 to 2023—who has served as one of 13 Elders on the Elders Advisory Committee of the Ministry of the Attorney General, who published my first book of poetry and who has been a valued and respected friend for nearly two decades; to participate in a reading at the Stephen Leacock Festival in Orillia with Tomson Highway as the guest of honour; and as a defender for Georgian Bay Reads in 2018, to champion Cherie Dimaline's post-apocalyptic YA novel, *The Marrow Thieves*. I sometimes wonder whether I would have developed such a keen interest in the First Nations authors' writing and culture if I had not read *The Temptations*.

I also continued to follow Wiebe's writing—novels, biographies, and essays. After reading Wiebe's essay, "Seven Words of Silence," published in the *Conrad Grebel Review* 31:2 (Spring 2013): 148–55, I understood that Wiebe's books had a lasting influence on me as a person and a writer. Reflecting on some of my writing,

I felt that my poem, "Sound of Stillness," although written earlier and published in 2009 in my collection, *Memoirs of a Praying Mantis*, may answer the call in Wiebe's essay—an invitation to readers and writers to discover their own words of silence. I would like to dedicate this poem, (post-publication), to Rudy Wiebe, in gratitude for sharing his words and images and thoughts.

Sound of Stillness

> —Dedicated to author, Rudy Wiebe,
> in admiration of his writing

Sound: merely a vibration as is sight.
    Apperceived by one of the senses,
    by the human ears, or any ears.
But a sound heard within
    is a voice of conscience,
    the sway of the God within,
    the resonance of Self.
Have you ever heard
    the lulling murmur of stillness,
    the echo of your inner voice
    guiding you what to do, or even
    more notably, what *not* to do?
Ego, soul, collective unconscious,
    anima, animus, archetypal images and all
    the rest of it. The One who guides us
    from some distant plane of existence
    where all feeling, all senses originate
    and where all about us returns.
Have you ever heard the sound of stillness?

INTRODUCTION
Rudy Wiebe's Works and Academic Life:
Changing Times in English Canadian Literature

· ·

Bianca Lakoseljac

Rudy Wiebe, one of Canada's most accomplished and prominent authors, is a two-time winner of the Governor General's Award for Fiction—for *The Temptations of Big Bear* (1973) and *A Discovery of Strangers* (1994). Wiebe won the Charles Taylor Prize for his memoir, *of this earth: a Mennonite Boyhood in the Boreal Forest* (2006). He also received the Writer's Trust Non-Fiction Prize for *Stolen Life: The Journey of a Cree Woman* (1998), which he co-wrote with Yvonne Johnson. In 2007 he was presented with the Leslie K. Tarr Award for his contribution to Christian literature. In 2009, he received Honorary Doctor of Letters from the University of Alberta. Wiebe is an officer of the Order of Canada.

With the publication of his controversial breakout novel, *Peace Shall Destroy Many* (1962), Wiebe became the unwitting founder of a new era in Mennonite literature and has since been an advocate of Prairie literary culture. His fiction often transcends culture and milieu and examines the struggles of societies and individuals. He has been called the first major Canadian writer to open his Mennonite community's experience to a wider audience. Wiebe has also been seen as the first major white Canadian writer to give voice to the First Peoples of Canada: his fiction reveals his sincere admiration of Indigenous Peoples culture and spirituality and its close links with nature and the natural world. Intriguingly, his writing has been regarded as somewhat impenetrable to traditional literary critical methodologies, and while it has been labeled as "brilliant" and "magnificent," it has also been seen as "challenging" due in part to his propensity for a rather Faulknerian turn of phrase and his use of multifaceted storymaking approaches, such as intertextual and intratextual dynamics, and the sociopolitical views and religious beliefs they embody.

Rudy Wiebe was born on October 4, 1934, in an isolated and ruggedly-picturesque community near Fairholme, Saskatchewan. His parents had escaped Soviet Russia in 1930—part of a Mennonite history of immigration and settlement as homesteaders in the Canadian West. Wiebe's family moved to Coaldale, a town east of Lethbridge in Alberta, in 1947. He received his B.A. from the University of Alberta in 1956, and then studied literature and theology at the University of Tübingen in West Germany. In 1962 he graduated with a Bachelor of Theology from Mennonite Brethren Bible College in Winnipeg, now Canadian Mennonite University. During his studies, he was an editor of the *Mennonite Brethren Herald*—which he was asked to leave after the publication of *Peace Shall Destroy Many*. This reaction to his work strengthened his belief in the power of the written word and reinforced his drive to write.

Wiebe's second novel, *First and Vital Candle*, was published in 1966; *The Blue Mountains of China*—seen as his first epic novel as it chronicles the Mennonite experience—in 1970; *The Temptations of Big Bear* in 1973; his fifth novel, *The Scorched-wood People* in 1977; *The Mad Trapper* in 1980; *My Lovely Enemy* in 1983; *A Discovery of Strangers* in 1994; *Sweeter Than All the World* in 2001; and *Come Back* in 2014—which Wiebe sees as a "most complex book ... in many ways" (Wiebe, Rudy. Email received by Bianca Lakoseljac, Feb. 12, 2020). He has also published biographies, collections of short stories, essays, and children's books. Wiebe's fiction has been translated into twelve European languages.

In 2008, Wiebe published *Big Bear*, a biographical account of the Plains Cree chief, Big Bear (1825–1888), who inspired Wiebe's 1973 novel, *The Temptations of Big Bear*. Both the novel and the biography are based on extensive research of government documents and interviews with the surviving descendants of the band and the community members.

From 1963 to 1967, Wiebe taught at a Mennonite college in Goshen, Indiana. He returned to the University of Alberta in 1967 and taught creative writing and English. He became immersed in Canadian literature. He wrote reviews and academic essays and mentored students some of whom became accomplished Canadian writers, among them Aritha van Herk, Myrna Kostash, and Katherine Govier—whose reflections on their work with Wiebe are included in this collection. He has also taught creative writing at colleges and universities in Canada, United States, and Germany. He has been Professor Emeritus at University of Alberta in Edmonton since 1992. He resides in Edmonton with his wife Tena and continues to write.

Wiebe credits his success as a writer to his professor and mentor, Dr. Frederick M. Salter (1895–1962). In 1959, as a student at the University of Alberta, Wiebe took an English course taught by Professor Salter. Little did he know that Dr. Salter's advice on the subject of Wiebe's thesis, "a good many people can write perfectly acceptable ... thesis on Shakespeare—but perhaps only you [Wiebe] can write a fine novel about Canadian Mennonites," was to forever shape his writing life.

I was introduced to Wiebe's novel, *The Temptations of Big Bear,* as a Master's student at York University in Toronto in the nineteen-nineties. I took a course entitled "Special Topics: Frog Lake 'Massacre'—1885." After reading Wiebe's novel, I was hooked on his writing. His engaging yet challenging storytelling drew me in, and my desire for those little-known segments of the Canadian past that seemed buried deep under the mounds of colonial history enticed me to expand my research. I read William Cameron's (1862–1951) book, *The War Trail of Big Bear,* which Wiebe credits as the source that propelled his drive to continue his research of the Plains Cree chief Big Bear's life. I was drawn in by Cameron's experiences during the Frog Lake 'Massacre' and his time spent in captivity as Big Bear's prisoner. Cameron expresses his admiration for Big Bear as a leader of the Cree Peoples and for his attempts to prevent the Frog Lake uprising. During Big Bear's trial in Regina in 1885, Cameron testified in support of the Cree chief. I read Wiebe's other novels which had been published by that time, as well as a number of his essays, and during my teaching years over the next couple of decades continued to follow his writing.

In October, 2007, Wiebe was a featured author at the Toronto International Festival of Authors at Harbourfront Centre. I attended his reading and discussion of his autobiographical text, *of this earth*, and we had a brief conversation during his book signing. At the time I was president of the Canadian Authors Association, Toronto Branch. I asked Wiebe if he would send a message of encouragement to our writers, and he simply wrote, "Keep writing."

Later, I photocopied Wiebe's note and included it in *Authors' Quarterly*, fall 2007 edition—a newsletter I edited at the time—and our writers were thrilled. I still keep that paper with Wiebe's message in my signed copy of his memoir. It reminds me how truthful and down-to-earth Wiebe's advice is, as is his writing.

Reading *of this earth* was especially meaningful for me. Wiebe's memories of growing up in the boreal forest in rural Saskatchewan drew me back into my own childhood in a village near Belgrade during Tito's socialist regime in the former Yugoslavia. Over the years I have wondered whether my captivation with Wiebe's writing has been in spite of his exploration of the controversial historical periods and the often contentious subjects and characters, or perhaps because of them. I am certain though that his fascinating storytelling, along with the magical landscapes and imagery that populate his fiction and imbue it with a spirituality that crosses ethnic, social, and religious borders and is difficult to define for it can only be felt, are all part of irresistible enchantment of Wiebe's writing.

Much has been written about Wiebe's fiction, but his nonfiction has been somewhat overlooked until his memoir, *of this earth*—which has been received with enthusiasm and praise, and has supplied an anecdote about Wiebe's "lucky shoes." During the ceremony for winning the Charles Taylor Prize, after a three-member jury praised Wiebe's memoir for its "spare and eloquent prose ... [which] finds universal truths amidst an isolated ... community," Wiebe was quoted as saying how he had to confess that he had an unfair advantage: "The shoes I am wearing I bought in 1974 to go to Rideau Hall to receive the Governor General's Award ... for *The Temptations of Big Bear*," Wiebe had said, to laughter from the audience. This is the witty side of Wiebe some of his colleagues can attest to.

Yvonne Johnson, Big Bear's great, great, granddaughter, with whom Wiebe teamed up and co-wrote *Stolen Life: Journey of a Cree Woman*, speaks, in her words, "with respect" for Rudy Wiebe. She explains that collaborating with Wiebe on writing her extraordinary memoir about her efforts to reclaim her history helped her to come to terms with a childhood of abuse, her descent into alcoholism, and later her struggle with the justice system. Wiebe read Johnson's seventeen notebooks of recollections, contemplated the letters they exchanged, and visited Johnson during her detention at the Kingston Prison for Women (no longer in use). Wiebe continued visiting Johnson after she was transferred to the Okimaw Ohci Healing Lodge in the

Cypress Hills. In a CBC interview with Sarah Scout (July 22, 2016), Johnson emphasizes the need for Indigenous voices to be heard "outside of our [Johnson's] own Peoples"—to be projected "to the larger world." She explains that writing the book helped her to face a painful past and to embrace the legacy she has inherited from her ancestors.

I thoroughly enjoyed compiling and editing the anthology: *Rudy Wiebe: Essays on His Works.* The collection is a mosaic of critical essays, literary journal and magazine articles, family histories, reviews, interviews and commentaries, depicting the life and work of a Canadian author who is among the most celebrated and prolific, albeit somewhat controversial. These pieces may not be available in essay collections aimed primarily for academic study at universities and colleges, which could be, in fact, a draw for scholars and readers interested in Wiebe's life as an author and an academic deeply involved with his Mennonite literary community, as well as with the English Canadian literary one. A prelude to the *Essays* is a witty and heartwarming cartoon, "Teaching Rudy to Dance ... all true events," by the iconic Canadian author Margaret Atwood. Rudy Wiebe's comment that Atwood was *trying* to teach him to dance, "Classic ironic Peggy [Atwood's name used by friends and family]—we've been friends since 1967" (Wiebe, Rudy. Email received by Bianca Lakoseljac, 28 March, 2021) attests to this literary giant's collegiality and good-humoured demeanour. The pieces featured in the collection are intended to create a dialogue with one another and serve as witness to changing times in English Canadian literature.

The collection opens with Miriam Toews's thought-provoking article, "Peace Shall Destroy Many,"—which echoes the theme of Wiebe's debut novel by the same title and, interestingly, his ongoing battle to help bring change to the Mennonite communities' ways. Toews, one of the most-respected Canadian female writers of her generation whose drive to expose the injustices of certain Mennonite communities has provided an impetus to her writing, discusses her time spent with Wiebe during a book tour in a Mennonite community in Germany. At the time, Toews was promoting her novel *A Complicated Kindness*—an insightful coming-of-age story about a 16-year-old girl's struggle with the strict dogma of her Mennonite community. After Toews' reading, a woman from the audience addressed her angrily, in Plautdietsch, or Low German, which Toews does not speak. However, through translation, Toews quickly understood that the woman's disapproval was her attempt to disgrace the author for daring to expose the wrongs within her community. Wiebe, who fully understood the woman's criticism, addressed the woman in Low German. He explained that Toews was "advocating for necessary change within the Mennonite culture" and justifiably holding the community accountable for its actions. In her essay, Toews explains that "on that day Rudy Wiebe stood up in front of a Mennonite 'congregation' and fought for me."

The next piece, Hildi Froese Tiessen's delightful essay, "Between Memory and Longing: Rudy Wiebe's *Sweeter Than All the World*," is a comprehensive discussion of Wiebe's ninth novel, *Sweeter Than All the World*. The essay opens a broad view into Wiebe's Russian

Mennonite heritage which has influenced and perme-
ated his work. It is important to note that although Wiebe
has been advocating for change, he has remained devoted
to his Mennonite community. The novel is a remarkable
odyssey into his heritage, a voyage of self-discovery that
follows the story of the Mennonite people from their persecution in the sixteenth-century Netherlands to their
emigration to Danzig, London, Russia, and the Americas,
and eventually to their settlement in Canada.

Another essay that presents a window into Wiebe's
background as an author is "Literary Genealogy: Exploring
the Legacy of F. M. Salter," by George Melnyk. It offers
a perspective into the early development in Canadian
literature and the work of Dr. Frederick M. Salter who
mentored Rudy Wiebe, W. O. Mitchell, and Robert
Kroetsch (who in turn would guide another generation
of talented authors). Melnyk's essay also reminds us that
in 1939, Professor Salter, who taught English at the
University of Alberta, launched a creative writing
course—the first in any Canadian University.

I am pleased to present my interview with Aritha
van Herk, a renowned author and a professor at the
University of Calgary, as it offers a witty and heartwarming glance into her work with Rudy Wiebe who
was her mentor and later her colleague and collaborator
on a number of publications. Van Herk's reflection on
her earlier work is also an instructive reminder for aspiring writers that an author's journey is a bumpy one with
much compromise and hard work.

Scot Morison's, informative piece, "The 'Rudy Wiebe
Room'," leads the reader to get to know Wiebe not only

as an author and an academic, but also as a friend. The essay also includes a photo of Wiebe with author Margaret Atwood—a tribute to their lifelong friendship. Morison, Wiebe's former student, describes his relationship with Wiebe as "centred on coffee and conversation every few months in a Second Cup several blocks from Wiebe's home in the Old Strathcona area of Edmonton." A staunch admirer of Wiebe's writing, Morison confesses, "We are friends now but he still intimidates me. Part of it is his talent and output. Wiebe is one of the finest writers this country has ever produced."

Reading Morison's account reminded me of my meeting Wiebe at Toronto's Harbourfront. This iconic writer seemed an imposing figure. If he had not mentioned his "lucky shoes" in his talk about the award, most likely I would have had my book signed and walked away quietly. About to do just that, I recalled how he chuckled good-humoredly as he told his story. And the next moment, the voice that croaked out of me surprised me: "As a Master's student, I wrote an essay on your characterization of Big Bear and got my 'A'." (It was actually, A minus; and it is the minus that drove me, all these years later, to revise it—not because of the grade, but because of the need to remedy a student-instinct to follow convention that felt like a pebble in my shoe.) Wiebe had looked up suddenly, his gaze intense. "I'm always glad to hear from students who did well," he had said. As an educator, I could totally relate to Wiebe's sentiments. As for my essay, I am including a revised, updated, version of the same essay in this collection.

Paul Tiessen, who authored "Memoir and the Re-reading of Fiction: Rudy Wiebe's *of this earth* and *Peace Shall Destroy Many*," has written extensively about Wiebe's work and is preparing a monograph investigating in broad terms the nature of the Canadian Mennonite Brethren community out of which Wiebe wrote his first, controversial novel. Paul Tiessen's in-depth knowledge of Wiebe's work and the history of the Mennonite community and culture enriches his essays and offers the reader an insight into Wiebe's fiction and nonfiction. And so does Hugh Cook's comprehensive interview with Wiebe in 2016, first published in *Image*, a quarterly literary journal—a far-reaching discussion of Wiebe's background and his lifelong commitment to writing.

Midway, I happily tucked in Olga Stein's insightful essay, "The 'Wistful, Windy Madness of a Gift': Rudy Wiebe's Books for Young Readers," which focuses on *Chinook Christmas* (1992) and *Hidden Buffalo* (2003), Wiebe's two books for children. Stein, who holds a PhD in English and is a university and college instructor, presents a succinct and vivid depiction of each plot and its characters, and entices the reader to examine yet another fascinating side of Wiebe's storytelling. In addition, Stein delineates certain main trajectories the books are part of, therefore offering valuable additional appreciation of Wiebe's writing.

Wiebe's innovative vision and his distinctive voice have led to his works being widely studied not only nationally but also internationally. Milena Kaličanin, Professor at the University of Niš, Serbia, in her eloquent essay, "Fact vs. Fiction in Rudy Wiebe's *Where is the Voice Coming From*," explores one of the central themes that runs through and simultaneously binds much of Wiebe's fiction—that of turning historical elements into stories by questioning their accuracy as a way of, in Kaličanin's words, "decoding the past." Kaličanin reasons that in Wiebe's story, "the narrator uses the reported facts and creates a work of art based on them, [which] testifies to Wiebe's ... desire to go beyond the crude and dubiously objective message of history in order to liberate an indigenous voice, visionary in its origin." In addition, Uroš Tomić, who teaches Anglophone Literature and Academic Writing in Belgrade, in his essay, "Is Grief Rational? Loss and Pain in Rudy Wiebe's *Come Back*," contemplates the nature of grief itself. Tomić concludes that, "Wiebe has shown us that there is *nothing* and *everything* rational about grief. ...that grief must be lived through and then subsumed into the core of our life force."

A selection of three book reviews offer valuable perspectives into Wiebe's writing at different points in his career, and into different genres. One is Hugh Cook's piece, "Salted with Fire"—an examination of Wiebe's novel, *Come Back*. The article expounds on certain vital aspects of this highly complex novel—complex in theme, structure and imagery. Yet this novel, one of Wiebe's most affecting, is brilliantly composed and not to be missed. The second is Myrna Kostash's 1973 review of *The Temptations of Big Bear*, which recognizes Wiebe's novel as a major step in English Canadian literature by depicting the wise Cree chief Big Bear with all his human strengths and weaknesses. In Kostash's words, "[the novel offers] the Peoples point of view, their version of events and their commentary on the experience—perhaps because we have never been instructed in it—which is the single most important accomplishment of the novel." The third review is Maureen Scott Harris' piece, "A Gift of Understanding"—a perceptive discussion of Wiebe and Yvonne Johnson's collaboration on Johnson's biography, *Stolen Life: The Journey of a Cree Woman*. Harris explains that Johnson's biography "... teaches about humanity."

Following this section are two articles. One is Katherine Govier's astute piece, "A Gentle Eye from Afar," in which Govier fittingly sees Wiebe as "an inspiration and a giver of insights into the shape of the world." The second is John Longhurst's intriguing, "Peace of Mind," which offers a window into Wiebe's perspective on his place as an author within his Mennonite community and his books about Indigenous Peoples in Western Canada.

George Melnyk's second essay featured in this collection, "The Other Wiebe: Decoding a Novelist's Nonfiction," offers a cross-discussion of Wiebe's nonfictional work. This essay is of particular interest for it makes a connection between Wiebe's fiction and nonfiction and the creative process involved. It also offers a glimpse into Wiebe's involvement with the writers' communities. In 1986–87 Wiebe served as chair at the Writers Union of Canada, and in 2005, he presented the Margaret Laurence Lecture at the Annual General Conference of the Writers Union—a literary organization of which Melnyk and I have been both members and board members. The Lecture, "A Writer's Life," is a reminder that Wiebe's writing, in Melnyk's words, "Has been framed by the meeting of cultures and peoples."

Wiebe's fiction and nonfiction, his essays and lectures, attest to his emphasis on the importance of the milieu which nourishes the creative process. At the Conference on Mennonite/s Writing at Goshen College in Indiana in 2002, Hildi Froese Tiessen, who has been Wiebe's long-time colleague and friend—Froese Tiessen is Professor Emerita at the University of Waterloo—offered valuable insight into the importance of a writer's life to the work created. Froese Tiessen, whose parents, like Wiebe's, immigrated to Canada from Stalin's Russia in 1930, spoke to an audience of mostly Mennonites:

> … Rudy Wiebe is ours! (And, I would add, Patrick
> Friesen and David Waltner-Toews and Di Brandt
> and Armin Wiebe and Sarah Klassen and Sandra
> Birdsell and Andreas Schroeder and Victor Jerrett
> Enns and John Weier and Ed Dyck and Jack
> Thiessen and Al Reimer and David Elias and David
> Bergen and Barbara Nickel and Miriam Toews and
> … .) I recognize myself and the people among
> whom I was nurtured in these authors' stories and
> poems. I believe that I share with these writers a
> greater than usual understanding of certain sub-texts.
> The tastes, smells, sounds of extended family
> gatherings, the inimitable rhythm of Low German
> and the tug of certain High German expressions of
> piety, the powerful force of four-part congregational

singing, the paradoxical sense of belonging—while living self-consciously on the margin of the dominant culture, the ambivalence about matters relating to faith and salvation, the memories of fragments of Bible stories, the compelling revelations of Mennonite history from the martyrs to the arrival in Canada of the poor post-World War Two refugees—all of these things, among others, the writers and most of us hold in common. (Tiessen, Hildi Froese. Email received by Bianca Lakoseljac, 25 Nov. 2020.)

Froese Tiessen's compelling account illustrates how the communities impact their writers, and in turn, how the writers and their stories impact the communities. It also affirms Wiebe's continuous involvement with the cultural and literary societies that shape the nature of his writing.

One of the highpoints of compiling and editing this essay collection is having the honour of interviewing Rudy Wiebe—this Canadian legend whose writing I've admired for decades. With the Covid-19 crisis and the distance between us (Wiebe lives in Alberta and I in Ontario) an e-mail interview seemed the best option. An exciting surprise and a bonus to our readers is Wiebe's inclusion of his four poems. "Everything," evocatively begins with Wiebe's friend, Robert Kroetsch's line, "I'm getting old now." The second poem, "hands in the time of pandemic," is a poignant reflection on the crisis caused by Covid-19. In response to my question concerning whether Wiebe continues to write during the pandemic, included are two poems: "Departure Level" and "The Question"—the author's profound contemplations on the current issues and our place in the world. Wiebe's masterful use of imagery is reborn in his verses, as seen in a stanza from "Departure Level:"

And then coyotes were howling. …
Their wild slivers of trickery
        bounced off the cliffs, shivered through bending
    willows and there came the moon, huge
    as a domed wildfire rising out of the trees.

I am certain our readers will find the poems enlightening. Wiebe, the 87 year old author, one of the most distinguished in Canada, explains: "I'm fading into poetry. … these are the first poem[s] I've published in over half a century" (Wiebe, Rudy. Email received by Bianca Lakoseljac, Oct. 1, 2020).

"Bibliography: Through the Eyes of Rudy Wiebe"—I set out to compile a comprehensive Bibliography of works by and about Wiebe, so far. I assembled just over 270 titles, as the body of writing by Wiebe and about his fiction and nonfiction is extensive, nationally and internationally. For certain essay collections, in addition to books, I also listed the essays by title to make it easier for researchers and scholars to locate them. I hope our readers will find the information useful.

Rudy Wiebe's literary work raises him to the status of a Canadian literary icon whose fiction and nonfiction are seen as major contributions to Canadian literature, and will continue to be enjoyed for generations to come.

In closing, I would like to pass on the message Wiebe had given me in October, 2007, at the Toronto International Festival of Authors. To all writers and aspiring writers: "Keep writing."

Teaching Rudy to Dance ...
all true events

Margaret Atwood

Margaret Atwood's cartoon, **Teaching Rudy to Dance ... all true events**, grew out of The Writers Union of Canada's Annual General Meeting held in Vancouver on May 31, 1986. Rudy Wiebe was the incoming TWUC chair. Wiebe explains that, "Peggy [Margaret Atwood's friends refer to Atwood as Peggy] thought a Union chair should know how to dance, so she decided to teach me! But I already knew ..." Wiebe and Atwood have been friends since they met in 1967. In Wiebe's words, "[S]he

[Atwood] and I have played jokes on each other; a wonderful life-long friend." (Wiebe, Rudy. Email received by Bianca Lakoseljac, April 25, 2022)

Peace Shall Destroy Many

Miriam Toews

> *It creates deep-seated wells of*
> *rage that find no release.*
> —MIRIAM TOEWS ON PACIFISM IN
> MENNONITE COMMUNITIES.

In 1962, a young scholar from Saskatchewan by the name of Rudy Wiebe caused outrage and scandal in Mennonite communities throughout North America when he published his first novel, *Peace Shall Destroy Many.* The title, taken from a verse in the Book of Daniel, encapsulated the contention of the novel—that pacifism and non-conflict, core tenets of the Mennonite faith, may in fact be sources of violence and conflict, all the more damaging because unacknowledged or denied.

Although the book was published two years before I was born, I can remember my parents discussing it at the kitchen table, conspiratorially, as if the topic was in itself dangerous. My mother would later tell me that she had driven herself to the city, Winnipeg, the day it was made available in stores—it would never have been sold in my little conservative Mennonite town—to find out what all the fuss was about. By the time I was buying books myself, I had learned to think of this novelist named Rudy Wiebe as controversial and heroic, as an *intellectual* whose work was *groundbreaking* and *revolutionary*. These were exciting words to me.

All the fuss was about the challenging questions posed by the novel's central character, Thom Wiens, an earnest young farmer living in a small isolated community in Saskatchewan (much like the community Rudy Wiebe grew up in). It is 1944, wartime, and the local men have either gone to conscientious objector work camps around Canada, or stayed behind to tend the crops and raise livestock. Wiens begins to wonder whether the Mennonite opposition to war may be self-serving. How can Mennonites stand aside while others are dying to protect the freedoms they enjoy? How can Mennonites justify selling their produce to the Canadian army, at a profit no less, and continue to preach peace and love for one's enemies?

Rudy Wiebe hadn't intended to stir things up with his novel. He was no Mennonite provocateur or self-appointed rabble-rouser. He wanted to write honestly and philosophically about the conflicts that arise from non-conflict. He also wanted to raise questions of sexuality and racism, and to test the established perception of Mennonites as a people 'in the world but not of the world'.

At the time, Wiebe was a devout Christian and respected member of the Mennonite establishment. After the book was published he was fired from his job as the editor of a Mennonite newspaper and denounced, by some, as a liar, an upstart and a traitor. Even worse, an atheist. Others, like my parents, were supportive, secretly though, as was and is the custom among dissenting Mennonites. When my mother said, 'Rudy Wiebe has aired our dirty laundry and it's about time,' she whispered. It was important to keep the peace in all matters, including the matter of *Peace Shall Destroy Many*.

'I guess it was a kind of bombshell,' Wiebe told an interviewer in 1972, 'because it was the first realistic novel ever written about Mennonites in western Canada. A lot of people had no clue how to read it. They got angry. I was talking from the inside and exposing things that shouldn't be exposed.'

Shouldn't be exposed. These are telling words. The conviction that certain realities *shouldn't be exposed* is what lurks behind the time-honoured Mennonite practice of avoiding conflict and refusing engagement. Everyday life in these remote towns and colonies is punctuated by conflicts, big and small—just like anywhere else—but Mennonites have a number of distinctive methods for dealing with them. You can, for example, whisper about them with your spouse late at night in bed and hope he or she doesn't betray you to the elders. Pray for resolution. Ask for guidance from your church pastor, who may also be the source of the conflict. Turn the other cheek, according to the words of Jesus. And, if it's bad enough, freeze out the individual creating the problem until they cease to exist in your thoughts, or even better, have that person shunned. (Shunning happens by order of the elders. It involves a complete denial of the individual's existence. It is a method of conflict avoidance that maintains the righteousness of the community while preventing any resolution or possibility of justice. It is murder without killing and it creates deepseated wells of rage that find no release.)

War is hell, it's true. *Shouldn't be exposed* is another hell. *Shouldn't be exposed* stifles and silences and violates. *Shouldn't be exposed* refuses and ignores and shames. *Shouldn't be exposed* shields bullies and tyrants. I have seen it in my own life.

When my sister was ten years old, she was grabbed off the street, driven around for a while by a group of teenage boys unknown to her or any of our family, doused in some brown, toxic liquid and dropped back off in front of our home. The white furry hat that she'd just received as a Christmas present was ruined and had to be thrown into the garbage. That's all I know about that. I don't know what else happened in the car. Police weren't called, nobody was called, it had happened and then there was silence and over time it seemed as though it might not have happened after all.

My grandmother, my father's mother, was a secret alcoholic. Our community was dry, drinking was a sin, but she shoplifted bottles of vanilla extract from the local grocer and drank them one by one alone in the darkness of her small apartment. My parents would let themselves in with a key that they kept, pick her up, clean her up and put her to bed. My mother had mentioned to me that she suspected that my grandmother had been assaulted by a group of local men when she was a young woman, but it was never spoken of, never investigated. Every few weeks, the owner of the grocery store where my grandmother stole vanilla would call my father and tell him the sum total of the missing bottles—he never confronted my grandmother directly—and my father would write him a cheque and that was that, until the next time, when the same process would be repeated.

My other grandmother, my mother's mother, was stood up at the altar twice by my grandfather until finally, on the third try, they were married. She had thirteen children, buried six of them as babies and spent a great deal of time praying. She would never even have suggested to my grandfather that his sexual desire was becoming an inconvenience. In fact, it was killing her, each pregnancy posing another threat to her life. At the onset of menopause and with the blessed end of pregnancies clearly in sight, she dropped dead of high blood pressure.

My father had a nervous breakdown at the age of seventeen and was diagnosed with bipolar disorder, then called manic depression. His family never spoke of it except to berate him for being weak and effeminate and not devout enough a Christian, even though he attended church relentlessly, taught Sunday school, prayed his heart out for relief and never missed a sermon.

When I was twelve, the car dealership next door wanted to expand their parking lot and they put pressure on my father to sell our house. My father didn't want to sell the house he had built himself for his new bride and the offspring that followed, and my mother encouraged him to fight, but he didn't once argue or put up any kind of resistance. Business was next to godliness in our town and if my father refused to sell his house and beautiful yard filled with chokecherry trees and Saskatoon trees and petunias and tiger lilies and home-made birdhouses painted with cheerful colours then he truly was a sinner. He sold the house for cheap and mourned his loss quietly. I remember my mother slinging her arm around my father's broad shoulders and whispering, 'Defend yourself, man,' and my father smiling mysteriously, with no words attached.

My mother's cousin received a Rhodes Scholarship to study at the University of Oxford and just a few months into the first term he died there, mysteriously, under suspicious circumstances, or according to God's will, in which case what was there to do about it? His parents chose not to hear any details of an investigation or an autopsy. What if their son had died from a drug overdose, or sexual misadventure, or suicide? If they don't know, then they don't feel obligated to condemn him as a sinner, and they can imagine their bright, young, beloved son in heaven.

My son's girlfriend told me a story about an Italian friend of hers. This Italian friend had an aunt who was absolutely furious with her brother for something they've all since forgotten. In order for her brother to know the extent of her rage she dragged a dead and bloodied deer carcass (I'm not sure where she got it from) onto his driveway for him to discover in the morning. That dead deer carcass said, 'Don't Fuck With Me!' Her brother got the message. He apologized. She made him prove he meant it. He convinced her of his contrition. They laughed. They clinked shot glasses of grappa and drank to peace. *Basta*! Well, I don't know exactly how it all went down but I've been so envious of this Italian brother and sister duo ever since my son's girlfriend told me the story.

During my twenty-year marriage, which ultimately ended in divorce and a tsunami of agony and madness and guilt for thinking that I had destroyed my innocent family out of pure selfishness and conceit, and with the thought that I should probably destroy myself before I could cause more damage, I would sometimes air my complaints to my husband after he'd been drinking and when he was just about to fall asleep. I knew that he wouldn't remember what I had said but at least I would have gotten it off my chest. It was a perfect arrangement. I could speak up but it wouldn't turn into a huge blowout. I would talk about mundane things, mostly, how it bugged me that we always had to have supper at 6 p.m. sharp, for instance, or that he didn't seem enthusiastic about my decision to join the Dakar Desert Rally, but I'd often get into bigger issues too; fundamental questions about our happiness and our compatibility. He would nod and smile, his eyes closed, and tell me we'd work it all out, he had to sleep, sorry. In the morning he'd have no memory of the conversation. In true Mennonite fashion, I had managed to take the edge off my disappointment and dissatisfaction (by saying a kind of prayer, pretending that someone was listening), without exposing myself, without provoking a big, ugly fight, and without changing a thing.

Between 2005 and 2009, in a very isolated Mennonite colony in Bolivia, 130 women and girls between the ages of three and sixty were raped by what many in the community believed to be ghosts, or Satan, as punishment for their sins. These girls and women were waking up in the morning sore, in pain, and often bleeding. These mysterious attacks went on for years. If the women complained they weren't believed and their stories were chalked up to 'wild female imagination'.

Finally, it was revealed that the women had been telling the truth. Two men from the community were caught in the middle of the night as they were climbing into a neighbour's bedroom window. The men were forced into a confession. They and seven other locals would spray an animal anaesthetic created by a local veterinarian through the screen windows of a house, knocking unconscious all occupants. They would climb in, rape the victims, and get out.

These Mennonite colonies are self-policed, except in cases of murder. The bishop and the elders came up with a solution to the problem of how to punish the offenders. They locked all nine men into sheds and basements, and the idea was that they would stay there for decades. Also, they would instruct these men to ask for forgiveness from the women. If the women refused to forgive these men then God would not forgive the women. If the women did not accept the men's apology they would have to leave the colony for the outside world, of which they knew nothing.

Eventually, this outside world was made aware of the Mennonite 'ghost rapes' and the perpetrators were arrested by the Bolivian police and put on trial by the Bolivian criminal court. According to sources within the community, the rapes have continued and no offers of counselling have been accepted by the elders on behalf of the women and girls. One explanation they made for refusing help was that, because the victims were sedated during the attacks, they couldn't possibly be suffering from psychological trauma.

Abe Warkentin, founder of *Die Mennonitische Poste*, the most widely read Mennonite newspaper across North and South America and whose headquarters are located in my home town, has called the Mennonites 'a broken people'. He has said that in our communities there continues to resound a 'deafening silence' when it comes to these crimes and issues, and he describes the scandal as 'little more than an enlargement of social problems, in which more energy is put into hiding them than confronting and solving them'.

My father, after politely inquiring as to when the next freight train was scheduled to pass through the tiny village he had walked to, killed himself by kneeling in front of it. Blank pieces of paper were found scattered next to his body. My sister killed herself twelve years later in an identical fashion. Earlier she had left a note that listed the many people she had loved and had added a plea for forgiveness and the hope that God would accept her into His kingdom. When I was a teenager my sister put her hands on my shoulders, as though knighting me, and told me that I was a 'survivor'. What does that mean? What does that require?

In 2008, I met Rudy Wiebe for the first time. A book tour had been arranged for the two of us in Germany. We would travel together from one small Mennonite village to the next, reading from our work and answering questions from audiences. A tall long-haired Lithuanian Mennonite living in Bonn drove us around from colony to colony and acted as our cultural attaché. He and Rudy Wiebe sat in the front seat of the car and told each other hilarious stories in Plautdietsch, the unwritten language of the Mennonites, and I sat in the back seat amazed that I was on a book tour with the guy who everybody had whispered about—the myth himself!

Rudy Wiebe was the same age my father would have been. They had a similar body type: tall, slightly stooped. He was formal and polite, like my father, with a way of looking up at things suddenly from a bowed head, so that in that instant, when he looked up or at you, his eyes were wide and his forehead was creased. He was a sort of folk hero in these communities, no longer condemned as a renegade traitor but sweetly embraced by these conservative Mennonites as a famous writer they could call their own, a prodigal son who spoke their language and who was no longer as harsh a critic of their culture as he'd been in his youth.

Rudy and I spent a week together on the road and had come to our last event in a tiny Mennonite town whose name I can't remember. Once again, the audience was overjoyed to hear Rudy speak and mostly puzzled or just indifferent when it was my turn. I don't speak Plautdietsch so a translator had to help me out when there were questions from the audience. I was reading from my novel, *A Complicated Kindness*, which is about a sixteen-year-old girl whose Mennonite family is torn apart by fundamentalism. My reading didn't leave a great taste in the mouths of these German Mennonites. Afterwards, an angry-looking woman stood up and asked to be given the microphone. Her question was directed at me. It went on for a long time, in Plautdietsch, and when she was finished the translator faltered, a bit reluctant to tell me what the woman had said. Rudy Wiebe had understood it all and was busy making notes on a pad of paper. The translator told me that the woman had said my book was filthy and that my characters' mockery of Menno Simons, the man who started the Mennonites in Holland five hundred years ago, was sacrilegious and sinful. She said that if she had a sixteen-year-old daughter she would not allow her to read my book. As the translator translated I smiled and nodded politely. When he was finished I thanked the woman for her comments. I was at a loss as to what to say next. Rudy Wiebe motioned for me to hand over the microphone. He walked to the edge of the stage and spoke directly to this woman in her language. After a minute or two, the woman stormed out of the room, dragging her mortified husband along with her. Rudy continued to talk for a while and then handed the microphone to the translator who translated everything back into English for me and the few other English speakers in the room.

Rudy had defended me. He had told this woman, 'No. You're wrong.' He said that the reaction to my book had reminded him of the Mennonite reaction to his first novel, *Peace Shall Destroy Many*. He told the people in the room that however they might feel about the swearing in the book, it was at least an honest book, and that the conversations it had generated were important ones and that it, in its way, was advocating for necessary change within our culture; it was holding us accountable as Mennonites to our humanity, our human-ness; it was asking us to be self-critical, to accept reality, and to love better. He may have said other things that weren't translated, I don't know.

What I'll remember is that on that day Rudy Wiebe stood up in front of a Mennonite 'congregation' and fought for me. My father would have approved. He may not have been able to do it himself but I know he would have appreciated the scene, this long-ago subversive hero defending his very own daughter.

Rudy and I took a train to Frankfurt the next day, where we were catching different flights home to Canada. The train was packed and, with the exception of one seat, there was standing room only. Rudy gestured for me to take the seat, but I hesitated. He looked tired and I knew the week had been hard on him. Again he reminded me of my father before he died, smiling valiantly, sadness in his eyes. I shook my head and gestured for him to take the seat. I was happy to stand, no problem. The train was moving fast and things, life, on the outside became a blur. I watched him as he gazed through the window out at the German countryside, pensive. Soon he was asleep and the train ticket he held in his hand slipped from his fingers and fell to the floor.

Between Memory and Longing:
Rudy Wiebe's *Sweeter Than All the World*

Hildi Froese Tiessen

Abstract: Rudy Wiebe's latest novel *Sweeter Than All the World* is, like his much-anthologized short story "Where Is the Voice Coming From?," a metafiction. Like the earlier, shorter work, the novel is a meditation on how an individual might—through the mediating forces of historical artifact and mystical experience—at once encounter history and discover something about oneself. In the novel Wiebe uses particular photographs from a 1981 collection entitled *Forever Summer, Forever Sunday: Peter Gerhard Rempel's Photographs of Mennonites in Russia, 1890–1919*. The photographs enable Wiebe to explore the transformative power of individual recollection (literally, re-collection: the taking up of the artifacts of the past one more time) and the role of the collective (the community and the commonly held stories and other representations of the past) in the articulation of longing and the realization of desire.

> *There are many ways to see us.*
> *We can look elsewhere; there are mirrors*
> *all around: let us begin with the Old Country.*
> —David Waltner-Toews, "A Word in the Nest"

We believed
it would be always summer
always Sunday. On Khortiza Island
we fell on our knees
searching reluctant undergrowth
for evidence of our having been there.
Our fingers trace names
once chiselled deep
in weathered stone.
　　　—SARAH KLASSEN, "ORIGINS"

Presumably all the parts of the story are themselves
available. A difficulty is that they are, as always,
available only in bits and pieces.
　　　—RUDY WIEBE, "WHERE IS THE VOICE COMING FROM?"

Actual photographs—testimonies to historical circumstance—inform some of the narratives of Rudy Wiebe's *Sweeter Than All the World*.[1] The following passage from the novel, and the accompanying photograph, illustrate what I mean:

---

1. Rudy Wiebe, *Sweeter Than All the World* (Toronto: Alfred A. Knopf, Canada, 2001).

Father, show me a picture.

Which one, sweetheart?

You know, you know.

You made me laugh, he says, laughing. So hard I
shook the camera under the hood. You and Greta
Isaak were perfect slender young men in trousers
and tied cravats, flat-brimmed hats, pince-nez and
twirled moustaches, superb, she in black, stood
leaning towards you in grey, seated in the round-
backed chair with your left leg perched at the ankle
on your right knee, each of you with a long
cigarette elegantly between your fingers, rolled
paper actually, such beautiful young men.[2]

---

2. Wiebe, 282. In contrast to other of Peter Gerhard Rempel's
photographs Wiebe invokes narratively in the text of his novel, this
re-inscription of Plate 74 of *Forever Summer, Forever Sunday: Peter
Gerhard Rempel's Photographs of Mennonites in Russia, 1890–1919*
is narrated as a personal historic event, not described as an artifact.
The narrator here (photographer Alexander Wiebe) takes pleasure
in the role-playing his subjects enact in his studio during their
photographic encounter with him and makes no reference to the
ambiguity and subversion implied in their cross-dressing perfor-
mance. That is, he does not seem to regard the tableau he describes
as evocative of any state beyond itself, and so, in effect, makes all
the more poignant the inscription of longing so palpably expressed,
as we shall see, in other descriptive evocations of other photographic texts in the novel. (All images reproduced in this essay are
from John D. Rempel and Paul Tiessen, *Forever Summer, Forever
Sunday: Peter Gerhard Rempel's Photographs of Mennonites in
Russia, 1890–1919* (St. Jacobs, ON.: Sand Hills Books, 1981) and
are used with permission.)

This essay investigates the relationship between literary fiction and the photograph. It probes the nature of collective memory. It suggests that, sometimes, cultural artifacts can engage our consciousness, invade our imagination, and lead us "home."

Members of my own generation of "Russian Mennonites," children and grandchildren of 1920s German-speaking immigrants to Canada from the Mennonite colonies of southern Ukraine (our parents called it Russia),[3] are cognizant of how far we have travelled from the richly-layered religious and social ethos our parents occupied, once, and of how little material culture we can gather around us to give us a palpable sense of how *they* lived and who *we* are relative to *their* past—our heritage. We find ourselves pondering the limited material inheritances our forebears have passed on to us (primarily photographs—evocative and in some sense, presumably, reliable). And we wonder whether these mementoes—these minor monuments—can offer us any meaningful access to a cultural and spiritual heritage we have come to know only second-hand.

---

3. "Russian Mennonites" is a descriptor used to identify Mennonites whose ancestors come from the northern regions of Germany and Holland; the term "Swiss Mennonites," on the other hand, identifies those whose ancestors come from the southern regions of Germany or Switzerland. "Russian Mennonites," who sojourned in Prussia before migrating further east, came to Canada by way of southern Ukraine; "Swiss Mennonites," by way of the United States. "Russian Mennonites" tend to be categorized as either "Kanadier" (those who came to Canada in the first wave of migration in the 1870s) or "Russländer" (those who migrated to Canada in the second wave, the 1920s).

In a very real sense people of my generation are engaging in what Marianne Hirsch calls "post memory"—"a 'second generation' memory characterized by belatedness, secondariness, and displacements."[4] The personal memories of our parents and grandparents are being "crowded out," Hirsch would observe, by the cultural memories that have taken their place and now tend to dominate. Such cultural memories are both enlarged and subverted when they are extravagantly re-constructed by Mennonite writers of historical fiction and metafiction like Sandra Birdsell and Rudy Wiebe.

"Cultural memory," Mieke Bal has observed, "can be located in literary texts because the latter are continuous with the communal fictionalizing, idealizing, monumentalizing impulses thriving in a conflicted culture."[5] Historical fiction informed by the photograph—like Rudy Wiebe's *Sweeter Than All the World*—has the capacity to posit at once the allure of "imaginary wholeness"[6] that collective memory would promise, as well as the unreliability of all the material means that would seem poised to deliver that wholeness. That is because the photograph—like the historical fiction itself—is essentially an unstable artifact, subject to diverse and contradictory interpretations.

---

4. Mieke Bal, citing Marianne Hirsch in Bal's "Introduction," in *Acts of Memory: Cultural Recall in the Present*, eds. Mieke Bal, Jonathan Crewe, and Leo Spitzer (Hanover: University Press of New England, 1999), xii. See, in the same volume: Marianne Hirsch, "Projected Memory: Holocaust Photographs in Personal and Public Fantasy," 3–23.

5. Bal, *Acts of Memory*, xiii.

6. Andreas Huyssen, "Monumental Seduction," in Bal, 198.

In fact, both literary fiction and the photograph offer incomplete and unstable renderings of what was and what might have been—of both memory and longing. The historical novelist gathers the fragments of what was, in order to construct a rendering of what might have been. And he knows, as he does this, that any material residue of the past—including the photograph—can invoke and represent a forgetting as much as a remembering. "The more monuments there are," Robert Musil has observed, "the more the past becomes invisible, the easier it is to forget."[7] Paradoxes like Musil's here speak to both the possibilities and the limitations inherent in the novelist's monumentalizing impulse. For the novelist knows—as Anthony Vidler has remarked— that "despite a yearning for a concrete place and time, the object of desire is neither here nor there, present or absent, now or then."[8] And so the novelist inscribes the gap—and invites his reader to inscribe the gap—between the historical evidence he has before him and the condition for which he longs. Sometimes that act of inscription, as Rudy Wiebe has so stunningly demonstrated in his powerful and much anthologized short story "Where Is the Voice Coming From?,"[9] serves to transport both writer and reader beyond the artifact, beyond the text and, in an instant of transcendence, to deliver them to the location of their desire.

---

7. Huyssen, citing Robert Musil, ibid., 193.

8. Anthony Vidler, *The Architectural Uncanny: Essays in the Modern Unhomely* (Cambridge, MA.: MIT Press, 1992), 66.

9. Rudy Wiebe, "Where is the Voice Coming From?," in Rudy Wiebe, *Where Is the Voice Coming From?* (Toronto: McClelland and Stewart, 1974), 135–143.

Among the facts and artifacts of history

Today we are experiencing, Svetlana Boym remarked in 2001, a "global epidemic of nostalgia, an affective yearning for a community with a collective memory, a longing for continuity in a fragmented world."[10] In the absence of "space which we [can] authentically occupy," Christopher Shaw and Malcolm Chase have written, we "fill the gap by manufacturing images of home and rootedness."[11] We might do well to take a cautious approach to nostalgia, as Mieke Bal has remarked. For nostalgia, Bal cautions, is "unproductive, escapist, and sentimental. It is ... the temporal equivalent of tourism ... It has also been conceived as longing for an idyllic past that never was."[12]

It could be argued that parts of both Wiebe's *Sweeter Than All the World* and Sandra Birdsell's *The Russländer*,[13] another novel dealing with the history of the Mennonites and also published in 2001, are, at least in part, expressions of nostalgia (even though, at the same time, they work to subvert that impulse). Certainly both novels offer investigations of an elusive past, expressions of "poignant yearning"[14] for a world that can never be recovered in its

---

10. Svetlana Boym, *The Future of Nostalgia* (New York: Basic Books, 2001), xiv.

11. Christopher Shaw and Malcolm Chase, *The Imagined Past: History and Nostalgia* (Manchester: Manchester University Press, 1989), 15.

12. Bal, *Acts of Memory* xi.

13. Sandra Birdsell, *The Russländer* (Toronto: McClelland & Stewart, 2001).

14. Nicholas Dames, "Austen's Nostalgics," *Representations* 73 (2001): 121.

entirety and yet is presented, in the very memorial artifacts constructed to invoke it, as more complete, more coherent than our own.

But these works reach beyond the romantic sentimentalism in which nostalgia trades. Questions about how the individual can gain access to the historical past —insert oneself within it—lie at the heart of Wiebe's work in particular. The search for the past that would confirm, say, Adam Wiebe's identity in *Sweeter Than All the World* becomes for Rudy Wiebe an analogue for any secular Mennonite's questions about what it means to make sense of or lay claim to a heritage from which one has become several steps removed. Adam's search, that is, becomes an analogue for the experience of many members of my own generation of Mennonites—people who know that the cultural and religious discourses that were, in another context, apparently sufficient for our parents' generation are not sufficient for us.

The structure of the novel itself, with Adam's quest complexly and unequivocally embedded in some seminal narratives of Russian Mennonite history, reinforces a central idea Wiebe seems to propose here: that in the very act of placing ourselves among the facts and artifacts that comprise our past, our personal history, we can make meaningful discoveries. In *Sweeter Than All the World* Wiebe returns to the issues he outlines in his great short metafiction "Where Is the Voice Coming From?," where, at the outset, he provocatively quotes Teilhard de Chardin: "We are continually inclined to isolate ourselves from things and events which surround us ... as though we were spectators, not elements, in what goes on."[15] As spectators, that is—and through the mediating force of what Wiebe (quoting Arnold Toynbee) speaks of as "the undifferentiated unity of the mystical experience"[16]—we, as readers and seekers, can become elements in what goes on.

From rupture and dislocation to collective memory

The tone of *Sweeter Than All the World* is markedly different from the often more astringent tone common to many of the Mennonite literary texts that preceded it.[17] Wiebe's *Sweeter Than All the World,* like Birdsell's *The Russländer*, published the same year, in 2001, opens up toward earlier Mennonite worlds with a more magnanimous gesture than one might discern in earlier texts. Whereas the mostly Manitoba-based authors of earlier Mennonite literary works tended to write against the grain of their immediate Mennonite experience, the late

---

15. Rudy Wiebe, "Where Is the Voice Coming From?," 135.

16. Ibid., 135.

17. Rudy Wiebe's earliest novels about Mennonites, *Peace Shall Destroy Many* (1962) and *The Blue Mountains of China* (1970), and subsequent writers' major early works dealing with the experience of Mennonites in Canada—Patrick Friesen's *The Shunning* (1980), David Waltner-Toews's *Good Housekeeping* (1983), Armin Wiebe's *The Salvation of Yasch Siemens* and Sandra Birdsell's *Night Travellers* (1984), Di Brandt's *questions i asked my mother* (1987), and Sarah Klassen's *Journey to Yalta* (1988)—tended to probe critically the ongoing value of rigid doctrines and patterns of patriarchal dominance that old world Mennonite immigrants from Russia had tried to transplant into their substantial settlements on the Canadian prairie.

twentieth-century protagonist in *Sweeter Than All the World*, Adam Wiebe, seeks to probe the nature of his own identity not so much among people he knows—among family and congregation—as in history, history preserved as artifact, the kind of history that can provide "unifying symbols and rituals that enable people to interpret common experiences."[18] The early works of Mennonite fiction and poetry published mostly in the 1960s and 1970s documented the disintegration of various elements of what some had hoped would become a Mennonite commonwealth in Canada. They revealed that the social, cultural, and religious practices and traditions that would once have allowed the Mennonites of any particular region of Canada (the prairies, for example) to refer to themselves as a community—or a "people"—no longer had coherence or sustaining power. For most of the early wave of Mennonite writers in Canada, that is, the coherent community came to be recognized as a deception, and the disintegrating cultural and religious ethos, as a trap. As the writers looked back on their own experience among their people, they saw themselves moving outward and away, while the urgent, but finally ineffectual, words of the Mennonites' ubiquitous, dominant patriarchs echoed in a hollow landscape.

The Mennonite community, its writers observed, had become a place where those who raised questions were shut out: "You criticized the church before *that*

---

18. See George Lipsitz, *Time Passages: Collective Memory and American Popular Culture* (Minneapolis: U. of Minnesota Press, 1990), 216.

group?" Deacon Block, in Rudy Wiebe's *Peace Shall Destroy Many*, demands of the author's primary spokesman, Joseph Dueck (as if anticipating the harsh treatment the 28-year-old author, Wiebe himself, would experience at the hands of powerful forces in his own community): "You took pains to speak a language [outsiders could] understand to slander our church?"[19]

This first wave of Canadian Mennonite literature reflected the disillusionment of a younger, Canadian-born generation reluctantly released by their communities into the world. Some among these writers who published major texts in the 1980s eventually recognized the extent of their growing detachment from Mennonite traditions and undertook the search for what George Lipsitz calls a "precious and communicable past."[20] Like Rudy Wiebe's Adam in *Sweeter Than All the World*, they began to explore, in collective memory, for example, the shared identity that might moderate their sense of cultural alienation. Like Adam, authors such as Wiebe and Birdsell and others began to probe, in what we might regard as gestures of optimism, their own relationship to the history and ethos of Mennonite religion and culture in the decades and centuries prior to the Mennonites' immigration to Canada.

---

19. Rudy Henry Wiebe, *Peace Shall Destroy Many* (Toronto: McClelland and Stewart, 1962), 60.

20. George Lipsitz, *Time Passages: Collective Memory and American Popular Culture* (Minneapolis: University of Minnesota Press, 1990), 36.

Sites of inscription

Two books lie at the heart of this essay. The first is Rudy
Wiebe's novel of 2001: *Sweeter Than All the World*. The
second is a collection of black and white photographs
published in 1981 as *Forever Summer, Forever Sunday: Peter
Gerhard Rempel's Photographs of Mennonites in Russia,
1890–1917*, edited by John D. Rempel, the photographer's grandson, and Paul Tiessen, husband to Hildegard E.
Tiessen (Hildi Froese Tiessen), translator of the book's
epistolary text and author of this essay.[21] The book was

---

21. John D. Rempel and Paul Tiessen's *Forever Summer, Forever
Sunday: Peter Gerhard Rempel's Photographs of Mennonites in
Russia, 1890–1919* (St. Jacobs, ON.: Sand Hills Books, 1981) was
some eight years in the making. Although it was not the first book
published by Sand Hills Books (a small press of which the Tiessens
are principals), the book was, in a very real sense, the reason for
Sand Hills' existence. After John Rempel and Paul Tiessen, both
young academics, had begun to talk about the glass plate negatives
Peter Gerhard Rempel had brought from Russia to Canada, they
could not imagine *not* placing the rich visual archive the photographs represented in the public domain. Rempel and Tiessen
found in these photographs, as their introduction reveals, the projection of a Russian Mennonite world-view later seemingly largely
forgotten or actively suppressed. The editors spoke of the book as
having community value as a documentary record of the dreams
and achievements of the Russian Mennonites at the apex of their
cultural and material development.

The book was published (with material support from the
Multiculturalism Program of the Government of Canada and the
Ontario Arts Council) in fall 1981, in an edition of 950 copies. It
was sold out in January 1982. Its primary audience turned out to
be Mennonites in Canada, among whom the book was favourably
reviewed in such prominent Mennonite periodicals as *The Mennonite*

known to most of the writers who maintained contact
with members of the Mennonite community, especially
writers like Rudy Wiebe and Sandra Birdsell, each of
whom also had a professional relationship with the
book's publishers. As one of the primary collaborators
on the volume and as an avid observer of the field of
Mennonite literature, I took notice when references to
Forever Summer, Forever Sunday began to appear in
Mennonite literary texts and elsewhere. This essay represents my first formal response to the emergence in that
body of literature of the trope of "forever summer, forever Sunday," which has found expression in both image
and text. Photographs from the book have appeared in
books and posters, for example, as well as in an etching
that forms part of a large metal sculpture depicting the
history of the Mennonites, by the metal artist Jo-Anne
Harder, installed on an atrium wall at Conrad Grebel
University College, the Mennonite college at the
University of Waterloo. Photographs or details of photographs from the book have graced the covers of other
major Mennonite literary works published around the
turn of the century—notably David Waltner-Toews' collection of poetry *The Impossible Uprooting* (1995):

Reporter (December 7, 1981), *The Mennonite Brethren Herald*
(December 18, 1981), *The Mennonite Mirror* (January 1982) and
(in the USA.) *Festival Quarterly* (Spring 1982). The mostly positive
reviews, on the one hand, praised the photographer and editors for
avoiding sentimentality and, on the other, cautioned readers not to
take the lifestyle reflected in the photographs as broadly representative of village life in the Mennonite colonies of Russia.

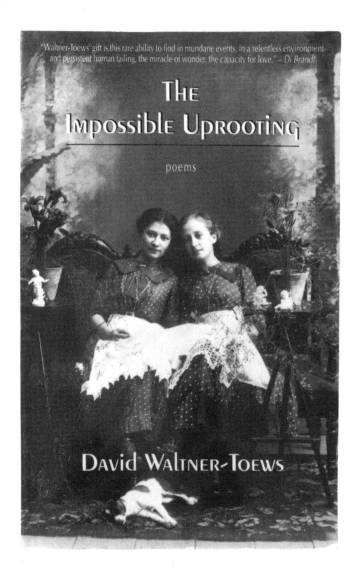

And Sandra Birdsell's Giller Prize-nominated novel, *The Russländer* (2001):

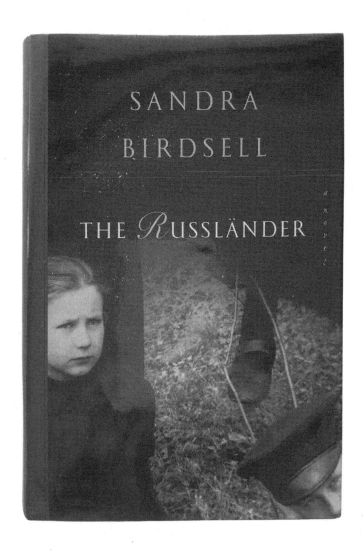

Forever Summer, Forever Sunday found its way, over the years, into various other "Russländer" texts as well, where its title evoked a contradictory landscape: a kind of palimpsest in which a utopian dream was overwritten by the shattering reality of revolution, disorder, plunder, and rape.[22] As monuments, photographs like Rempel's do not provide final, fixed meanings, of course. A photograph is always open to interpretation. Thus, they do not so much transport their audience into particular narratives as provide sites of emblematic inscription: places where longing can be both observed and registered, perhaps even mystically realized; places where questions can be framed.

In *Sweeter Than All the World*, for example, the descriptions of specific photographs simultaneously evoke and erase the complex world of the Mennonite colonies

---

22. Photographs from the book were featured in Volume 2 of Norma Jost Voth's *Mennonite Foods & Folkways from South Russia* (Intercourse, PA: Good Books, 1991). They figured prominently, also, in David Dueck's documentary film entitled *And When They Shall Ask* (Dueck Films,1983), which was widely distributed among Mennonite audiences in a campaign of special screenings. *And When They Shall Ask* was, upon its release, screened to large audiences in the Mennonite communities of Canada. The narrative and visual images of the film allude to Rempel's photographs but, in parts of the film at least, the trope of "forever summer" is inverted. In Dueck's film the Mennonites' aspirations to material success and cultural refinement fairly innocently foregrounded in Rempel's photographs tend to be debunked and de-valued as signs of moral degeneracy. That is, Dueck offers a fairly straight-forward moralistic interpretation of the world Rempel's photographs evoke, unlike Wiebe, for whom the photographic images invoke aspiration and longing and remain more open to interpretation.

of Russia as they seem to have existed in the early years of the last century. The world these photographs represented was finally not so much a particular time and place as an abstract and evocative landscape, an ethos in which, it would seem, individuals could find—or project—meaning and share it with others. Rudy Wiebe's protagonist, Adam, (along with the author himself) is asking, "How can one insert oneself into such a cultural landscape? Such an ethos, a community? If those were my people, how might I find my way back to them?" As metanarrative, *Sweeter Than All the World* foregrounds questions like: "What access do secular Mennonites have to their ancestral past? What form might acts of cultural reclamation take, and what might they reveal? Is it possible to gain entry to the world beyond the cultural artifact? How might I appropriate that world—or it me? What would be the cost of attempting its recovery?"

It is not surprising that a great Canadian historical metafictionist like Rudy Wiebe should explore in an historical novel—a rich memorializing artifact in its own right—how difficult it is to engage the past in a meaningful way. How fact and artifact fail to provide a secure and reliable entry into an ancestral past; how they suggest something about what the past might have been but fall short of conveying what it was and what it meant. How every monument—from the photograph to the work of literary fiction—is an expression of longing towards that place beyond the image, beyond the text. How sometimes miraculously, in a moment of epiphany as readers, we realize what we've longed for and sneak beyond the artifact in an instant of transcendence. How that epiphany we experience might stretch well beyond any actual lived history—any facts of existence—and how that doesn't matter.

Everyday mental property

It was some years after *Forever Summer, Forever Sunday* appeared that the compelling trope the title evoked[23] gradually began to capture the Mennonite imagination. The photographer's daughter, Tina Rempel, recalling with immense pleasure around 1980 the early twentieth-century period of her own life, pronounced that era a wonderful, idyllic time, when every season seemed like summer, every day like Sunday. "Bei uns war es immer Sommer, immer Sonntag," she declared. Tina Rempel's words, which—along with the idealizing photographs themselves—came five decades after her family's immigration into Canada from Russia, were deftly adapted by a number of Mennonite writers who made of the compelling phrase, "forever summer, forever Sunday," a trope suggestive of a time and place when the cares of the world seemed remote from the everyday life of the Mennonite colonists, an era that seemed now almost a fantasy, a period that ended when the Mennonite commonwealth was shattered by the violence of revolution and anarchy. The trope "forever summer, forever Sunday,"

---

23. This volume of pictures, reproduced from glass plates made in Russia by Peter Gerhard Rempel (1872–1933), projects, in studio portraits and the adjacent text, a seemingly untroubled world of languor and luxury in the Mennonite colonies of pre-revolutionary Russia.

that is, eventually became a kind of hinge connecting the all-too-present discomforting complexities of twentieth-century Mennonite immigrant experience in Canada with the apparently more stable and more coherent culture of the earlier, late-nineteenth and early-twentieth-century, pre-revolution Russian Mennonite commonwealth. Indeed, these photographs, suggestive of harmonious and—to be sure—idealized variants upon a way of life, played a part in helping to construct among the Russian Mennonites of Canada what Alon Confino, in his study of collective memory, refers to as "common denominators" that function "to create an imagined community."[24] Such a collection of photographs, that is, contributed to allowing, or stimulating, Mennonites in general—and, eventually, writers of historical fiction like Birdsell and Wiebe in particular—to "construct a past through a process of appropriation and contestation."[25]

During the 1980s and 1990s the trope "forever summer, forever Sunday" emerged in the larger Mennonite consciousness as a kind of cultural icon. For many it became what Confino calls "everyday mental property."[26] Most Mennonites knew what it meant. It functioned, furthermore, to construct for many members of the "Russländer" audience—no matter how disenfranchised from their cultural and religious heritage they had come to feel—the possibility of realizing themselves "as historical subjects with a common past."[27]

---

24. Alon Cofino, "Collective Memory and Cultural History: Problems of Method," *American Historical Review* 102 (1997): 1399.

25. Confino, 1402.

26. Confino, 1402.

27. Lipsitz, 32.

Hence, a complex historical and cultural construct was evoked for the "Russländer" reader when she read, in Sarah Klassen's collection of poetry *Journey to Yalta* (1988), for example:

> Mennonites
> having come a long way
> like to return
> in herds like lemming
> to places of death.
> Frozen forests declared out of bounds
> we surround the old oak tree we owned
> once. We stretched warm limbs
> along its rough-ridged branches,
> its roots
> loved the same rivers we loved. We
> believed
> it would be always Summer
> always Sunday …".[28]

Or in David Waltner-Toews' sixteen-page poem, "A Word in the Nest," which begins:

> Rummaging through an old
> trunk in the attic
> I pulled out yellowed, crinkled
> pictures; My five-year-old mother with a cow,
> my four-year-old father on a horse,

---

28. Sarah Klassen, "Origins," *Journey to Yalta* (Winnipeg: Turnstone Press, 1988), 3.

the long, warm day before the Revolution,
forever Summer, forever Sunday,
forever seen through the sepia of suffering."[29]

Birdsell and Wiebe, through their fictional reconstruction of cultural history in their most recent work, play self-consciously both within and against the trope of "forever summer, forever Sunday." In Birdsell's case, the central character Katherine (Katya) Vogt is based on the image that appears on the dust-jacket and paper covers of the novel.[30]

---

29. David Waltner-Toews, "A Word in the Nest," *The Impossible Uprooting* (Toronto: McClelland & Stewart, 1995), 37.

30. Birdsell has on several occasions identified also other central characters in her novel with the figures in Plate 40 of Rempel's collection of photographs (for example, Lydia and Greta), and has suggested the presence of a rich texture of relationship between Rempel's photographs (and by implication the utopian—and ironic—trope they represent) and various of her novel's characters.

As for Rudy Wiebe, in *Sweeter Than All the World* he, too, "quotes" (if I may use that term figuratively and suggestively) Rempel's photographs. For him, a photograph from Rempel's volume has the power to evoke the gestures and tone of another age.

More than this, when Elizabeth Katerina Wiebe speaks, her words invoke the vast realm of longing and emotion beyond the photographic (and narrative) text.:

> I remember my mother always slender and pale ... In the finest portrait [my father, Alexander Wiebe] ever took with his large studio camera, she is half turned, half kneeling on a chair, her left leg almost doubling her long skirt under her and her arms crossed on the chairback; strands of her hair stray back down to her waist, and forward over the lace-trimmed blouse on her breast. She is looking right, serene as glass with the painted studio backdrop behind her, her eyes raised as if anticipating a vision from heaven; it is coming, yes. Her lips will open in adoration.[31]

Peter Gerhard Rempel's photographs function for both Birdsell and Wiebe as what David Lowenthal calls "emblems of communal identity, continuity."[32] They simultaneously draw upon and serve to shape collective memory; they unite these writers' present-day audience by alluding with some degree of literalness to self-representing artifacts from the past. As if to say: this is how it was; this is what we knew; this is who we were.

---

31. Wiebe, *Sweeter Than All the World*, 261–62.
32. David Lowenthal, *The Past is a Foreign Country* (Cambridge: Cambridge University Press, 1985), xvi.

The transformative power of individual recollection

One of the epigraphs to Wiebe's novel is taken from the Russian poet Joseph Brodsky: "You're coming home again. What does that mean?"[33] *Sweeter Than All the World* explores, among other things, what it might mean for a secular Mennonite to probe his ancestral past, to come home. It begins with a mother "calling into the long northern evening. 'Where a-a-re you?'"[34] Adam Wiebe's life, it would seem, begins in a kind of garden, and the novel proceeds to document his attempt to recover some variant of paradise lost, an imagined community. The language describing worlds imagined, lost, and yearned for evokes the "forever summer" trope:

And then, ahh then! Adam and Eve lived together in the most beautiful garden on earth, eating fresh fruit and playing with the gold and sweet gum and pearls and onyx stones that were in the four rivers that flowed out of Eden, and bathing in them too. It was always the perfect seventh day of creation, forever rest, forever summer.[35]

In the hands of Rudy Wiebe, the photographs of Peter Gerhard Rempel are narrativized. By incorporating the photographic images into the text as narratives that inscribe home and family and loss, Wiebe reveals how, when we take the material culture of history into the

---

33. Joseph Brodsky, quoted in Wiebe, *Sweeter Than All the World*, [epigraph].
34. Wiebe, *Sweeter Than All the World*, 7.
35. Ibid., 9.

present, we must take possession of it in a very personal way. The monument (be it photograph or story), although it both shapes and reflects collective memory, is available to be inscribed (to have its meaning established) by every individual who encounters it.

Yes, Papa. Now, please, can I see a picture?

Which one?

Of Enoch and Abel, my beautiful brothers. Not
where they are four and six and looking from under
broad, black-brimmed hats, their small hands
clutching the railing of a fake bridge set over a
stream that does not exist on your sunny studio
floor; not the picture where they sit in a cardboard
boat with sailor hats to sail across a paper-painted
sea, no, show me the sweetest portrait of all, the
one I watched you and mother arrange so carefully,
together. There is a background of bushy shadow
on the right, and wide scrolled and flowered steps
leading upwards, left. Enoch, aged three, stands in
his striped summer shirt and shorts looking into
the distance while he holds the large china family
chamberpot at his side. And just under his gaze,
facing into the camera and bare to the waist,
beautiful Abel, aged one, sits with his chubby legs
bent, on the smaller, rounder chamberpot that was
first mine, then Enoch's and now his, Abel's eyes so
enormous and his face as blank and perfectly sad as
any small animal's—O my brothers, O Enoch, O
Abel, Abel, my lost brother Abel ... .[36]

---

36. Ibid., 278–79.

Peter Gerhard Rempel's photographs would seem to partake of the very world they represent in those early years of the twentieth century. Yet they are, from their inception, contrived and ultimately unstable, unreliable. Like all the facts and artifacts of history, they might lie strewn at the threshold of the past, but we cannot apprehend them as though they were the past itself. We can only place ourselves among them (as Wiebe's characters do) and inscribe them with narratives of our own. And sometimes when we do that, we find ourselves transported both into and beyond these fragments of history.

The mystical experience or aesthetic insight that might ensue is parallel to what happens at the end of Rudy Wiebe's compelling metahistorical fiction, "Where Is the Voice Coming From?" In a manner reminiscent of that story, Wiebe's novel *Sweeter Than All the World* explores the relationship between cultural artifact, memory, and longing. For Wiebe, the photographs of Peter Gerhard Rempel serve as representations (however unreliable in any literal sense) of a lost era. At the same time they are expressions of desire, icons that invoke the coherent community of Mennonite life and culture for which characters like Adam Wiebe, along with so many of us, members of his generation, Mennonites dislodged from an ethos and a tradition that once seemed to hold together our world, yearn. Like Wiebe's character Elizabeth Katerina, we look to the artifact, the photograph, the novel. We seek refuge in it, and even more, hope it will have the capacity to transport us home.

Father, show me a picture.

The summer picnic on the banks of the Dnieper River. Mother, on the right in her broad hat and long white dress, leans back against the cliff; your five friends lounge on the grass and against the rocks between you; and you sit on the left by the basket, the picnic blanket and the samovar. Everyone except you holds a glass, lifting them towards you as if in a toast. Father, why are you holding a guitar, the finders of your right hand curled as if you were playing it? Did you, could you ever, play the guitar? Sing?

But he does not answer me. Finally I must continue for myself. I tell him: I am in the picture too, even if no one—not you, perhaps not even Mama— knows it. I am there below her heart, hidden, untouchable, safe.[37]

In "Where Is the Voice Coming From?" the narrator surrounds himself with cultural artifacts that contradict each other and would seem to lead to no one place. When the narrator finally gives in to the incompleteness of the fragments of history he uncovers, he is transported, by an embracing act of the imagination, into the realm of his own desire. He hears a voice emerging from the ruins—a voice as incomprehensible as it is compelling. A voice that is at once mysteriously intangible and deeply

---

37. Ibid., 287.

satisfying. In this passage from *Sweeter Than All the World* Elizabeth Katerina seeks shelter in the shards of memory represented by her father's album of photographs. Like the narrator in "Where Is the Voice Coming From" she finds herself submerged among the artifacts she ponders. She is as insistent as the narrator in Wiebe's story in declaring that she is *there*—where the actions of history take place. She is, at the same time, aware that she cannot, by any conventional means, communicate to others the essence of her experience. She simply declares it, and through Wiebe's skilful rendering of her personal narrative, the fortunate reader is transported with her to that other realm.

Sweeter Than All the World is not an exercise in simple nostalgia, which tends, as Nicholas Dames has observed, to replace "stubbornly individual pasts with communal pasts."[38] Instead, the novelist (who is palpably present as a structuring force behind the novel's multiple narratives) celebrates the insertion of personal memory into history.[39] Wiebe, that is, reclaims, recovers collective memory that has, in large measure, as Susan A. Crane has remarked, been "besieged, deformed and transformed by history,"[40] and gathers it into the realm of literary fiction, of art. In *Sweeter Than All the World* he celebrates the transformative power of individual recollection (literally, re-collection: the taking up of the

---

38. Dames, 131.

39. See Susan A. Crane, "Writing the Individual Back into Collective Memory," *American Historical Review* 102 (1997): 1375, passim.

40. Crane, 1379.

artifacts of the past one more time) and so, also, the power of the individual imagination. At the same time he recognizes that it is the collective (the community and the commonly held stories and other representations of the past) that makes the personal articulation of longing—and the realization of desire—possible.

And so in *Sweeter Than All the World* Wiebe embraces the historical photograph, with all its inherent indeterminacies, along with the imaginative narratives of the past, and posits an inclusive vision which holds that any one individual might place herself among the artifacts and narratives that would give testimony to her heritage and possibly find among them a place sufficient to be called home.

Literary Genealogy: Exploring the legacy of F.M. Salter

George Melnyk

April 1, 1998, *Alberta Views*

"How do you grow a poet?"

Robert Kroetsch was asking how a new land, like Alberta, nurtures literary creativity, what a colonial society needs to do to grow its own stories. Kroetsch asked the question because he wanted to write those stories. In 1945, just a kid out of Heisler, Alberta, he signed up for a course in creative writing at the University of Alberta. It was taught by F.M. Salter, easily the most influential figure in creative writing in Alberta. Salter was committed to helping his students become successful writers. Single-handedly, he coaxed two generations of writers out of the Alberta soil.

In his memoir, *A Likely Story: The Writing Life*, Kroetsch recounts how he felt out of place on the first day of Salter's class; returning war veterans were talking about their very adult war experiences and he felt completely inexperienced as a kid fresh out of high school. "I had been nowhere, I felt. I had done nothing, I felt. After class, I went and dropped the course and registered in a course called Victorian poetry." Kroetsch preferred to use the province as a psychic reservoir for his writing rather than a place to live. After graduating from the U of A, he chose to go north to gain the experience he felt he needed to become a writer. It was 20 years before his first novel, *But We Are Exiles*, the story of his northern adventures, was published. With works such as *The Studhorse Man*, which earned him the Governor General's Award in 1969, he went on to an illustrious literary career; but what if he had stayed in Salter's class?

Frederick Millet Salter (1895–1962) first came to the U of A in the 1920s to lecture in the English department, returning at the end of the 1930s. Originally from Chatham, New Brunswick, he helped shape a department whose context was primarily British literature, part of Canada's colonial heritage. But Salter, himself an early English scholar, challenged this emphasis on the old country by launching in 1939 the first creative writing course offered by any Canadian university. He was able to get it approved by calling it English 65 or composition.

Salter grew writers the way gardeners grow roses. A short, stocky man with a distinctive little moustache, Salter enjoyed reading Shakespeare aloud as he paced around his office. He loved the English language, the very sound of it, as well as its writing. "He had a wonderful reading voice," Rudy Wiebe, one of Salter's students, remembers.

"In the classroom he read to us from our own work or from other sources either good or bad, and through comparison and example he passed on to us his love of the right word and accurate detail, his ear for apt expression, his impatience with anything shoddy," says Robert

74

Blackburn, another of Salter's students. "He used to say that our university on the northern frontier was the last which could enrol some students who had never before seen electric lights; he knew that most of us had never seen palaces or pirates or skylarks or maple trees or many other exotic things we had read about, and he taught us that the most important things to wonder at and write about were those within our own experience." Salter knew how to motivate students. If they wrote something excellent he read it over the university radio station—the forerunner of CKUA. The work was brought alive by that impressive voice for all the world to hear. Salter was instrumental in launching the career of Alberta's pre-eminent postwar novelist, the late W.O. Mitchell. Originally from Weyburn, Saskatchewan, Mitchell had enrolled at the U of A in 1940 to become a teacher. His future wife, Merna, was then a member of the original group of CKUA Players who did radio dramatizations. Salter took an interest in the work of local dramatists performed by the CKUA Players, and it was through Merna he met Bill, who had been working on his writing since the late 1930s.

After reading some of Mitchell's short stories, Salter was convinced the young writer had tremendous potential. He wrote to Jack Patterson, fiction editor of *Maclean's*, encouraging him to publish this outstanding new western talent. In the fall of 1941, Patterson wrote to Mitchell accepting one of his stories (he was paid $85) and ended the letter with "best regards to yourself and your sponsor, Mr. Salter." *You Gotta Teeter* appeared in *Maclean's* August, 15, 1942, the very day of Bill and Merna's wedding, at which Salter gave the toast to the bride. Next, Salter wrote to Edward Weeks, the editor of *Atlantic Monthly*, to suggest that the stories being published by the illustrious gentleman were of a lower quality than those being written by his students. The editor wrote back asking to see this work and subsequently published Mitchell's *Owl and the Bens* in April, 1945.

Mitchell acknowledged his indebtedness to Salter's promotional efforts when he wrote to Weeks that he appreciated the confidence *Atlantic Monthly* showed in his work and "in Mr. Salter's judgement, which I have never questioned for the five years that he has helped me." The closeness generated by the mentoring role Salter played was evident July 11, 1943. "That night," Merna Mitchell recalls, "Bill was sleeping on a couch in Salter's home not far from the University Hospital, and Salter woke him to tell him that he had a son."

Mitchell's venerated classic, *Who Has Seen the Wind*, was published in 1947. With its combination of humour and insight, its ear for the spoken word, and its embracing of the essential drama of human life, *Who Has Seen the Wind* is one of the great works of Canadian literature, the male equivalent of *Anne of Green Gables*. Mitchell valued the close protégé/mentor relationship he had with Salter, and he used that model in his own career as a writing teacher. In the 1970s, Mitchell taught creative writing at the Banff School of Fine Arts, where he introduced Mitchell's *Messy Method of Writing*, or freefall in which writers mine their memory for landscape, images, stories, characters and situations.

Salter died in 1962, while only in his 60s. His book on writing, *The Way of the Makers*, was published by The Friends of the University of Alberta in 1967, followed by a trade edition, *The Art of Writing*, in 1971. The book was dedicated to his creative writing students. "If I really have blazed a new path toward excellence in writing, others will be able to make the path easy and straight," Salter wrote in the preface. It was not only Mitchell who carried Salter's legacy forward, but the equally distinguished novelist, Rudy Wiebe.

Wiebe is the winner of two Governor General's awards for fiction and a professor emeritus of Canadian Literature and Creative Writing at the U of A. As a student of Salter's in the mid-50s, he wrote a short story that won a national contest and was published in *Liberty* magazine. Wiebe was furious when the story was published. "The title was changed from *Eight and the Present* to *The Midnight Ride of an Alberta Boy*, he recalls. "It wasn't even set in Alberta as far as I was concerned, it was set in Saskatchewan. Anyway, Salter said: 'Just calm down. Take the $100 you got paid and buy a Canada Savings Bond.' I did buy the bond because I listened to him a lot in those days."

Wiebe listened to Salter in many ways. For his master's, he talked to Salter about doing a thesis on Shakespeare. "You could probably do a good thesis on Shakespeare, but so could many others," Salter replied. "Only *you* could write a good novel about Mennonites."

"That made a lot of sense to me," Wiebe says. So he wrote *Peace Shall Destroy Many*. Salter was sufficiently impressed by the novel that he told the young student to send it to "the very best publisher in the country." Along with the manuscript, Salter sent a letter to publisher Jack McClelland, of McClelland & Stewart, praising the work. *Peace Shall Destroy Many*, the first novel about Mennonites in Canada, was published in 1962. The more conservative element in the Mennonite community was unhappy with the book's frank discussion of community conflicts, but this didn't stop Wiebe from embarking on an illustrious literary career. His 1973 novel, *The Temptations of Big Bear*, which dealt with the second Riel Rebellion and the tragic figure of the Cree chief, Big Bear, won a well-deserved Governor General's award.

Wiebe's achievement as a writer is based on the view that writing is a hard slog. "You end up struggling with one thing at a time, one story at a time," he says. Without Salter, "a guy like me living out in the boonies would never have had the nerve to do this."

Wiebe began teaching Canadian literature and creative writing at the U of A in 1967, inheriting the mantle bequeathed by Salter. Numerous students went on to literary success under Wiebe's tough guidance. In 1977, NeWest Press published its first fiction title, *Getting Here*, an anthology of women's fiction edited by Wiebe. Most of the contributors were or had been students in his classes. Among them were Caterina Edwards, Helen Rosta, and Aritha van Herk whose lead story was *A Woman of Moderate Temperament*. "Often you can't tell if a person sitting in a class with you may turn out to be, in the long run, a much better writer than you are," Wiebe says.

If Salter launched Mitchell and Wiebe on a trajectory to the pantheon of CanLit, then Wiebe in turn launched van Herk, the first woman writer in the Salter tradition to make it to the top of the Can-Lit charts. Under the supervision of Wiebe, van Herk's creative writing thesis, *Judith*, won the Seal First Novel Award in 1978. The prize was $50,000, at the time the most valuable literary prize in Canada. The novel was published in Canada, the United States, and Europe. Set in rural Alberta, *Judith* is a powerful expression of the feminist consciousness that captured women in the 1970s. At age 23, van Herk became an instant celebrity. She drove about in a white Porsche bought with the prize money, *Judith* on its vanity licence plate.

Looking back to 1978, when her career took off as fast as Donovan Bailey in a 100-metre dash, she realizes that, as a young woman and writer, she was sitting on a volcano. "In some ways it was the best thing that could happen to a writer and in other ways it was the worst thing that could happen. Everyone looked at the money and the fame and thought I was becoming a spoiled little ingenue. All I had really done was to be a studious kid who read everything I could and wrote a novel under Rudy's guidance." In 1983, van Herk joined the English department at the University of Calgary as a professor of creative writing, replacing W.P. Kinsella, who had decided the academic life wasn't for him. As the mover and shaker behind Canada's first PhD in creative writing, she committed herself to the Salter tradition. She has worked tirelessly on behalf of new writers, especially in the area of publishing. In the 1980s, she and Wiebe edited two anthologies of stories from Western Canada. In the 1990s, she edited three further collections of fiction—*Alberta ReBound*, *Boundless Alberta*, and *Due West*. "We have responsibilities as writers," van Herk explains. "I'm not just a writer out to write books and be famous and make money. I have a responsibility to my colleagues and to my readers and to my culture. I owe something to this community."

That sense of obligation and sharing is evident in the number of new writers she has shepherded since she began teaching at the university—Joan Crate, Rosemary Nixon, Suzette Mayr and Hiromi Goto. Looking back on her apprenticeship with Wiebe, she realizes that mentoring is not always a gentle process. "Rudy was my teacher and he was wonderful to me. He was an excellent supervisor but I had incredible fights with him. You have to fight with Rudy. That's the only way to have a relationship with him. He won' t respect you if you don' t fight with him." Although Wiebe was her *de facto* mentor since he was her official supervisor, she considers Robert Kroetsch, the writer who fled Salter's class, to be her "spiritual mentor."

While acknowledging the influence of Wiebe and Kroetsch on her, van Herk is modest in her assessment of her own influence on the younger generation of writers. Younger writers, she says, are not going "to see me in the same kind of power as my generation saw Rudy and Robert." Her modesty may be endearing but not accurate. In the past decade, she has nurtured a whole new generation of Alberta writers, including the acclaimed Calgary novelist, Hiromi Goto.

A Canadian of Japanese descent, Hiromi Goto won the Commonwealth Writers' Prize in 1995 for the best first book in the Caribbean and Canada region. Her novel, *Chorus of Mushrooms*, went on to win a second international prize, The Canada-Japan Book Award, the following year. The jury described *Chorus of Mushrooms* as conveying "an authentic sense of the difficulty experienced by a young Japanese-Canadian woman caught between the pull of assimilation and the hunger to come to terms with her Japanese heritage." Born in Chiba-ken Japan in 1966, Goto immigrated to British Columbia with her family at the age of three. They later settled in southern Alberta, where her father operated a mushroom farm. After taking her bachelor of arts at the U of C, she began taking creative writing classes, first with Fred Wah and then with van Herk. Goto considers this a time when her writing became politicized in terms of racial and feminist politics. "Taking those courses was a big influence," she says, "because suddenly I was working in a group and a community of writers."

Goto began *Chorus of Mushrooms* in the last fiction writing class she took with van Herk. Like *Judith*, it reflects the formative experiences of the novelist in which place, cultural identity and gender intertwine in a psychological drama. Like Wiebe's *Peace Shall Destroy Many*, Goto's first book has the author's ethnic background as its subject. And just as Salter helped Wiebe get published, van Herk was there for Goto. "I ended up with about 50 pages that I could actually keep from the manuscript when Aritha's class was over," Goto says. "Then I was talking to her outside of class and she said there was a deadline for NeWest coming up and why don't I hurry and finish it and hand it in. So I did, and they liked it."

In Salter's day, promising writers had to turn to Toronto for their first step on the road to fame, but now Alberta writers can garner international recognition right here at home. A case in point is Thomas Wharton, who studied writing at the U of A and is now a PhD student at the U of C. Wharton's 1995 novel, *Icefields*, about a turn-of-the-century mountaineering expedition, won a bevy of honours: the Commonwealth Writers' Prize for Best First Book in the Caribbean and Canada Region; the Writers Guild of Alberta Henry Kreisel Award for Best First Book; two awards at the Banff Mountain Book Festival; and a 1997 nomination for the Boardman-Tasker Award for mountain literature. *Icefields* sold well in Canada, the U.S., and Britain. As a native Albertan raised in the Rockies, Wharton's writing represents the Mitchell side of Salter's legacy in the same way that Goto's work and Wiebe's are symbolic of the ethnic and immigrant identity. Salter looked to both polarities for creative energy and literary achievement. In this sense, he was very much a Canadian seeking to define the distinctness of our character.

The nurturing of Alberta writers in university creative writing classes that Salter started in 1939 is still going strong nearly 60 years later. The U of A and the U of C have nationally renowned programs that produce talented writers. Both universities have writer-in-residence programs which bring nationally and internationally known writers to Alberta, enabling the tradition to be continually refreshed with new perspectives. The university's association with creative writing may bring the theoretical and ideological concerns of academia to bear on the writing. But this may also be a way of keeping the writing current and contemporary. The large number of award-winning writers to come out of both universities are a sign of the excellence of the work done there. The fundamental vision of how to grow writers through university programs—brought to Alberta by F.M. Salter—remains unchanged. The seeds that Salter sowed have grown into tall trees that continue to bear magnificent fruit generation after generation. Salter believed passionately that enthusiasm and good work went hand in hand. That his own enthusiasm for the written word continues to resonate after so many years is a tribute to his passion and the literary achievements of his students, their students, and students to come.

Interview with Rudy Wiebe:
CanLit in Time of COVID-19

Bianca Lakoseljac

April 20, 2022

Introduction: The following interview with author Rudy Wiebe—this Canadian legend whose writing I've admired for decades—was specially arranged for the collection, *Rudy Wiebe: Essays on His Works*. With the Covid-19 crisis and the distance between us—Wiebe lives in Alberta and I in Ontario—an e-mail interview seemed the best option.

Question 1. Bianca Lakoseljac: You have lived almost your entire life in prairie Canada, but your stories take place all over the world, from Canada's High Arctic and around the globe on four continents. Could you explain why this is so?

Answer 1. Rudy Wiebe: "Where is the Voice Coming from?" (Written in October, 1970, while I was working on *The Temptations of Big Bear*) is my most widely read story, and, I think, one of the most revealing about my writing instincts. The English word "where" demands "place"; in a lifetime of writing, the stories of people have come to me from places all over the globe because I have travelled, deliberately and widely, to look for them. To mention the most obvious novels only, and the main journeys that shaped them:

First and Vital Candle (1966): in particular, two months of travel, summer 1964, from Indiana, USA, to Winnipeg and on to Red Lake, Northern Ontario and the isolated Cree/Ojibwa settlements of Pikangikom, Deer Lake, Poplar Hill. Also the Cold War NATO Defense Headquarters deep in the rock mines below North Bay, Ontario. Journeys made by car and float plane; the daily journals both written and dictated are now in the University of Calgary Archives.

The Blue Mountains of China (1970): four months travel for our family of four, 1966, from Indiana USA to Asuncion, Paraguay and the various Mennonite Colonies and Indigenous people of the Gran Chaco—in particular with my Mennonite cousins in Village # 5 in Fernheim, and the Ayoreo bands of the northern Chaco desert— and shorter trips to Peru, Argentina, Uruguay, Brazil. Journey by train, jet plane, bus, jeep, horse and buggy, truck. Original autograph daily journal Sept. 1-Dec. 22, 1966 and notes, recordings, pictures, Ayoreo spears still in my possession.

The Temptations of Big Bear (1973): in Edmonton, spring 1970, I converted a used school bus into a travel home for our family of five and, whenever possible, throughout 1970–72 we explored the physical world where Big Bear's Plains Cree people lived hunting and trading until

1885: Alberta and Saskatchewan, from the Beaver River and Turtle Lake south through the Great Sand and Cypress Hills to the Missouri and Musselshell Rivers of Montana. Very detailed daily journals (esp. July 1—Aug 10, 1970), pictures, maps of roads/highways/trails travelled; including memories indelible beyond written record. For example: one midsummer night in 1971 I slept alone beside the Tramping Lakes and awoke into moonlight and the thunder of buffalo running deep in the earth, shining buffalo charging up out of the water of that long, slender lake in the Cree glory of their creation. All written files still in my possession.

A Discovery of Strangers (1994): July 5–25, 1988: a six-person three-canoe expedition retracing the 1821 route, through Dene lands, of the first Franklin Arctic exploration disaster between the Coppermine River and the tree-line site of Fort Enterprise. Detailed journals kept by me and son Chris of our journey from the tundra height of land at Obstruction Rapids and Starvation Lake to Winter Lake: tundra and eskers and ptarmigan and delicious Back's grayling and 21 triple or double portage carries and relentless bloody mosquitoes and runnable rapids and ptarmigan and Dogrib Rock and unending lake paddling—we saw no people nor a single caribou, though we heard a wolf howl—and the immense Snare River Falls and then, suddenly, out of the water horizon of Winter Lake we beheld the spires of a Gothic cathedral, rising. Struck dumb, we paddled furiously and the vision transformed itself into thick spruce crosses over three grave mounds on a tiny island, looming in the brilliant morning sky. Autograph daily journal, files, pictures in my possession.

Sweeter than All the World (2001): In 1929 my parents Abram and Katerina Wiebe with their 5 children were the only members of either family to escape Stalin's "paradise", but as the USSR began to disintegrate in the 1980's, year by year more of my relatives managed to emigrate to West Germany as Umsiedler (resettled). In June 1995, 8 of us Canadian Wiebes met over 300 Wiebe Umsiedler in Detmold to celebrate our amazing family's global heritage; in May—June, 1997 Tena and I flew to Orenburg, USSR, and visited the places of Mennonite settlement there and in Neu Samara where our ancestors once lived. The long steppes surrounding Village # 8, Romanovkva, where 70 years ago my brothers brought lunch to the Baskir horsemen herding village cattle— huge collective farm barns, original Mennonite house-barns (including Tena's father's and my uncle's), graveyards, KGB dungeons from which no one ever returned—pictures, scrawled notebooks of places, unreadable Russian maps, interviews in my possession.

To sum up: writers are often advised: "Write what you know." I agree, but, what I "know" is not merely what happens to me; it is also what I deliberately dig for. And often, when I do, I find worlds of story so rich there is no need to "make up" anything ... well, not much.

Q2. BL: Fire imagery runs through most of your writing. In your essay "Flowers for Approaching the Fire," a complex and powerful meditation on martyrdom, the fire image is explored from yet another perspective. I find myself fascinated, and yet perplexed, by the juxtaposition of flowers and fire imagery (Where the Truth Lies 281–298). The essay ends with a message to the reader: "When you are approaching the fire, remember this: flowers are your best, your only protection" (298). Could you explain?

A2. RW: The essay you mention was first given as a lecture to commemorate the martyrdom of Christians throughout history. This image of "flower" grows out of the 1527 story/legend [Martyrs Mirror, 1660] of the Anabaptist believer Leonard Keyser, whose body the prosecuting Austrian officials could not burn to death because, while being transported to the stake, he leaned down and picked a road-side flower to protect himself. That is: to be utterly, straightforwardly, imagistically simplistic about it, in Keyser's story, the seemingly fragile beauty of faith overcomes the church/state's brute physical power of fire and sword.

Q3. BL: In "Unearthing Language: An Interview with Rudy Wiebe and Robert Kroetsch," recorded by Shirley Neuman in April 1980, you use the term, "apprehension of perfection." Here is the sentence: "I think [a human being] is an animal capable of the apprehension of perfection" (AVITL 234). Could you explain the meaning of the term?

A3. RW: "Apprehension" is a marvellous, almost contradictory word, and it makes me happy to know that in a conversation long ago I found this perfect word for what I still feel very deeply. "Apprehension" can be a verb, a noun, or an adjective: here, spoken as a verb, it explains that we humans can both understand and grasp a vision of perfection, but at the same time we are anxious, fearful about it. Forty years after that talk with Bob, this "apprehension" (noun) is still with me: perfection is possible; dare I face it? I long for, and face that possibility every day of my life.

Q4. BL: In your novel, *Sweeter than All the World,* your character, Trijntjen, daughter of Weynken Claes (who was charged with heresy and burned to death in The Hague in 1527) describes the arrival of the Spanish soldiers who will arrest her mother:

> It was deep sunset when the Spanish soldiers in their steel helmets hammered on the gate of our farmstead. We had watched for them through the outside window. They came marching along the road on the dike, and the evening light burned red around them. They looked like one huge, thick monster that bristled spears and heads, different heads lifting out of it and pulling back in, heads human, then horse, then steel human again. Growing larger so fast. I had looked out on the dike road all my life, but they seemed to be coming low, flat, on a burnished sea of shining blood. (Wiebe 30–31)

How do you go about creating such powerful scenes—at once visual, emotional, and foreshadowing?

A4: RW: When you have been writing slowly, steadily on some long piece for many days (novels = years), there can be moments (lovely) when suddenly the words shift: from slow, laborious construction … change … more construction and tear-down—suddenly they shape-shift into something as it were blossoming out of themselves; when you can barely keep up typing with the flow. If that ever happens, well … let it stand: "STET" as an old-time proofreader would jot in the margin. Just be happy and thankful and shut up and type.

Q5. BL: Has the COVID-19 crisis affected what you write?

A5. RW: Didn't someone once say, "Old writers never die—they just fade away"? Well, in these unending months of dying I seem to be fading away into what might be poetry. The first, "Everything," begins with a line from my friend Bob Kroetsch; the second, "Hands," is written in a form I am trying to develop as unpunctuated "rectangular" poems. It appeared in Alberta Views Magazine, September 2020—the first poem I've published in over half a century.

Everything

"I'm getting old now," she said.
I had to laugh, "What do you get,
when you get 'old'?"
But she would not laugh.
"Life's so short," she eluded me,
    "there's never enough time to

forget everything."
"And you want to? Every thing?"
"Not every <u>thing</u>—everything."
"Why?"
"Then I'd even forget to want to remember."
"Good," I say, "forgetting is good at times …
        I just can't remember which times."
Now it is she who laughs, "But then you
        know you've forgotten … something …"
"What?"
We look at each other. This may well be
no laughing matter. Perhaps
both of us have already
gotten more than
enough
old.

        *****

hands in the time of pandemic

whyte avenue is a raw march photograph   nothing
moves   a pickup mutters at the intersection   no
person visible on blocks of sidewalk   only grey light-
wired trees only me held erect by my hands wobbly
search for two-cane balance so this is the world and
here i   the pickup leaps at the light

go home and stay home wash your hands droplets
physical distancing do not

the 104 street green light is long enough for my
shufobble walk a long one-cane man coming fast
shirtsleeves in the cold his right arm dangles like a
limp hose its bare hand flapping madly good
morning i say   good he says too near my left ear
good and miserable i turn slowly he strides on into
red o dearest god will my hand sink into that
trembling-aspen shudder

not touch your face self isolate COronaVIrusDisease
2019 *sanitize ppe stay*

mayday on 106 street offers three distanced joggers
also two dogs white bristle and tan smooth tugging
a brown girl reading her phone i rest in my wheeled
walker watch bristle's nose sweep the grass and stop
he pounds his shoulder down his paws claw him into
the smell of that spot while tan anoints an ash and the
girl's thumbs fly texting my blue hands inter-lace
themselves the infinity of things hands can do
beyond paws unimaginable

*stay the blazes home alta crude 3.72 a barrel work
from home we're all in*

yes sixty years ago i worked from home searching
for my first novel in a manual typewriter inside one
windowless room of our basement apartment on 109
street but today even in viral isolation a brown girl
with dogs can hold the known world in her hands
pocket it handy and snug on her buttocks

in this together flatten the curve 7 of 10 deaths in care homes face masks the

incredible   seven weeks shufobbling in old strathcona an hour a day and the change in my pocket is unchanged   but immeasurably more important is home   my scheene Taunte *lovely lady* in my first language in our 3 storey house where our daughter and granddaughter whose own house is 9 feet from ours excellent physical distancing come laughing to our back porch and hand us home-baked bread and groceries and the front-yard apple tree will bud with the first droplets of spring rain and we lift our hands to each other in love and wave the song without the words and never stop at

the new normal testing elbow bump caremongering ventilator virtual care

pestilence no human sense can find it all you need do is breathe you can also bow your head into your hands and pray o creator have mercy on us

MAYDAY 2020 COVID-19 PEOPLE edmonton 498 infected 12 dead alberta 5,573 infected 92 dead canada   55,573 infected 3,346 dead   world 3,420,000 infected 239,603 dead

no   these **countless** numbers shall never have the last word

trust   work   compassion   hope

Q6. BL: Do you continue to write?

A6. RW: Here are a couple of poems I've been working on. "Departure Level" was published in Brick 108. Inter 2022.

Departure Level

We are shaking hands at the Departure Level
door when Ove, the Norwegian translator,
leans close and breathes into my ear, "Remember.
Stay ahead of the wolves."
He already said that, yesterday, when we lay
along a log on a gravel bar in Strawberry Creek
         watching a beaver unroll its supper of white bark
off an aspen branch, its front paws turning the stem
between its bent teeth as if it were a four-foot corncob.
And then coyotes were howling. One pack
up the valley began to bark, yowl its mockery
         at a pack laughing high and franticly near the river.
We were surrounded. Their wild slivers of trickery
         bounced off the cliffs, shivered through bending
 willows and there came the moon, huge
as a domed wildfire rising out of the trees.
So I tell him again, "I've never heard a wolf
 in our valley." And he says, now, "I think
for you, here, Coyote is enough."
The airport door turns him inside. He will catch
a flight home to Tromso,
beyond the Arctic Circle.

         *****

The Question

Do you believe in God?

Why not?

That's my question: why would you?

Maybe because we need one?

God? Who needs that?

Maybe you do, you just don't—look, there's
the full moon rising out of the trees .... do you
need the moon?

It's beautiful, I'd miss it, ... but I don't
need it like I need water, or air or—

Maybe you do need it, very much, you just don't
know. My grade 9 granddaughter could tell you:
without the moon's gravity pull, the earth's spin, one
day, would last only about 6 hours, there'd be over
a thousand days in a year, we'd never get enough sleep to—

Hold it! If there had never been anything but a 6-hour
day, human beings would have evolved to fit that pattern
and it wouldn't bother us one little bit if—

Okay okay ... but what if it weren't there, now?

What?

What if, say, some human clumping around on the moon
accidently triggered a nuclear—

Accidently? More likely deliberate.

Okay … a nuclear chain reaction that in 5 minutes
13 seconds explodes the entire moon into space dust.
Nothing.

The orange moon is brooding on the molten tips
of the aspen. Someone, somewhere, is singing
wait and worship while the night
  sets her evening lamps alight
  through all the sky

I ask, again, Why not?

He says nothing. He is
staring at the moon.

Q7. BL: Your novel, *The Temptations of Big Bear*, is among
the most powerful stories I have read. During my graduate studies at York University, I took a course, Special
Topics: Frog Lake "Massacre"—1885. In addition to *The
Temptations*, I also read William Cameron's (1862–1951)
book, *The War Trail of Big Bear*, which you credit as the
source that propelled you to continue your research of
the Plains Cree chief Big Bear's life. In your essay, "With
the Flow," published in your collection of essays, *Where*

the Truth Lies (2016), you refer to the historical Big Bear as "a power in my life … [whose] … spirit began to live in my imagination beyond my knowing; and would remain" (18). Could you explain?

A7. RW: My relationship with the historical Big Bear has been one of the major thought/writing pilgrimages of my long life. Here's what I articulated about that in 2009; and I say now: let that stand: STET.

–Big Bear: the wise and brilliant Plains Cree chief who in 1876 refused to "touch the pen" to Treaty 6 because he recognized it gave the Canadian government control ("it was not given to us to have the rope about our necks") over everything Native (Morris 192). His complex life, and that of his many descendants to this day: the story of the continuing creation of our shared homeland Canada, and of justice for all, especially the Aboriginal People, from sea to sea to sea.

Oh, Big Bear; a power in my life. As if I continuously dreamed him—though I have never been conscious of that dreaming in my sleep; only when awake. As though, once I had climbed Bull's Forehead Hill above the confluence of the Red Deer and the South Saskatchewan Rivers—the place where in 1838—39 he was given his bear vision—and Elder John Tootoosis of the Poundmaker First Nation had shown me the place where his body was buried in 1888 on the bank of the Battle River, and in New York's American Museum of Natural History had held in my hands the core of his sacred bundle—the great bear paw complete with claws he had, as instructed in the vision, sewn onto a bib of red stroud—and I had been forgiven for opening the bundle cloths without knowing the proper songs to sing, nor prayers to prey, and alone, without a circle of believers to assist me: after that, his spirit began to live in my imagination beyond my knowing; and would remain. (18)

CONCLUSION: I would like to express my gratitude to Rudy Wiebe for agreeing to an interview which offers a broad perspective into his life as a distinguished author, academic, respected professor, and mentor. I feel privileged to have had the opportunity to get to know Rudy Wiebe (through our correspondence during the pandemic crisis and now the Russian invasion of Ukraine) as caring, supportive, and accommodating, always engaged with and concerned about the state of the world. I will always value the insights garnered from Wiebe's books and his wise words.

Fact vs. Fiction in Rudy Wiebe's
Where is the Voice Coming From

Milena Kaličanin

Abstract. Rudy Wiebe's collection of short stories *Where is the Voice Coming From* was first published in 1974. The mere fact that this collection has seen numerous new editions at the turn of the 21st century reflects its credibility in depicting contemporary indigenous phenomena. Apart from exploring the complex relationship of document, history and fiction, the well-known title story depicts two contrasted views on experiencing reality: the one that perceives it as a mysterious, almost mystical experience and is generally related to the oral culture of the Indigenous peoples, and the other that rests on the allegedly objective factual evidence of the white settlers. In his exploration of the conflict between the 'Almighty Voice' and the NorthWest Mounted police, which has been the subject of various conflicting accounts, Wiebe examines the process of turning events into stories and expresses his doubts about their historical accuracy. In that, he comes close to the view of various postcolonial literary critics, who generally oppose the trend of falsifying reality by relying on the objectivity of historical reports as the only way of experiencing and decoding the past.

In 1968, the Kenyan novelist, Ngugi wa Thiong'o, demanded the abolition of the English department at the University of Nairobi. This appeal, quite unexpected and revolutionary for the historical moment it originated in, was further approved by a great number of the Kenyan intelligentsia, university professors, creative artists and critical thinkers, who passionately recommended marginalizing British writing in a European survey course and encouraged students to attend instead the course in Modern African Literature. Behind this proposal, as Marx rightfully claims, "lay the idea that literature is a privileged representative of custom and belief that anthropologists call culture" (Marx 2004, p. 85). The insistent reference on the African literary perspective would enable students "to recover distinctly African ways of seeing which habituation to European texts had corrupted" (Marx 2004, p. 85), that afterwards became a rather compelling argument in Ngugi's highly influential study *Decolonizing the Mind* (1986), where literature is perceived as a "collective memory bank of people's experience in history ... that creates a whole conception of ourselves as people" (Ngugi 1986, p. 15 quoted in Marx 2004, p. 86). Since literature mediates our relationship to the world, it is logical that if we read about it in English, we will eventually perceive it differently than if we read it in one of the African languages or dialects. It was precisely this reason that Ngugi had on his mind when he strictly proposed that all English Departments in Africa should be abolished and that English should be avoided as a medium of literary expression on the part of African writers.

These claims, later rightly acknowledged as the crucial part of postcolonial literary and critical outlook, came along with the constant questioning of the relationship between the Western literary canon and postcolonial texts in the 1980s and 1990s worldwide. Most common conceptions regarding this problematic relationship relate to the notion that any instance of postcolonial writing basically repudiates the canon; "accordingly, readers have become well practiced in treating work from Europe's former colonies as the antithesis of canonical writing and as an instrumental component in efforts to recover oral and print traditions that imperialism threatened to obliterate" (Marx 2004, p. 83). Apart from this well-spread notion, there is yet another popular belief that postcolonial literature mostly deals with the revision and rewriting of canonical texts in order to emphasize the marginalized Other, usually not given enough space or simply misinterpreted in the dominant literary canon.

The frequent reliance on imperial remainders is definitely a common trait in postcolonial writing. Ngugi was, of course, not the first writer and critic from the colonial world who established the foundations of postcolonial writing and criticism, but his work in this sphere can rightly be given the epithet of pioneering. Bearing all these notions in mind, this paper focuses on the work of Rudy Wiebe, or the title story from his short story collection *Where is the Voice Coming From* first published in 1974, to be precise. The mere fact that this collection has seen numerous new editions at the turn of the 21st century reflects its credibility in depicting contemporary postcolonial, as well as indigenous phenomena.

Although a descendant of the Russian Mennonite family in Canada and thus a true-born Canadian himself, Wiebe was deeply influenced with the white settlers' treatment of Canadian indigenous population, and, as a consequence, his writing is tremendously affected with the vivid depiction of postcolonial issues. This is probably due to the fact that as an offspring of a Mennonite family, Wiebe himself felt basically isolated from the mainstream trends in Canadian culture and education; namely, for thirteen years he lived in an isolated community of about 250 people, as part of the last generation of homesteaders to settle the Canadian west, and did not speak English until the age of six. It is no wonder, therefore, that Wiebe intuitively recognized the closeness to Yvonne Johnson, an Aboriginal woman, who provided inspiration for his stories about the Aboriginal past of Canada. Wiebe's obsession with his personal Mennonite heritage and Canadian Aboriginal past represent the main spheres of his literary interest, with a particular emphasis on the potent urge to understand and make sense of the common trait of both cultures—the gloomy fact that they are almost extinct nowadays.

Considering the previously mentioned characteristics of postcolonial literature as the one that repudiates and revises the canon by mostly recovering oral testimonies of the colonized, the ones whose voices have not adequately been represented in the Western literary canon, Wiebe's story, *Where is the Voice coming From?*, commences with his frank confession that "the problem is to make the story" (Wiebe 1974, p. 92). By deliberately breaking all the valid conventions in short story writing, especially the existence of logical data such as a proper beginning, middle and end of the story, as well as an appropriate setting, characterization and plot, Wiebe shares with the readers his insights into the problem of story making. The relevant quotations from the French philosopher de Chardin (his claim that people in general tend to perceive themselves as mere spectators and not elements in the events that surround them) and English historian Toynbee (his shrewd observation that reality represents the undifferentiated unity of mystical experience) are masterfully inserted at the very beginning of Wiebe's story in order to portray the author's personal dilemma related to the way he tells the story of the Almighty Voice and his conflict with the NorthWest Mounted police: the tension between his task as a historical reporter of the given event or its artistic interpreter, creative story-maker.

By using this literary technique, Wiebe deliberately engages his readers in the narrator's challenge thus making them not mere observers, but active participants in the act of story-making. The readers are supposed to use the existing story fragments and perceive them as pieces of a puzzle whose final design still remains mysterious, whereas the narrator basically functions as a catalyst for the conclusion in this universal quest for truth and meaning:

> Presumably all the parts of the story are themselves available. A difficulty is that they are, as always, available only in bits and pieces. Though the acts themselves seem quite clear, some written reports of the acts contradict each other. As if these acts were,

> at one time too well-known; as if the original
> nodule of each particular fact had from somewhere
> received non-factual accretions; or even more, as if,
> since the basic facts were so clear perhaps there were
> a larger number of facts than still simply told by
> this mouth to that ear, of course, even less can be
> expected. (Wiebe 1974, p. 93)

"The bits and pieces" of the conflict between the Almighty Voice and the NorthWest Mounted police are gradually revealed: the narrator starts his inquisitive search for the genuine truth and meaning of this almost forgotten story, in the fashion of a proper journalist dissatisfied with the given evidence and factual recordings of the event, intuitively sensing that there is a great shady area in the story left for him to explore and finally decode. The seemingly objective course of the tragic event is officially explained in the following manner: a Cree Indian got accused of stealing a cow, he was evading arrest and was eventually machine-gunned in a shallow trench from which he was defending himself.

However, the narrator genuinely perceives a striking antagonism between the two separate versions of the identical event; on the one hand, there is the factual evidence that would be seriously considered in every Western court of law: official documents from the trial to the undisciplined "Injun", the museum in which the remaining objects of the tragedy are exhibited (samples of skull, weapons of the police officers involved in the plot, old photos, etc.) and the policemen's cemetery nearby; on the other hand, the narrator becomes aware of the significant indigenous oral tradition (Cree songs and legends dedicated to the brave resistance of the Almighty Voice) and the interesting fact that the rebel's grave is surprisingly nowhere to be found. Thus, the potent discrepancy between the European and indigenous point of view in description of the identical event basically points to the significant difference of the given cultures, their inconsistent comprehension of history, oral and written tradition, etc.

A dominant trait in Wiebe's story represents the notion that the white settlers unquestioningly assume the superior position in their recording of history, while the narrator bravely probes the version of truth they unanimously offer and simultaneously offers its new versions. The mere fact that the narrator uses the reported facts and creates a work of art based on them, testifies to Wiebe's initial desire to go beyond the crude and dubiously objective message of history in order to liberate an indigenous voice, visionary in its origin. Apart from the relevant issue of the objectivity of recorded historical events, a very important postcolonial question of appropriation is thus raised in Wiebe's story.

The white settlers' assumption of the superior position regarding the authenticity of the given historical event in Wiebe's story can be connected with the basic theses in Said's postcolonial theory. Edward Said, in his study *Orientalism* (1994), claims that Orientalism presents a Western style of dominating, restructuring and having authority and power over the Orient or 'Other'. (Said 1994, p. 3) As a result of this unfair power balance, the Orient is not a free subject of thought or action.

(Said 1994, p. 3) In effect, the unequal relationship between the Occident (the West) and the Orient (the 'Other'), causes the white-European culture to gain in strength and identity by setting itself up against the orient culture. (Said 1994, p. 3) The Oriental is seen as being irrational, depraved, childlike and 'different', whereas the European is seen as rational, virtuous, mature and 'normal'. (Said 1994, p. 40) This constructed binary opposition contains a warning against the so called 'innocent' representation of cultural differences on the surface level, and points to various acts of falsifications, exclusions and selections carried out by the colonizers, usually perceived as invisible, and thus, allegedly non-existent.

A good illustration of Said's claims is in Wiebe's story portrayed through the complete discrepancy between the official description and remaining photo of the indigenous fugitive. Namely, according to the official documents, the Almighty Voice is depicted as a plain Indian, approximately 22 years old, with "complexion inclined to be fair, wavy dark hair to shoulders...sharp features and parrot nose with flat tip, scar on left cheek running from mouth towards ear, feminine appearance" (Wiebe 1974, p. 95). "The ultimate problem in making the story" (Wiebe 1974, p. 95), as the narrator wisely informs us, lies in the fact that the Almighty Voice's photo shows a totally different figure than the one described in the official documents:

> ... nothing can be seen of a scar, the hair is not
> wavy and shoulder-length but hangs almost to the
> waist in two thick straight braids worked through

with beads, fur, ribbons and cords...and no face is more *man* than his face. The mouth, the nose, the clenched brows, the eyes—the eyes are large, yes and dark, but even in this watered-down reproduction of unending reproductions of that original, a steady look into those eyes cannot be endured. It is a face like an ax. (Wiebe 1974, p. 95)

In his influential study *Culture and Imperialism* (1993), Said suggests that it is often the postcolonial society that tends to oversimplify the intent of past imperialistic powers. By this oversimplification, there are attempts to justify the view of European hegemony that was used as a mechanism to bring about colonial rule, therefore separating the colonial intent from colonized impact. In other words, the process of colonization is mostly presented as a justified act, because it is undertaken for the sake of spreading civilization to savages, civilizing the brutes, converting the heathen, or, to borrow Alice Miller's phrase— it is undertaken "for their own good" (Miller 2002).

If we apply this idea to Wiebe's story, the utter inconsistency in the Almighty Voice's official description and remaining photo fits into Said's calculated colonial intent scheme: in the colonizer's appropriation of the native land and culture, no resistance on the part of the Aboriginal population is approved of since it would represent a valid recognition of the white settlers' illegitimate claims. Accordingly, any attempt at heroic and honorable opposition to them should be obliterated, or, at least, diminished, legally twisted, historically forged and formally ridiculed. Hence, instead of realistically portraying the dignified, warrior-like posture of the Almighty Voice, the official data put an emphasis on his alleged feminine appearance. Furthermore, the derisive song of the officials, the policemen who arrested the rebelling Indian *("hey Injun you'll get/hung/for stealing that steer/hey Injun for killing that government cow you'll get three/weeks on the woodpile hey Injun",* Wiebe 1974, p. 96) is purposefully left out from the official historical recordings.

Thus, apart from exploring the complex relationship of document, history and fiction, the well-known title story depicts two contrasted views on experiencing reality: the one that perceives it as a mysterious, almost mystical experience and is generally related to the oral culture of the Indigenous peoples, and the other that rests on the allegedly objective factual evidence of the white settlers. In his exploration of the conflict between the 'Almighty Voice' and the NorthWest Mounted police, which has been the subject of various conflicting accounts, Wiebe critically examines the process of turning events into stories and expresses his doubts about their historical accuracy. In that, he comes close to the view of previously mentioned postcolonial literary critics, who generally oppose the trend of falsifying reality by relying on the dubious objectivity of historical reports as the only way of experiencing and decoding the past. The process of falsifying reality is usually successfully achieved by introducing negative stereotyping regarding the indigenous population. The stereotypical one-sided perception of the Native American population that basically legitimizes and justifies the process of colonizing the Other actually boils down to the feature that Terry Goldie described as 'fear' (Goldie 1989, p. 215). The hypocritical projection of the colonizers' own cultural values and customs onto the Other (including the mere falsification of truth, exclusion of facts and selective legality), has suitably complemented the fearsome, raw, unrefined and unsophisticated aspect of the Indigenous peoples that was utterly difficult to be accepted by the civilized, refined and sophisticated Europeans.

The narrator in Wiebe's story gradually becomes aware of this sharp inconsistency in the official representation of truth. Experiencing a sort of a moral dilemma of whether to conform to the official version of the truth or to offer his artistic insight into what actually happened to the Almighty Voice, he resorts to Aristotle for help. One of the most famous quotations from Aristotle refers to the difference between the historian and the poet, the former relating what has happened, the latter what may happen. The narrator realizes that these statements cannot truly explain the storyteller's activity since, as he claims,

> despite the most rigid application of impersonal investigation, the elements of the story have now run me aground. If ever I could, I can no longer pretend to objective, omnipotent disinterestedness. I am no longer *spectator* of what *has* happened or what *may* happen: I am become *element* in what is happening at this very moment (Wiebe 1974, p. 96).

In other words, the narrator/the author becomes personally involved in the tragic event and finds it necessary to offer the indigenous perspective on it, to give voice to the Indian fugitive, ominously lacking in the official documents. Therefore, he concludes that "the sound of his speaking is there even it has never been recorded in an official report" (Wiebe 1974, p. 96). Finally, the story ends with the image of the Almighty Voice, ambushed in the gully, singing his rebellious and dignified warrior song (*"We have fought well/You have died like braves"*, Wiebe 1974, p. 97). The narrator of the story is completely taken in by his creative vision of heroic indigenous resistance and presents it as the authentic vision of the tragic event:

> And there is a voice. It is an incredible voice that rises from among the young poplars ripped of their spring bark, from among the dead somewhere lying there, out of the arm-deep pit shorter than a man; a voice rises over the exploding smoke and thunder of guns that reel back in their positions, worked over, serviced by the grimed motionless men in bright coats and glinting buttons, a voice so high and clear, so unbelievably high and strong in its unending wordless cry...I say 'wordless cry' because that is the way it sounds to me. I could be more accurate if I had a reliable interpreter who would make a reliable interpretation. For I do not, of course, understand Cree myself. (Wiebe 1974, p. 97)

Through "the wordless cry" of a courageous Indian who jumps out of the ravine and sings a powerful song of defiance, the narrator brings together all the important themes in his story: the white settlers' and indigenous relationship towards the imperialist past, progressive dying of an Aboriginal nation, utter loss of the First nations' community and, finally, the unwilling alienation of an individual. The end of the story also gives a powerful expression to a striking paradox that the narrator gradually becomes aware of—the sense that while the act of turning historical events into stories, supposed facts into fiction, may be falsifying (the way historical records can be, as already discussed in the paper), it may be our only way of experiencing the past.

This is precisely the reason why the journalist leaves his version of the story open-ended: he purposefully projects himself into an unreliable narrator, who cannot speak and understand Cree, thus implying that the story he described represents only his private version of the historical event. The potent implication in his conclusion is, of course, that his version of the story should not be regarded as the sole, unequivocal and indisputable truth about the Almighty Voice's personal rebellion (the way the official historical recordings professed), but only a single variant of a given event that may lead to its further diverse interpretations. The common ground for the future (postcolonial, among others) decipherments should unquestionably represent the prophetic and visionary voice of the defiant Indian, obstinately resisting appropriation, finally liberated and ready to be heard.

However, the mere fact that the story of defying appropriation on the part of the indigenous population in

Canada is told by an offspring of the white settlers has triggered off a great amount of negative criticism and legitimate questioning. This notion brings us back to Ngugi's argument, dealt with at the beginning of this paper, about frequent misrepresentations of indigenous population in postcolonial writing if it solely relies on the English language as a medium of its expression. For instance, E.F. Dyck offers a definition of the phrase "appropriation of voice" as it is used in Canadian literary criticism: "it almost always refers primarily to 'theft' of an ethnic group's 'story' by an outsider" (Dyck 1998, p. 30 quoted in Dueck 2001, p. 147). This definition, quoted in the paper "From Whom is the Voice Coming? Mennonites, First Nations People and Appropriation of Voice" by Jonathan Dueck from the University of Alberta, insists on the notions of "voice" and the idea of story as an ethnic property. Relying on the idea that social identities are always defined in the relation to an Other (Rew and Campbell 1999, p. 13 quoted in Dueck 2001, p. 147), Dueck further claims that:

> while stories themselves may flow freely and in objective terms may seem to be without an "owner", they are centrally implicated in the construction of social identity, and as such, groups lay claim to the stories which seem to lay claim to them. That is, a story by which First Nations identity is narrated seems to be the property of the First Nations people, since it is a part of the act of asserting identity and thus not distinct from that identity, at least in the act of narration (Dueck 2001, p. 147)

It remains a question, then, whether or not *Where is the Voice Coming From?* is seen "from the inside" (Dueck 2001, p. 147), to use Dueck's phrase, as Wiebe's appropriation of the indigenous story. Finally, Dueck expresses his genuine belief that this issue is basically non-essential and far from universal and benevolently concludes that "while ideas of appropriation of voice...can be applied strategically—that is, speaking concerning a particular construction of ethnic boundaries at a specific time, rather than speaking of essential ethnic characteristics— these formulations must be subjected to specific historical and material critiques" (Dueck 2001, p. 155). Dueck's constructive reasoning in this sphere definitely corresponds to the interpretation of Wiebe's story offered in this paper: namely, what is important is the fact that contrasted versions of the identical historical event are represented, various voices are uncovered and heard, thus deliberately leaving an empty space for its future interpretations, bearing in mind the author's intentional use of the medium of unreliable narrator and the story's open-ended conclusion. After all, as a contemporary Scottish novelist James Robertson has rightfully noticed, "you should trust the story...the storyteller might dissemble and deceive, the story can't: the story can only ever be itself." (Robertson 2010, p. 34)

References:

Dueck, J. (2001). From Whom is the Voice Coming? Mennonites, First Nations People and Appropriation of Voice. *Journal of Mennonite Studies*. Volume 19, pp. 144–157.

Dyck, E.F. (Nov. 1998). Thom Wiens to Yvonne Johnson: Rudy Wiebe's Appropriate Voice? *Rhubarb* 1: l, pp. 29–33.

Goldie, T. (1989). *Fear and Temptation: Images of the Indigene in Canadian, Australian and New Zealand Literatures.* Kingston, On: McGill-Queen's UP.

Marx, J. (2004). Postcolonial Literature and Western Literary Canon. In Neil Lazarus (Ed.), *The Cambridge Companion to Postcolonial Literary Studies.* Cambridge: Cambridge University Press.

Miller, A. (2002). *For Your Own Good: Hidden Cruelty in Child-Rearing and the Roots of Violence.* New York: Farrar—Straus—Giroux.

Rew A., & Jolin R. C. (1999) Political economy of Identity and Affect, pp. 13–20, in Alan Rew and John R. Campbell (Eds.), *Identity and Affect: Experiences of Identity in a Globalising World.* London: Pluto Press.

Robertson, J. (2010). *And the Land Lay Still.* UK: Hamish Hamilton.

Said, E.W. (1994). *Orientalism.* New York: Vintage Books.

Said, E.W. (1993). *Culture and Imperialism.* New York: Vintage Books.

Wa Thiong'o, N. (1986). *Decolonizing the Mind: The Politics of Language in African Literature.* London: Heinemann Educational Books.

Wiebe, R. (1974). *Where is the Voice Coming From?* Toronto: McClelland and Stewart.

Memoir and the Re-reading of Fiction: Rudy Wiebe's *of this earth* and *Peace Shall Destroy Many*

Paul Tiessen

> *We shall not cease from exploration*
> *And the end of all our exploring*
> *Will be to arrive where we started*
> *And know the place for the first time.*
> —T.S. ELIOT, "LITTLE GIDDING"

"That was so long ago, it is almost no longer so," is the English version of the "Mennonite proverb" that Canadian novelist Rudy Wiebe (b. 1934) uses as one of the two epigraphs to his award-winning 2006 memoir, *of this earth: A Mennonite Boyhood in the Boreal Forest*. The epigraph is rooted in the Low German of Wiebe's people, people who in the late 1700s moved from the Vistula Delta (where they had moved 200 years before from the Netherlands) to Russia and (as in the case of his parents) to Canada between 1923 and 1930: "Daut wia soo lang tridj, daut es meist nijch meea soo." His second epigraph is from "Conversation #2," taken from Robert Kroetsch's *The Snowbird Poems*: "What do you do for a living, I asked. / I remember, she replied."[1]

---

1. In a Foreword to his novel *Peace Shall Destroy Many*, Wiebe

provides a one-page description of the historic origins of the Mennonites in the novel, who stem from early Anabaptists: "The Anabaptists of the sixteenth century were the extreme evangelical wing of the Reformation movement. The name 'Mennonite' was early attached to them, after Menno Simons, their sole early theological leader to survive persecution.... They were driven from Switzerland to America, from Holland and northern Germany to Prussia, then Russia, finally to North and South America. Wherever they went they carried peculiar customs, a peculiar language, a peculiar faith in the literal meaning of the Bible.... The Mennonites portrayed in this book ... could belong to any one of several groups that came to Canada from Russia in the 1920s." These are also the Mennonites of *of this earth*.

In 2007 Wiebe won the $25,000 Charles Taylor Prize for Literary Non-Fiction for *of this earth*. During his career Wiebe, who has received many honours, has twice won the Canadian Governor General's Award for Fiction: in 1973 for his novel *The Temptations of Big Bear*; in 1994 for his novel *A Discovery of Strangers*. This year (2009) Wiebe, who lives in Edmonton, Alberta, received the $30,000 Lieutenant Governor of Alberta Distinguished Artist Award. Wiebe is a Member of the Order of Canada.

My essay is based on my presentation to a special session on Canadian Mennonite Literature organized by the Christianity and Literary Study Group and held at the annual meetings of the Association of Canadian College and University Teachers of English in May 2009 at Carleton University in Ottawa. It echoes some of the concerns about subjectivity, identity, and naming in my earlier essay, "The Naming of Rudy Wiebe," *Journal of Mennonite Studies* 7 (1989): 115–22 (which was published also in *Short Fiction in the New Literatures in English*. Ed. Jacqueline Bardolph. Nice: 1989. 133–39). It is a companion essay to my recently-published "[T]here are certain things Mennonite children are kept from seeing': Sexuality, Seeing, and Saying in Rudy Wiebe's *of this earth* and *Peace Shall Destroy Many*," *Journal of Mennonite Studies* 26 (2008): 133–42. There I explore, in part, Thom's yearning for a discourse concerning matters of sex and romance: "Words about sex in *Peace Shall Destroy Many* emerge, when they emerge at all, only indirectly, in fits and starts, sometimes furtively and slyly, sometimes obscenely and vulgarly. Any

With these epigraphs drawing attention to remembering and narrating, Wiebe invites the reader to move forward into the warm subjective interiority of his memoir, where he recounts his growing-up years, from birth to age thirteen. It is a memoir suffused in fantasy-like beauty and delicate softness, with the adult "rememberer" (re-)constructing the sensate freshness of a child's ways of seeing, touching, and, not least, hearing. It is, at the same time, a memoir of a Christian community of a sort that is ideal for a growing child: safe, sensitive, generous, supportive, hard-working, spiritually and socially stimulating, emotionally warm and accepting.

---

tender words about sex, about sexual attraction, are sought in vain by the protagonist, Thom Wiens, for the language of tender expression remains an inexpressible fantasy. When Thom wants to speak with his pal about a girl he finds attractive, 'to merely talk about her in an uninhibited manner as about anyone else,' he finds that the social presuppositions of his world do not admit the structuring or expression of that kind of talk: 'If people would just mention things about her,' he thinks to himself, his mind on the beautiful Annamarie Lepp; 'but single Mennonite men did not talk at length about girls to one another.' Though 'longing desperately' to speak of girls, the two male friends, automatically censoring what they say, turn quickly to 'talking casually about the harvest.' In this first of his major works beginning to write a Mennonite history of sex as a word, a word that can not be spoken, Wiebe represents the word with a dash, the dash—cold, stiff, detached—providing a chasm representing that which cannot be said. There is, here, no revelling in a liberated sense of the spirit or the senses."

For a detailed study of Wiebe's language, especially his interest in "monoglossic" and "heteroglossic" discourses, see Penny van Toorn, *Rudy Wiebe and the Historicity of the Word* (Edmonton: University of Alberta Press, 1995).

Surprisingly, however, and without overt warning of any kind, with these epigraphs Wiebe, in taking us forward, simultaneously invites us to look back. Through gestures of intertextuality within the memoir, he nudges us into considering one of his literary worlds that has largely bypassed readers' attention, most crucially the world of the child in his first novel, *Peace Shall Destroy Many*. It has bypassed readers' attention because it is a world that he hinted at yet simultaneously held in abeyance forty-four years earlier, in that 1962 novel. I am thinking of the barely-glimpsed world, in that novel, of young Hal Wiens. The virtually sinless and prelapsarian world of the memoir is a large version of the wondrous world of the idealistic young Hal, but Hal's world is sharply constrained, his voice pinched back. Further, Hal's is a world that is overwhelmingly eclipsed by the severe world of the novel's troubled protagonist, Hal's nineteen-year old brother, Thom Wiens. Thus, we get to know Hal's world fully, as it were, only in the memoir.

The memoir provides us with ingredients and signposts that implicitly or explicitly direct us to that 1962 novel, the meanings of which Wiebe in essence urges us to understand anew. In its entering into conversation with the novel, the memoir gives us the sense that a vital if barely-noticeable subjectivity teems beneath the jagged surfaces of the sternly programmatic bulk and thrust of that austere early novel, a novel concerning the blind language of power and control in a small religious community in a remote corner of Saskatchewan. There, most of our attention is taken up by bitter and confrontational moments along its spiritually stark vistas where cacophonous confusion and conflict of various adult voices prevail.[2]

Whether we let the epigraphs deliver us forward into the 2006 memoir or, in effect, back to selected portions of the 1962 novel, they carry us to the rhythms and cadences of an idyllic world that tugs at our own yearnings for innocence. It is true that Wiebe recognizes that such a world can belong only to the child, and then, to be sure, only to the child recalled by the adult—but nonetheless it is a world that, without irony, he presents and realizes in its fullness in the memoir. It is a world suffused with the wonders of language, and shaped by the sounds of the voice.

Wiebe explains his understanding of a child's relation to language—first the sounds, then the meanings—at many points in the memoir. He suggests that a child at birth falls into a kind of language bath, an "immersion of words" (*of this earth* 131). Wiebe as memoirist revels in the texture and aura that his family and community and

---

2. The blurb on the back cover summarizes the concerns of *Peace Shall Destroy Many*: "Fleeing from privation and hardship in Russia, a small group of Mennonites have settled in the rich farming lands of Saskatchewan during the years of the Depression. The community has thrived, while still adhering to its ancient traditions and beliefs. / Then comes the year 1944, and into the lives of a people dedicated to peace and non-violence come the increasingly powerful threats and challenges from the war-torn world outside. Through a careful weaving of events, Mr. Wiebe reveals the violence that lurks just beneath the surface in the lives of this Mennonite community. The ebb and flow of times and events and their effect on this intensely religious people are described in passages of power and great vibrancy."

church produced with the lavish soundscape of their words and songs. He uses limpid layers of language to let words from the past sift through and mingle with his play of words in the present. "Herr, Gott, du bist unsere Zuflucht für und für" he writes in his prologue, "Lord, God, you have been our refuge in all generations." Words such as these from Psalm 90 he heard, read aloud and recited, at home and in church, "before [he] could speak any language" (3). Words were at the heart of the sensory net into which he fell as a child.

In *Peace Shall Destroy Many*, a parallel soundscape is intermittently present in the ethos that defines young Hal. But it is the mainly world of Thom that we hear and feel in the novel. However, Thom has difficulty in hearing and feeling his own world, so bereft is he of any language that he might require for such understanding. Tragically, the dynamics of the community in which he lives have stripped him of a complexly nuanced and subtly analytical and humanely critical language that he only fumblingly seeks. Hal, younger and not yet any kind of threat to the power structures in the community of the novel, can get away with expressing an excess of unbridled and undisciplined language. For Thom, the community's strict dogma and discipline have led him to a scarcity of words, a shortage of linguistic expression, a paucity of narrative choices, and have reduced the range of his emotional life.[3]

---

3. That the dominant trajectory and tone of *Peace Shall Destroy Many* offer a world at odds with those of the memoir is established by its epigraph, which stands imperturbably and

What makes an examination of the novel in light of the memoir particularly compelling and urgent (and, to be sure, ironic) is the essentially autobiographical nature of both texts. The novel's material setting—its place in Saskatchewan, its time, its demographic, and, implicitly, many of its people—is more or less identical to that of the memoir, published 44 years later. Hence, if we come to the exuberant memoir after having read the acerbic novel, we might at first wonder at Wiebe's uninhibited sense of rejoicing—of his awe at the very nature of the grandeur and mystery of existence even in physically difficult times—that is sustained throughout the very long text of the memoir.

But some of the memoir's details—the overlapping subjectivity with the "Hal" portions of the novel, or allusions to parallel images or events in the novel—make clear that Wiebe would have us re-read those portions of the novel and, in the end, re-read and understand afresh the novel as a whole. With the memoir, then, Wiebe provides a bold and dramatic invitation to re-think his controversial first novel with which he came to public prominence nearly a half-century ago. It is an invitation to re-enter and explore again certain lyrical layers of the novel where plot and story and narrative trajectory seem to come to a stop, and where poetic utterance, an

---

starkly at odds with the epigraphs of the memoir. Embedding the words of the novel's title, the epigraph is an Old Testament passage, drawn from Daniel 8: "And in the latter time, a king / shall stand up. / And his power shall be mighty / and he shall prosper. / And he shall magnify himself in his heart, / and by peace shall destroy many: / But he shall be broken without hand."

unbridled embrace of the joy of sensual existence within a natural idyll of sky and tree, wind and water, begin.

* * *

Thom Wiens's interior world, which dominates the novel, is one of painful edges. It is objectified in whatever causes him to stumble when he "feel[s] something abrupt against his boot" (*Peace* 82) rising out of a swamp just beyond the slough where he and his friend Pete Block are cutting hay. Pete, seeing Thom trip, offers a dully pragmatic response: "'Shouldn't be any rocks here in the swamp'" (82). It is, in fact, not a rock, but a skull. Thom, who surmises that it must come from a wood-buffalo, imagines, too, that it might fit in to the story of some unknown Indian hunter decades ago (83). He laments that the words to tell such a story are not accessible to him nor, seemingly, to anyone in Canada: "Not one remembered word of how generations upon generations [of Indians] lived and died" (83). Thom is aware that about "white men" (82) there is a plenteous supply of words in the "'stacks of European history books to read'" (83).

Pete, at ease with the community's prejudices against Indians, challenges Thom's would-be imaginative flight through space and time and a possible—perhaps golden—Indian past by reducing the focus to the here and now. He scoffs at Thom's yearning for story-telling by scoffing at the Indians on the neighbouring reserve who, he says, would stoop to any kind of subterfuge just to steal five chickens from his dad. Thom is shocked by the incommensurability of the two themes, the infinite vastness of a unique but unknown history against the "conventional triviality" summed up by Pete's anxiety over missing five chickens. But he cannot find the means—the story, any story—to respond to Pete's reductive criteria for understanding an Other. Frustratedly recognizing his incapacity to respond with words, "Thom hurled the skull as far as he could" (*Peace* 83), so that it might lie safely in the still-unmown hay on the next piece of land, which belongs to his own family, and await the arrival there perhaps of some new language. Pete, held back by his dull imagination, only snorts at Thom, telling him that it will ruin his mower when he runs over it. Thom is filled with anger, but is trapped in his claustrophobic feeling of inarticulate confusion.[4]

When Thom's own hay mower later gets caught not on that skull but on the root of a tree, his neighbour, the kindly Pastor Lepp leaves his own mower to come over to help Thom. Suddenly: "Without warning, without looking up, Thom said, "What are the traditions of the

---

4. The recently departed schoolteacher, Joseph Dueck, who is present in the novel in epistolary and flashback formulations, does provide a model of eloquent articulation and visionary thought. His spirit hovers over the novel, but he is absent from the narrative diegetic.

It is interesting to note that already in *Peace Shall Destroy Many* Wiebe alluded to the story of Big Bear (111). In *of this earth* Wiebe marvels at his ignorance at travelling, without knowing the significance, at age eleven and a half, on a bus alongside Indian lands where Big Bear had been born 120 years before. Yet Big Bear would, says Wiebe, bringing to mind much of his work, including his *The Temptations of Big Bear*, "someday inhabit half a century of my personal, my writing, life" (*of this earth* 325).

fathers?" (*Peace* 86). The pastor is startled, but nonetheless sympathetically engages Thom in a lengthy conversation about the beliefs and actions of the local church community. Privately, he claims that he wishes for Thom an effective English-language mission in teaching children from the Indian community. However, he declares that, when he speaks from the pulpit on a Sunday, and speaks exclusively in German, he must side with the rigid structures of that community. Thom is startled by the gentle pastor's capacity for moving so illogically and tight-heartedly against his own private sensibilities.

Pastor Lepp and Pete Block, like other adults of Thom's religious community drawn inexorably into the tight orbit of the church, are obsessively controlled by Pete's father, Deacon Peter Block, who polices both the language and the silences in the community. Although both Pastor Lepp and the young Pete Block are at intervals close to the serious and sincere Thom Wiens, they demonstrate soon enough that they belong to the fear-driven camp of the "massively domineering" Deacon ("An author speaks" 65). Thom is endlessly stymied by these people who are controlled by Deacon Block, people who produce in him his seething crisis of spirit and conscience, and so alienate and isolate him inside his own tormented mind and body. Wiebe uses the "uncertain ... confused ... ambivalent" Thom to pursue what is for him the "quest for truth" at the heart of the narrative ("An author speaks" 65), but it is a quest that Thom does not have the language to fulfill.

Speaking to an audience at the University of Manitoba's St. John's College twenty-five years after the publication of *Peace Shall Destroy Many*, Wiebe provided touch-stones in the novel that I shall pick up in this essay. He alluded repeatedly to the episode of Thom standing in the hay slough and contemplating the buffalo skull, and seemed to intimate that there was something of the novel-ist—of an early version of Rudy Wiebe himself, as it were—in that moment. It was a moment that included, for Thom, the rudiments of story-telling, for, as Wiebe put it, "that half-rotted skull does suggest greater possibil-ities." That moment, with the skull in his hands, lets Thom begin to sense something beyond "mere bone," beyond even the once-massive body of the beast, right to an incipient sense of a world made up of "that surround-ing landscape, that air, those particular people [on the reserve] with their desires, their endless human necessi-ties" ("Skull" 20). Wiebe claimed that Thom begins to catch a glimpse, however faint and fleeting, of life beyond the reductively programmed religious absolutes of his community: "Thom in the swamp does what a novelist can do: lends us eyes, ears, tongue" (20). But, overall, the dangerous swamp with its sucking mud and seeping water becomes an image for what keeps Thom from breaking outside the so-called Christian dogma that clings to him and entraps him. For all Thom's seeing, he cannot ad-vance to any kind of significant saying. As Wiebe pointed out to his Winnipeg audience, Thom remained trapped inside a conflict-ridden and claustrophobic world, para-lyzed by "suppression and avoidance" (*Peace* 238).[5]

---

5. Wiebe could not prevent himself from pointing out that Thom, holding the skull, does not attempt to evoke Hamlet, nor

When Thom, in some desperation, does cast about for stories by which he might seek some kind of redemption and release, he finds little solace in his searching. His mind flashes back to stories he read in some "pale-blue booklets" buried on the bottom shelf of his scrawny school library—stories of Greek mythology (*Peace* 84). When the story of Prometheus flashes to mind, he can only see himself as both the giant who has carried the divine fire to man and the eagle eating the giant's liver, "daily ravaging … the writhing body" (85).

Along with the skull, two other grim images and motifs that leap from the pages in *Peace Shall Destroy Many* include the story of Elizabeth and her father and of the Christmas pageant that is juxtaposed to the violent episode in the barn. In his twenty-fifth anniversary recollections, Wiebe identified all three—the skull episode, the Elizabeth/Deacon Block relationship, the combination of Christmas-nativity childlike sweetness and futile violence—as belonging to a string of "broken suggestions of stories" that he had written during his student

---

the jester Yorick, with an "Alas, poor Bison, I knew him … " ("Skull" 20).

During that anniversary lecture in Winnipeg Wiebe confessed that, once it had appeared in Canada, *Peace Shall Destroy Many* provided even its author with lessons about words, and became for him "both an exaltation and a trauma" ("Skull" 8): "With my wife and two infant children, I was living in Winnipeg and editing a weekly church paper when *Peace Shall Destroy Many* was published in September, 1962. By March, 1963, I was no longer editor and by August we had left Canada. O, words have power, power beyond what I had imagined in three years of wrestling with them [while writing that book]" (8).

days of the 1950s for Professor F.M. Salter's writing classes at the University of Alberta.

But Wiebe identified also a fourth, that of the two young boys' frog hunt so evocatively told in the first Prelude of the novel. The description of the two young boys, one fair, one dark, on their spring hunt for frogs' eggs (9–10), stands in sharp contrast to the other three. The rhythms are more relaxed, a spirit of lightness and brightness hovers over all.

Wiebe, contextualizing that Prelude in his 1987 recollections, said alluringly: "Perhaps only those who have lived through the cold, the darkness of a northern prairie winter can comprehend the miracle of warm earth and water and spring green leaves and frogs singing; can comprehend the incredible feeling that the bright morning spring air fondling your nostrils releases you into" ("Skull" 11). With those words Wiebe was, in effect, not only summarizing a minor strand of attentiveness in the novel, but also anticipating his memoir— for the spirit and tone, the rhythm and temper, of the opening Prelude of the novel are, so to speak, carried over into *of this earth*, where they are vastly expanded. Indeed, in the memoir, it seems like we are held in a carefree world of "lookin' for frogs' eggs again." Descriptions like this one, of the coming of spring—as though taken from *Fern Hill*—suffuse the entire memoir: "one morning the world had rolled over into bright green to the music of frogs singing between the rushes of every flooded slough. The creeks ran loud as ducks gabbling under the plank culverts, and before I was aware of it my creased pants were crumpled from not having been rolled up far enough when I waded in the mossy, sinking slough, muddy and slimed with frogs' eggs" (209).

* * *

In the memoir, gone is the anxiety that knots the stomach—never mind the spirit and the soul, the mind and the heart—of the 1962 novel's protagonist Thom Wiens. Gone is Thom's clumsy groping for truth with his awkward mix of "sincerity, uncertainly, confusion, mistakes, and renewed attempts" ("An author speaks" 65). For example, although the troubling heft and burdensome weight given to the five stolen chickens are hinted at, they now romantically link local Indians to the nomadic Bashkirs of Russia. Mildly bothersome details about chickens now become lost in the haze of silly gossip of a "talky" neighbour (*of this earth* 311).

Gone too, or rather, transformed into lightly-handled vestigial residue, are those three dark elements, wrapped in dour sourness, that I have already taken (if somewhat arbitrarily) from Wiebe's 1987 list.

First: gone altogether is what Wiebe has called "the fiction that determines the entire body of the novel … the story of Elizabeth and her father" ("Skull" 11). In the novel, Elizabeth dies in the pangs of her secret pregnancy, the result of her sexual union with the Metis hired hand, that she has kept hidden from her hyper-patriarchal father. There are deaths in the memoir, certainly. Especially significant to Wiebe is the death of his dear sister Helen, a death that is described with a sad melancholy, but not with any kind of hopelessness or despair. In the memoir, a conversational Wiebe—relaxing in his own deep sense of personal being, of spiritual and material rootedness—simply trusts his audience with the details of his life. Comfortable with his own control of language, he gives the sad tragedy in the family a cradle for coming to rest within the folds of his gentle recollections. By contrast, in the 1962 novel, Thom's—and by implication, the reader's—route to knowledge is brutal, confrontational, filled with shock, with disgust, and hypocrisies, with false taboos and manufactured fears of transgression.

Second: the pale-blue booklets with their terrifying images of Promethean self-violation are back, but are now filled with the narrator's hilarious day-dreams of Theseus and the Minotaur (203), or his happy experiences of reading and re-reading of "laughing, golden Aphrodite, the irresistible goddess of love and beauty," in love with the "bent and blackened" Hephaestus (212).

Third: a Christmas program followed by violence in a barn (recalling the Christmas program at the end of *Peace Shall Destroy Many*) is now but a shimmering speculation among nostalgic memories about whether in fact there had been an actual Christmas program during the fall when Wiebe was nine years old. Perhaps there was no teacher at all that term—perhaps because there had been some kind of trouble. "It might be that the Christmas concert went wrong, something happened between a soldier on leave and the teacher, in the barn, while Santa Claus was handing out Christmas bags to us little kids," Wiebe says with a deliberate and teasing vagueness (213). For Wiebe—offering readers the persona of a slightly bemused and wise elder statesman, or of the well-tempered memoir writer—there is now no sense of sexual tension, no pained exploration of hypocrisies, power, dogma. Only this casual reflection that includes his hinting at connections between 2006 memoir and 1962 novel: "that may well be a shadow incarnation of the ending of my first novel—but the fact is I can remember neither teacher nor problem" (213).

Wiebe has liberated and revealed and explored fully in his memoir a spirit that only lingered along some of the happier edges of *Peace Shall Destroy Many*. In the memoir he in effect offers a recuperative reading of the spirit of Thom's younger brother Hal, to whom early reviewers remained, as Hildegard E. Tiessen points out, oblivious. His name, an abbreviated form of Helmut, suggests, in the German, "bright spirit" (Tiessen 171). Hal is a positive force representing renewal for the community and, at the end, announcing the end of its isolation, she observes (Tiessen 171–72).

Language flows freely and non-judgmentally for Hal, as it does not for his brother Thom—who is earnest, searching, quick to physical anger, slow to find generous spaces where words can grow and flourish. Hal, playing hooky from school, is the first speaker in that opening Prelude, where he cries out with a jubilant, "Let's go!" (*Peace* 10). This certainly is not Eliot's "Let us go then, you and I." Racing along barefoot in the field that the agonized Thom is ploughing, and transforming himself from "Indian" to fighter-plane as he runs lightly on the earth, Hal is the first speaker in the narrative proper, too, carrying himself forward in an embodying gush of words. Even a word like "half-breed," commonly used negatively by people in his community, holds no ethical or moral value for Hal (15). And it is Hal, ever ready to brim with words (on those occasions when we encounter him), who offers the novel's closing benediction. As the Wiens family, Thom at the reins of the cutter, heads home through the icy, clear, anguish-riddled December night, Hal chirps up with his unselfconscious "Wish it was spring so we could go lookin' for frogs' eggs again" (238). "'Yes,' Mrs Wiens said, holding her little boy tightly." At the same time she imagines, with some kind of desperate hope, that Thom, who is "staring skyward," might be "driving them toward the brightest star in the heavens" (*Peace* 238–39). Wiebe puts strong limits on Hal's wish for spring and Mrs. Wiens's fantasy; right after they have been expressed, he closes the novel by referring to the World War Two backdrop that informs the tone and the issues of the whole work: "Around the world the guns were already booming in a new day" (239).

Wiebe's memoir lets things float more open-endedly and buoyantly in its closing pages. If the idyllic images at the heart of *Fern Hill* offer continuities with Wiebe's edenic memoir, the mournful ending of *Fern Hill*, capturing an adult's perspective, does not. Wiebe's memoir ends with affirmations of its celebration of story and word, with him at age thirteen looking ahead to a new phase of life on the southern Alberta prairie where—as in the manner of young Hal's life in *Peace Shall Destroy Many*—there seems to be space adequate for expressing an infinitude of words: "A seemingly endless land forever open to the visitation of wind. Bracing myself into

that breathing wind, I would grow to feel it: a land too
far to see, fathomless to the looking eye—but, perhaps,
touchable by words ... words forged and bolted together
into the living architecture of story" (387).

* * *

Wiebe's memoir becomes a kind of blueprint that maps a
re-reading of his first novel. In a metaphoric sense, the
memoir is a kind of coming into language for the Hal of
the novel. Its open joy in language, from the opening to
the closing page, makes all the more palpable and poignant the language crisis that Thom experiences in the novel.

The memoir lets Wiebe explore the dynamic by
which a child and words, language, story grow into
each other, intuitively, as it were, become as one with
each other. It is a child who embodies a fullness of religious insight, absorbing and conveying it in innocence
and without question, and—in keeping with the spirit
of the Mennonite/Christian community overall, including, astonishingly, all of its adults—certainly without
the pain of tormented questioning and questing that
Thom endures in *Peace Shall Destroy Many*. In writing
a memoir that enters into the kind of conversation with
his first novel that I have here been suggesting, he has
written an exhilarating work that a reader of that novel,
even a reader attentive to the Hal of that novel, might
not have expected, for the memoir is so much more
spirited and free-wheeling at multiple levels even than
the episodes involving Hal in the novel. In the memoir,
Wiebe has found a way of expressing how a culture

produces a Christian way of life that is readily accessible to all its members.

Why should Wiebe's 1962 novel be so troubled—with Hal, its "bright light," barely visible—and his 2006 memoir so untroubled? Why should the two works manifest such astonishing differences—in tone, attitude, and content, in textures and tensions, in how Wiebe negotiates the spaces involving himself, his material, and his audience?

The differences have something to do with Wiebe, without telling anyone, having conflated two historic venues in his novel. Although the novel is manifestly set in the remote Saskatchewan boreal forest of the 1934–47 memoir, it in fact draws also on the politics of the Mennonite church and community to which the Wiebe family moved in May 1947, when Wiebe was thirteen, and where Wiebe grew up as a teenager and young adult. The astringent world defined of Deacon Block of the novel, for example, is actually drawn from Wiebe's bitter experiences of church elders that he observed in southern Alberta, where his family moved in May 1947. Spiritually speaking, it is essentially the "Hal" portions of the novel that conform with the broad outlines and the delicious depths of the very place where the memoir is set.

But the differences are partly a function also of the passage of time—for example, of the respective eras in which Wiebe is writing. Thus they are a function, possibly, of the late modernism still exerting its assumptions in a novel that was written during the late fifties and early sixties, and of the postmodernism informing the leisurely and non-judgmental recollections of memoir.

The differences are partly a function, too, of the change in genre and the concomitant change in centres of subjectivity. These are a function of conventions affecting literary forms, as Wiebe moves from the urgently programmatic novel written in the third person and centring on an earnest and anxious young adult to the reverie of first-person memoir. The memoir as genre invites the author to respond to his place as a child in an exotic world of strange immigrants at great remove from the typical Canadian reader. Indeed, it is almost a world of an "Other," for in many ways it is remote even from Wiebe's own place in the urban and urbane world of city and university, and of national and international reputation. In reality, his "Mennonite" life has become grafted onto his professional life in a very wide world. Yet, too, signifier and signified seem to stand close together and their differences seem almost to dissolve in Wiebe's memoir, and so the exotic "Otherness" is simultaneously made intimate, just as ironic distance between the world of the child and adult is muted.

The differences partly have something to do with the status of the writer, with the changed socio-cultural position of the writer within various public (including literary and religious) spheres, with Wiebe himself having graduated, as it were, from the role of a "young theologian" (to quote from jacket blurbs) in his twenties when he wrote his first novel as a kind of angry young man to what reviewers now regularly call "one of Canada's most gifted writers," a tried and true writer who is now in his seventies, a writer known for his interest in pursuing empathetically the remote and hidden voices of the unknown Canadian—in the memoir, vividly pursuing his own formative voice.[6]

The differences have something to do with Wiebe as a master artist now free of and easy within an apparently tension-free world untouched by debilitating rancour and obsessive control, where he has time to follow the dramatic rhythms of satisfying reflection, of shapes of beckoning images awaiting attention in old family photo albums. He is demonstrably performing being at ease now, unfazed by bits of forgetting, happily prepared to announce a memory gap as a memory gap. Even though Wiebe is known for work saturated in his meticulous historical research, for work that draws (although sometimes not without irony) on "fact," he foregoes the illusion of managing an air-tight mastery of facts in the memoir. His emphasis on an infant's inevitable immersion into a bath of language notwithstanding, he avoids absolute readings of the self as child.

The differences have something to do, too, with Wiebe's own longing. Wiebe clearly takes enormous joy in playfully creating the world of the child. In his memoir he explores the child to give vast scope to his reading of the human subject more generally. For him, as for Carolyn Steedman, writing on autobiography, childhood provides a privileged entry point into "the human subject,

---

6. Wiebe's famous short story, "Where Is the Voice Coming From?", provides his paradigmatic summation of his stance as a writer in pursuit of silenced—and only partially and complicatedly retrievable—voices.

of locating it in time and chronology, and 'explaining' it." And through his 2006 exploration of a Mennonite childhood, Wiebe finds a means of connecting subjectivity—and his own history of subjectivity—to the broader culture, one that foregrounds his Mennonite culture (Steedman 11, 13).

Eventually, the young child of the memoir presumably will gather up some of the language keys that, if he enters a world (even a religious world) close to what Wiebe understands today, will eventually make life (and religion) comprehensible to him in generous and gentle linguistic terms. He will get there by a circuitous and leisurely route, happily and unselfconsciously inviting the adult reader along—even if the adult reader chuckles knowingly at the touches of innocence that he/she, but not the boy, can understand as provisional. It is a meandering and easy-going route that is unlikely to bring the boy of the memoir into the tense confines of that a Thom Wiens portrays in the 1962 novel.

Works Cited:

Steedman, Carolyn. *Past Tenses: Essays on writing, autobiography and history*. London: Rivers Oram Press, 1992.

Tiessen, Hildegard E. "A Mighty Inner River: 'Peace' in the Early Fiction of Rudy Wiebe." *The Canadian Novel: Here and Now*. Ed. John Moss. Toronto: NC Press, 1978. 169–81.

van Toorn, Penny. *Rudy Wiebe and the Historicity of the Word*. Edmonton: University of Alberta Press, 1995.

Wiebe, Rudy. "An author speaks about his novel." *A Voice in the Land: Essays By and About Rudy Wiebe*. Ed. W.J. Keith. Edmonton: NeWest Press, 1981. 64–68.

---. *of this earth: a Mennonite boyhood in the boreal forest*. Toronto: Alfred A. Knopf Canada 2006.

---. *Peace Shall Destroy Many*. Grand Rapids, MI: Wm. B. Eerdmans Publishing Company, 1968 [1964]. (First published: Toronto: McClelland and Stewart, 1962.)

---. "The Skull in the Swamp." *Journal of Mennonite Studies* 5 (1987): 8–20.

The "Wistful, Windy Madness of a Gift": Rudy Wiebe's Books for Young Readers

Olga Stein

Children's books and stories are often written not just for children. Some of the best are written as literature that adult readers can enjoy and share with young listeners. In such cases, the themes, characters, language, and illustrations of a work are all facets that can be appreciated—indeed, savoured—individually and in combination. Older readers may understandably be more aware of the beauty of some features, while youngsters will naturally be drawn to others. A good example of such literature is *Chinook Christmas*. The story is one that Rudy Wiebe wrote in 1978. It has appeared in a number of his story collections (the most recent, *Collected Stories, 1953–2010,* was published in 2010 by the University of Alberta Press). However, *Chinook Christmas* was not produced as a children's book until 1992, when Northern Lights, the children's books imprint of Red Deer College Press, brought it out in a very attractive format, with fine and evocative illustrations by the artist David More.

Chinook Christmas begins with a passage so vivid that one is transported to a blustery 1940s town in the Canadian Prairies:

The winter I turned nine was our first in southern
Alberta, and the snowy scars of irrigation ditches
circling lower and lower into the long, shallow
hollow of our town seemed to me then like the
trenches of some besieging army. The grey, wrinkled
snow lay driven there off the tilted fields, long, long
welts of it carved in parallels below the square top
of Big Chief Mountain sixty miles away where the
implacable General of the Winds stood forever
roaring at his troops: *Advance!*

What follows are equally redolent descriptions of a small
farming town and its community, mostly Mennonites
speaking Low German. Wiebe's story is replete with eye-
catching characters, like Mrs. Cartwright, who sells meat
at the counter of Oncle Willm's butcher shop. As Eric,
the main character, reveals with innocence befitting a
nine-year-old boy, "Mrs. Cartwright was always dressed
so perfectly, her face as careful as a picture ... [W]hen she
leaned over the counter, laughing," after telling a joke
(though Oncle Willm also cracked jokes "unlike any
other Mennonite grown-up"), "I always wanted to laugh
with her, like every man who bought meat there did—
though I never saw a woman do it—her lips and teeth so
red and white and marvelously, smoothly exact."

The town, with its three parallel streets running north
and south, unpaved, and navigated mostly by horse-
drawn drays, is nevertheless a whole and fascinating
world for Eric. It is the adult Eric who recollects the
story of one unusually warm Christmas, but it is a child's
sense of wonder and curiosity that flavours the telling.

What captivates the young Eric? Apart from the beguiling scents of his mother's Christmas baking, and the surprising development of a Chinook—that is, "a touch of warmth; very nearly a flare of mad possibility in the cold"—it is Eric's older sister Anni, who is fourteen at the time, and has already been "kissed once or twice under a full moon." Anni is full of laughter, songs, hijinks, and a certain kind of knowing, and it is Anni who makes things happen when she declares that she wants a Christmas tree. "Anni always knew what she wanted," Eric states with a degree of admiration.

The problem, and one that Anni is determined to solve, is that unlike the bush homestead in northern Alberta, where the family lived before moving to a town, evergreens aren't simply available for the taking. Spruce that have been harvested cost a dollar, according to Mrs. Orleski, whose hardscrabble life includes selling Christmas trees (when she isn't selling copies of the *Lethbridge Herald* for a nickel). One dollar, however, makes a Christmas tree a luxury that Eric's parents cannot afford. Yet in the spirit of throwing caution to the wind, Anni and Eric set out for "downtown," hitching a ride on Mr. Ireland's dray, to find Mrs. Orleski and her trees. They spot her with just three remaining ones on a lot next to the Doerksen Brothers' hardware and grocery store. The lot is now "thick with needled aroma like the mountains where Mrs Orleski said her son worked deep in the Crowsnest Mines." Diligent Mrs. Orleski had a successful day, and as the children approach her, she makes a gesture that is remarkable—something Eric did not expect from a woman who is known for her parsimony.

It may or may not be one of the strange, mollifying effects of the Chinook. Here as elsewhere, Wiebe condenses character and voice into a small amount of text:

> "You kits still lookin'?"... And abruptly she
> wheeled: her nostrils flared into the Chinook,
> opening huge like gills in fast water.
>
> "Here, Here! They leave it, the leetle branch,
> they leave it lotsa ..." and she stopping, gathering
> with the swift, inevitable hands of workers,
> "Sometimes stumps, have it too much branch ...."
>
> And she thrust them at me .... Mrs. Orleski's
> two stubby arms filled with spruce boughs like a
> proffered squirrel's nest stuffed fat and full and
> warm for the winter,
>
> "You take it, is good, hang it some places,
> Mama happy, so ...."
>
> Offering the wistful, windy madness of a gift
> Anni said, "I'm sorry," and I stared at her in
> horror. "We still have no money."
>
> "Wha? I no take it, your money ... give for
> nutting. You take!"

Years ago, when I reviewed Wiebe's second children's book, *Hidden Buffalo* (published in 2003, also by Red Deer Press), I omitted any mention of Wiebe's other writing—his contributions to our developing body of national literature, and to regional and Mennonite literature in particular. My review of *Hidden Buffalo* is appended below, but I wish to take the opportunity to rectify the foregoing omission here.

As many critics who are knowledgeable about Mennonite literature in Canada already know, Wiebe broke ground with his 1962 novel, *Peace Shall Destroy Many*. He cleared the way for other Mennonite writers, and along with them, turned this writing—which emanated from Anabaptist communities in Canada and the United States—into a genre or what used to be seen as an instance of minor literature. Wiebe went on to publish another eight novels, several collections of short stories and essays, and a volume of memoirs, *Of This Earth: A Mennonite Boyhood in the Boreal Forest* (published in 2007). He was awarded the Governor General's Award for Fiction twice: in 1973 for *The Temptations of Big Bear,* and in 1994 for *A Discovery of Strangers.* In 2007, he received the Charles Taylor prize for his memoirs. I mention the Governor General's and Charles Taylor awards because I wish to make a point that goes beyond the plain biographical facts of Wiebe's literary career. Major literary awards, as I've come to understand them, select books for celebration, but such distinctions do not merely endow winning and nominated books with cultural prestige; literary prizes confer on works and their authors a special type of value (or symbolic capital). This recognition effects the shift of authors, their books, and the communities they represent from the cultural margins toward a nation's centre or literary mainstream (in terms of production/publishing and consumption). Wiebe, I hope to stress, played a decisively role in this process—whereby authors of Mennonite provenance ceased being producers of minor literature and became part of the canon of Canadian literature.

There is abundant scholarship and critical writing on Wiebe's fiction and memoirs. One can easily gather a few examples of what has been written about Wiebe's work. All demonstrate recognition of Wiebe's contribution to Canadian literature, as well as his growing reputation as a writer. For example, in a review of *The Scorched-Wood People*, published in 1979, Delbert E. Wylder observed:

> Like William Faulkner, who created the Yoknapatawpha County, and Frederick Manfred, who staked out his own Siouxland, Rudy Wiebe is developing as the spokesman of the Canadian great plains area. The Scorched-Wood People is a novel set in the same area as his Governor General's Award winning novel, *The Temptations of Big Bear.* It is the tale of the loss of the Canadian West by the Metis to the dominantly Scottish and British Canadians, and it centers around two of the most fascinating characters in Western Canadian, or American for that matter, literature. (Wylder 237–238)[1]

In a review of *Rudy Wiebe: Collected Stories, 1953–2010*, penned by Neil Querengesser in 2012 and published in the Autumn issue of *Canadian Literature*, we find references to a much-expanded oeuvre. Querengesser sums up the collection with the following: "[Wiebe's] storytelling

---

1. Wylder, Delbert E. Review of *The Scorched-Wood People*, by Rudy Wiebe. *Western American Literature*, vol. 14 no. 3, 1979, p. 237–238. *Project MUSE*, doi:10.1353/wal.1979.0081.

gifts are evident throughout this remarkable collection of one and fifty tales, which offers a substantially complete and satisfying retrospective of his published short fiction." More importantly, Querengesser's review furnishes a lens that proves useful for assessing *Wiebe's* accomplishments in stories like *Chinook Christmas*.

> In what continues to be an oft-quoted passage from Rudy Wiebe's "Speaking Saskatchewan," a shy young boy during his first day in the rural schoolhouse is introduced by his teacher to shelves full of books that will lead him throughout his life to a blessed continuing epiphany, hearing "human voices speaking from everywhere and every age," to which "[h]e will listen ... now for as long as he lives." Wiebe has of course not only listened to those voices over the years, but also augmented their number abundantly through his own many works of fiction and non-fiction, speaking as "himself" and through a rich variety of narrators and narrative personae (Querengesser 191).[2]

Finally, and apropos of those voices—that multiplicity of different histories, languages, cultures, and beliefs to which Wiebe's writing gives expression—Larissa Petrillo's

---

2. Querengesser, Neil. "Those Voices Speaking Now." *Canadian Literature/Littérature Canadienne: a Quarterly of Criticism and Review* (Univ. of British Columbia, Vancouver), no. 214, The University of British Columbia—*Canadian Literature*, 2012, p. 191–.

essay, published in the *Encyclopedia of Post-Colonial Literatures in English,* informs us: "[Wiebe] challenges the biases of mainstream history by presenting multiple points of view. He does so, however, using a literary style that is exemplary in its experimentation. He highlights the act of fictive translation and unsettles the division between history and literature; he also urges readers to be critically aware of their position in reading a multi-voiced text" (Petrillo 1).[3]

Chinook Christmas is likewise a multi-voiced text, and one whose sophistication and literary craft transgress categories that pertain to readers' age or literary genre. The same can be said of many of *Wiebe's* shorter narratives and novels. Additionally, these tend to reflect either his Mennonite heritage, or the personal experience of living in proximity to and keenly observing Indigenous peoples. Wiebe's two books for children represent precisely this binate absorption and regard. Yet what interests me also are the narratives built on adventure, romance, and large-than-life protagonists—fare that is likely to appeal to young adults. It is pertinent, I think, that the latter is terrain that Wiebe shares with a number of important literary predecessors.

Wiebe's personal history does not entirely account for some dimensions of his work. Hence, it might be

---

3. Petrillo, Larissa. *Wiebe, Rudy (1934–)* Edited by Eugene Benson, and L. W. Conolly. Routledge, Taylor & Francis Group, Abingdon, 2005. *ProQuest,* https://ezproxy.library.yorku.ca/login ?url=https://www-proquest-com.ezproxy.library.yorku.ca /encyclopedias-reference-works/wiebe-rudy-1934/docview /2137903268/se-2?accountid=15182.

fruitful to look closely at the books that helped shaped him as a writer. It is surely relevant that before *The Temptations of Big Bear* and *The Scorched-Wood People* there was John Richardson's *Wacousta*, published in 1832, and Wallace Stegner's entire oeuvre. In a lively conversation with Hugh Cook, in issue 90 of *Image* magazine, Wiebe mentions that as a boy he read "violent Zane Grey" and *The Spirit of the Border,* first published in 1906.[4] Can we not assume consequently that some of Wiebe's writing draws on a tradition to which American writers and social activists, James Fenimore Cooper and Jack London, also contributed? These literary lines of descent, some of which transgress regional and even national categories, are worth investigating.

Lastly, I wish to draw attention to the importance Wiebe attributes to community in both *Chinook Christmas* and *Hidden Buffalo.* This lesson—in valuing and respecting every member, young or old—is one of the most instructive and pleasing aspects of these books. Community, empathy, and the generosity and faith in others this entails, can explain all manner of miracles.

Review of *Hidden Buffalo*

Olga Stein's review of *Hidden Buffalo* first appeared in Books in Canada, in 2006. http://www.booksincanada .com/article_view.asp?id=3683

---

4. "Conversation with Rudy Wiebe." Hugh Cook interviews Rudy Wiebe. *Image* 90 (Fall, 2016), pp. 63–76. Accessed 6 Apr 2022. https://imagejournal.org/article/conversation-rudy-wiebe/

Hidden Buffalo is Rudy Wiebe's wonderfully crafted tale of Sky Running, a young Cree boy from a time "long past but not forgotten." Sky is helping his tribe look for the much-needed prairie buffalo herds. He has stood all day on the higher ground overlooking Sounding Lake and the endless expanse of grassland to see whether the animals could be spotted. It is the time of "Changing Leaves," and unlike previous autumns, the buffalo are nowhere to be seen. Wiebe's story recalls a time and way of life that held no guarantee of survival. Sky, despite his young age, is fully conscious of the peril his people face if they fail to find the buffalo in time to dry the meat —food that would see them through the long months of winter.

That evening, gathered around the fire, Sky's grandmother tells the children a story about how the Creator brought forth the Buffalo. She explains that the Creator made a pact with the animals, promising to make them plentiful if they gave of themselves to the people in exchange. Underlying this story is the Cree's profound faith in nature's capacity to sustain human and animal life, to maintain a rewarding symbiosis.

After the storytelling is over, Sky wanders along the lakeshore and finds a stone shaped like a buffalo, and when he falls asleep with this talisman-like object at his side, he dreams of a herd of buffalo grazing by a river that is surrounded by "layers of black and light brown and white cliffs." Sky's dream prompts the entire tribe to make a long and arduous journey to the place along the Red Deer River that matches the scene in the boy's vision. Approaching the river with its surrounding cliffs, the tribe is greeted by the sight of "numberless" buffalo.

The Chief invites Sky to ride with the hunters. The boy's marvelous dream has saved the tribe and he is suitably rewarded. "Sky cannot speak for happiness."

Rich and vivid artwork by Michael Lonechild combine perfectly with Wiebe's text in this lovely book for young readers aged 7 to 10.

Interview with Aritha van Herk:
Rudy Wiebe, a Mentor and a Critic

Bianca Lakoseljac

November 20, 2020

Introduction: Aritha van Herk is a celebrated Canadian author who wrote her first novel, *Judith*, as a Master's student working under Rudy Wiebe's supervision. The novel won the Seal First Novel Award in 1978, at the time the most prestigious literary award ($50,000) in Canada. A professor at the University of Calgary, van Herk is the author of five novels, numerous non-fiction books, and essays. Her writing explores feminist themes and depicts the culture of western Canada. This interview was arranged specifically for the anthology, *Rudy Wiebe: Essays on His Works*, and was conducted through email by editor, Bianca Lakoseljac.

Q1. Bianca Lakoseljac: Your creative writing thesis, *Judith*, became an instant success. What was the most valuable aspect of writing your novel with Wiebe's guidance?

A1. Aritha van Herk: It wasn't exactly instant. I worked on the novel over three years, and revised the work considerably before it was published. In many ways, the most valuable aspect of writing with Wiebe's guidance was learning how to gain confidence in my own ability and my own ideas. He was encouraging about producing writing, but he made some suggestions that genuinely puzzled me, and that I had to sort out creatively in terms of what I would follow and what I would not. His interests were very different from mine—and although we both came out of a rural, immigrant background, our social and political trajectories were radically different. So, the most valuable aspect of working with him was figuring out what mattered to me, in terms of writing and language.

Q2. BL: What was the most challenging part of writing your first novel?

A2: AvH: The most challenging aspect of undertaking a novel as a young writer is finding the assurance needed to tackle a longer work, one that needs to be built and developed over a longer period. For me, the most challenging element of writing fiction was then and continues to be creating convincing dialogue. I suspect I don't want people to talk, and so my characters can be quite taciturn.

Q3. BL: Could you identify one writing approach you inherited from Wiebe and were glad to pass on to your students?

A3: AvH: It's an old but useful piece of advice, which has circulated for years: "Write what you know." Wiebe was an adamant advocate of writing about what is familiar, investigating the ways that we can write about the world we understand, or perhaps need to understand what we do not understand about what we take for granted. I departed from that advice, but I have come back to it, and have honed it as a useful tenet regarding writing that focusses on place, and how place inhabits the imagination alongside geographical and historical temperament as tonal accompaniment to landscape. My ambitious students often want to write fantasy, but quickly learn that world-building can be daunting. So, I begin with the familiar that they may have overlooked as writing material. And, as Wiebe did, I encourage them to explore their obsessions.

Q4. BL: In Scot Morison's article "The Annotated Rudy Wiebe" published by *New Trail*, University of Alberta, autumn, 2016, you are quoted as saying that Rudy Wiebe "... was generous with his attention and, as a teacher, mostly interested in the quality of writing." You also mention that Wiebe "... didn't suffer fools gladly." Would you care to elaborate on these statements?

A4. AvH: Wiebe was interested in language and the texture of writing, but he was suspicious of experimental writing, especially in terms of deconstructionist language play. His well-known comment to his friend Robert Kroetsch, "Bob, you are always horsing around with language" (Shirley Neuman, "Unearthing Language: An Interview with Rudy Wiebe and Robert Kroetsch," in *A Voice in the Land: Essays By and About Rudy Wiebe*), expressed his combined annoyance and fascination with those who understand that language is a place of transgression, not a vehicle for persuasion. As for the sufferance of fools, Wiebe had justifiably scant patience for trendiness, for laziness, for tardiness, or for excuses. You met your deadlines—or else.

Q5. BL: As a professor and mentor for three-and-a-half decades, you have supported a number of your students and helped propel their writing careers. Would you say that you committed yourself to Wiebe and his mentor, Frederick Millet Salter's (1895–1962) tradition of working tirelessly to shine a light on new writers?

A5. AvH: I pragmatically recognized, very early, that making a living as a writer would be difficult, and so I began to teach writing. I had some disquiet about that, because artists have a strong sense that they must dedicate themselves to their practice. But two crucial elements changed my mind. The first is that if you teach at a university, you have access to what is the biggest and best library in the area. The resources that a fine library provides are essential for a writer—every writer must read and read. The second was again a conversation with Robert Kroetsch, where I was lamenting that I would write more if I were not teaching. Kroetsch's wisdom was often dispensed in pithy comments, and he said, "Aritha, nobody can write all the time." He was right, of course, the art of living needs to be combined with the practice of art. And my students are part of my life of imaginative discovery and energy. I have, in my own particular tradition, mentored a long list of "students," although I prefer to think of them as writerly colleagues. They include—and these are just a few: Anar Ali, Anita Badami, Dawn Bryan, Rob Budde, Weyman Chan, Joan Crate, Marika Deliyannides, Mark Giles, Jessica Grant, Jaqueline Honnet, Barb Howard, Adrian Kelly, Jani Krulc, Yasmin Ladha, Lisa Murphy-Lamb, Peter Oliva, Roberta Rees, Anne Sorbie, and Andrew Wedderburn.

Q6. BL: You have been quoted as saying that, although Wiebe was a wonderful teacher, you had numerous disagreements. Can you give some instances where disagreements occurred?

A6, AvH: We had many disagreements about literature and approaches to writing. For example, my heroes were Marian Engel and Robert Kroetsch, his were Frederick Philip Grove and C.S. Lewis, which I could not fathom. And we have always had strenuous arguments about women and sexism. Wiebe is very much shaped by patriarchy, and he tended to be dismissive of women's fight for equality. We had intense clashes about that—and I credit his benign chauvinism with strengthening my own particular brand of fierce feminism.

Q7. BL: Wiebe was your official supervisor. Was he also your spiritual mentor? Your inspiration?

A7. AvH: Wiebe and I diverge considerably on what might be considered spiritual. I am a committed agnostic, and we disagree about Christianity, which he embraces. Imagination is my spiritual refuge. But he was a creative and literary mentor in the sense that he reiterated pride in the regional, what William Carlos Williams calls in *Paterson* "a local pride." Dennis Cooley too (a wonderful and underrated writer) addressed this power of the local in his *The Vernacular Muse*. So, Wiebe was an inspiration in tandem with the other prairie writers, and especially Robert Kroetsch, who persuaded me to pursue my own ideas of place and language here and now. He first made our Battle River country in Alberta a place of mischief and misdeed.

Q8. BL: As the author of many works, where does your creative vision emerge from?

A8: AvH: The horizon; the many hidden stories of women and those who are forgotten; the parkland of Alberta; the Calgary chinook.

Q9: BL: What is the most useful skill a writer should nurture?

A9: AvH: Digression and dreaming. To quote Don DeLillo, "May the days be aimless. Do not advance action according to a plan."

Q10: BL: Wiebe, your mentor when you were a student, became your colleague at the beginning of your writing and teaching career, and your joint accomplishments were highly acclaimed. You co-edited two anthologies with Wiebe: *More Stories from Western Canada*, in 1980; and *West of Fiction*, in 1983 (with co-editor Leah Flater).

What was the most beneficial aspect of working with Wiebe as co-editor?

A10: AvH: Wiebe was well-read in 20th century Canadian short fiction, and so brought to the editing of the anthologies we did excellent knowledge of different stories and how they would work in dialogue with one another. I was more knowledgeable about contemporary writers. Our main point of convergence was that we were both interested in raising the profile of writing from western Canada, often peripheral in anthologies published out of central Canada. Perhaps more significant, although now not accorded much mention, was our imagining, initiating, and beginning Nunataks, the First Fiction series that continues to be published by NeWest Press. We were once on a road trip, and driving on Highway 40, at the Highwood Pass stopped for a break. There, at that wonderful viewpoint, we found a description of Nunataks, peaks that rose above the ice sheet, and consequently were never glaciated. It struck us as a marvellous name for a series of works by new writers. As editors of the series, we published Joan Crate, Hiromi Goto, Thomas Wharton, Lauralyn Chow, and many others.

Q11: BL: Were there challenges as well, and if so, could you explain?

A11. AvH: Wiebe was less aware of contemporary writers, women writers, writers who were not canonical or mainstream. And he was as a reader and person always in search of the heroic. In fact, he was a determined sizeist

—he valued magnitude, as per his quote in "Passage by Land," which reads, "You must lay great black steel lines of fiction, break up that space with huge design, and like the fiction of the Russian steppes, build giant artifact." I was more interested in detail. We had some "great" arguments about who was "important," and who was "good." I won only half of them.

Q12. BL: What message would you give to Wiebe today?

A12. AvH: Keep reading. Write shorter sentences. And stop trying to change history.

—ARITHA VAN HERK, UNIVERSITY OF CALGARY, ALBERTA, NOVEMBER 20, 2020.

Conclusion: Many thanks to Aritha van Herk—a Canadian writer, critic, editor, public intellectual, and university professor whose work has been translated into ten languages—for the interview and for providing a perspective into her work with Rudy Wiebe who was her mentor during her studies and later a colleague and collaborator on a number of publications. Van Herk's introspective discussion is an instructive reveal of the challenges and rewards of being a writer.

Is Grief Rational? Loss and Pain in Rudy Wiebe's *Come Back*

Uroš Tomić

> *Nowhere, beloved, can the world exist but within us.*
> *Our life is spent in changing. And ever lessening,*
> *The outer world disappears.*
> —RUDY WIEBE, *COME BACK* (71)

Personal understanding of the world is essentially a closed loop, a fixed circuit: one is forever bound by the meagerness of one's own sensory and intellectual perceptions of an image that is, like visible colors of the spectrum, just a fraction of what there might be. Reality, therefore, becomes a deeply individualized concept, refracted through a prism of subjective beliefs, experiences, emotions, and discrete comprehensions. Dependable on the vagaries of restless life, reality as we humans perceive it, is in constant state of flux; an Oldman river, although one that too often fails to find a larger body of water into which to flow. Rudy Wiebe's 10th novel, *Come Back*, published in 2014, nestles into this murky space between personal reality and the unknowable outside world, inhabiting the ice-capped, slippery region of no man's land between memory and actuality, between profound loss and its acceptance. Suffused with autobiographical impulses like rivulets of darkness in veined marble, the novel examines the stubbornly, solipsistically internal, non-verbalized experience of personal pain that blossoms perpetually after the death of a loved one.

The novel begins in 2010, with Hal Wiens depicted as a "presumably dignified middle-class seventy-five-year-old male" (14), a retired university professor, grieving the passing of his wife Yolanda and leading a largely solitary life, away from his two surviving children and their families. He is also an aged version of a character readers have met before in Wiebe's first novel, *Peace Shall Destroy Many*, published in 1962. This connection is pertinent: Wiebe is inviting us to witness and minutely observe the life span of a man whose existence has been shaped by the uneasy and at times forceful intrusion of the outside world into his personal, closed-off space.

The ghost of Thom Wiens, Hal's eldest brother and the protagonist of Wiebe's first novel, haunts the pages of *Come Back* in many ways, bringing with him Hal's early understanding of pain and death. Thom's silent presence echoes Hal's devout Mennonite upbringing that brooked no deviation from the straight and narrow path—a profoundly religious experience that still delineates Hal's grasp of reality and the way he is able to perceive and justify the reasons for human suffering. Thom is also the first of several key losses in Hal's life, none more profoundly perplexing than the death by suicide of his 24-year-old son Gabriel (Gabe) in 1985, in a car parked near the family's peaceful cabin in the countryside. Hal's compulsion to understand Gabe's reasons and fully confront his death after 25 years becomes the thematic linchpin of *Come Back*, and a way for Hal to face and accept his own life force that at times seems to mock painfully the dead that surround him.

It is significant to note that just as Hal's character echoes Rudy Wiebe's Mennonite and educational background, so does Gabe's death crucially mirror the demise of Wiebe's own eldest son, Michael, who committed suicide that same year and at the same age. The novel can thus be seen to function as more than a personally informed piece of fiction: it is Wiebe's public reckoning with his own private grief and a way of exploring the question of the rationality of grief in its widest implication.

As the plot evolves, Hal spends most of his time in a Double Cup café (which "doubles" for Wiebe's favorite haunt, the Second Cup café on the corner of Whyte Avenue and Calgary Trail in Edmonton), passively observing the "unending scarf woven of movement" (7) cocooned in this passivity as in a protective armor, and "comforted because he needed none" (7). Hal is seriously mistaken; the illusion of solace is about to dissipate, leaving the elderly man naked before the onslaught of old *fresh* pain. On a seemingly ordinary day, one that "cracked wide open to that remorseless memory always poised to strike" (18) through the coffee-shop window overlooking the sidewalk, in a sudden flurry of motion, Hal believes to have observed a tall, slender passerby sporting his long deceased son Gabe's signature orange down-filled coat. The young man's distinct stature and gait, as well as the "exposed forehead curved to a widow's peak of light-brown hair fluffed back with snow—ends curled ......the long strides, the shift of shoulders inside the tight orange"(7), all closely resembled Gabe's. Hal runs mindlessly into the street in pursuit of an apparition, causing a traffic accident, then retreating into his fenced-off reality, a changed man.

Wiebe has prepared us for this event by interlacing the narrative with the motif of a lone raven, whose rare sighting in Edmonton's urban area invokes the biblical raven, the first named bird in the Old Testament, the one that Noah sent into the void after the flood to seek land, the one that never flew back, lost forever. In a similar fashion, Hal embarks on a journey without hope: he trawls through Gabe's diaries, letters, and notes, searching for his son's presence and, more importantly, for a rational explication of his own grief. By degrees, this grief becomes universal in its specificity, his son's suicide a focal point for all the losses in his life.

By opening the pages of Gabriel's diaries to the reader, Wiebe allows us to look into the past life of a young man whose sentiments are exposed to the point of transparency: Gabe's personal reality is fraught with obsessive thoughts, guilt, and a generalized sense of purposelessness. Observing Hal reading his son's words enables the reader to glimpse into the complex mind-set of those who have died by their own hand: the repetitions, the culpabilities, the loops of memory, the lacunae filled with fantasy.

Hal enters into a complex dialogue with his dead son and, more significantly, with his own past self, searching for *a posteriori* knowledge, for the elusive hindsight that might offer a glimpse of comprehension. Ironically, Gabe's diaries offer just that: his whole intellect bared to its core, as the young man traces the road to his death openly and almost shamelessly, flaunting his depression with adolescent abandon. His words are not ambivalent, even if his feelings are. The diaries outline Gabriel's darkly felt fascination with young girls, especially Ailsa, the 13-year-old daughter of family friends, for whom the young man develops a sensual fixation, creating a fantasy of mythical proportions. Gabe asks himself: "Why have I created her (with those incredible green eyes) into this legend?" (178). Austrian poet Rainer Maria Rilke, the articulated voice of early 20th century lyricism and mystic beauty, becomes Gabriel's sole companion—and one could say a companion to his inner self—his poetry a frequent expression of Gabe's innermost feelings, at first nascent and enveloped in embryonic pretensions, then, by degrees, blossoming into unbearable obsessive compulsions.

In an attempt to understand the depths of Gabriel's despair, possibly for the first time fully, Hal experiences a fresh wave of longing and sorrow for his dead son. Wiebe's authorial choice to follow several of Gabe's entries with passages of lyrical prose, creating an assemblage of associative impressions rather than narration puts us directly in the path of Hal's process of negotiating and bargaining for Gabe's legacy. Hal's thoughts become almost a prose poem, a long dirge mixing images of what his son's last moments were like with Hal's pointless desire to have known his son better. The old man takes stock: at 25 Van Gogh was creating art that led him directly to grasp the idea of Godly presence; Hal himself was studying theology at Winnipeg Mennonite College, exploring his understanding of the spiritual world, and his son was already dead, having concluded that "Existence is an ugly pain" (164).

Hal himself obsesses over a figure unreachable, paralleling Gabe's obsession with girls as objects of half-understood yet irresistible fantasy: from the grace of gymnast Nadia Comaneci to the innocence of young Nastassja Kinski in *Tess* and *Paris, Texas* to the ethereal beauty of soprano Emma Kirby. They all lead Gabe inexorably to Ailsa, who "comes across as an extremely typical very young teenager with childish traits. She is lovely, more rounded breasts and buttocks, her bare feet perfect and her lower lip so full" (176). Within the same breath, he creates a realistic appraisal of too young a girl and builds up an image of a deadly siren to his untethered imagination. Similarly, Hal's compulsive perusal of Gabe's writing leads the old man to the only possible (and crucially unfinished), taunting, question: "you had such unimaginable strength to come here to park among the trees, why couldn't you use that strength to …" (267).

The stark clarity and the brutal un-deniability of Gabe's death has always been too much for his father to accept, having decided that, "Gabe would now be the black hole in his universe of memory" (25). Wiebe manipulates contrasting images of blackness and whiteness throughout the novel, and the absolute absence of color as well as its opposite play a significant role in the novel's structure. The dichotomy of light and darkness, the whiteness of the snow and the blackness of the premonitory ravens, Gabe's diaries that change from burgundy to black as his mental state deteriorates, echo the persistent contrast between Hal's vitality and his son's death wish, the land of the living and the realm of the dead, the force of memory and the void of absence. Even Hal's grief is a sure sign of his aliveness, his ability to withstand the pain of loss a mark of his life energy, as opposed to Gabriel who writes, "why God why do I have to feel things so intensely" (94), which portrays him as incapable of bearing the weight of life. In this sense, the assault of memories that descends upon Hal in the novel proves that, even as he struggles to understand Gabriel's decision, he recognizes he must relinquish the fabricated, preferred memory of his son as he seemed in life and accept Gabriel in death after 25 years of careful, deliberate elusion.

Come Back is Rudy Wiebe's novel of transitional, liminal states that exist in between the psychological structures that maintain our sense of self in a world too large to be fully grasped. If it is also his way of dealing with his son's suicide, then it is an effort that transcends personal and individual for the sake of the collective, shared experience of life and death, loss and grief. In constructing a deeply and universally emotional story from the catalyst of personal pain, Wiebe has shown us that there is *nothing* and *everything* rational about grief. He has also shown us that grief must be lived through and then subsumed into the core of our life force. Even Gabriel agrees:

"Quit reading this, trying to find clues to who I am. Shut the case and go on with your lives" (144).

References:

Giesbrecht, Herbert. "O Life, How Naked and How Hard When Known." *A Voice in the Land*. Edmonton: NeWest Publishers, 1981.

Van Toorn, Penny. "*Peace Shall Destroy Many*: Breaking Open the Capsule." *Rudy Wiebe and the Historicity of the Word*. The University of Alberta Press, 1995.

Van Toorn, Penny. "The Politics of Narrative Practice." *Rudy Wiebe and the Historicity of the Word*. The University of Alberta Press, 1995.

Wiebe, Rudy. *Come Back.* : Toronto: Random House, 2014.

Wiebe, Rudy. *Peace Shall Destroy Many.* Toronto: McClelland & Stewart, 1962. Vintage Canada, 2001.

The "Rudy Wiebe Room"

Scot Morison

PHOTOGRAPH OF RUDY WIEBE BY JOHN ULAN.

Introduction: Writers Mentoring Writers for 40 Years

The article, "The 'Rudy Wiebe Room'" was first published in Autumn 2016 issue of New Trail, *University of Alberta's alumni magazine, as "The Annotated Rudy Wiebe," upon the 40th anniversary of the creative writing program at the U of A which was headed by Rudy Wiebe.*

As an author, Rudy Wiebe stands among the one-name heroes of Canadian literature: Atwood, Munro, Wiebe. At the helm of the University of Alberta's creative writing program for many years, Wiebe's "writing is hard" out-look and wry sense of humour helped forge successful authors and stoke a passion for language.

Forty years ago, English professor and author Rudy Wiebe led the establishment of a writer-in-residence program at the University of Alberta. Since then, many eminent novelists, short story writers and poets have come to Edmonton to mentor aspiring and emerging writers in the community. The program, the longest continuously running offering of its kind in Canada, provides a distinguished writer a year's salary, time to write, and an office, in exchange for mentoring other writers. The ripples of effect created both by the writers who mentor and those who are mentored reach across the country and beyond, to readers and writers around the world.

In March, 2016, 22 former writers-in-residence returned to campus to celebrate the 40th anniversary of the program. Special events included an announcement that the creative writing room, Room 4–59, in the northeast corner of the fourth floor of the Humanities Building is now named the "Rudy Wiebe Room."

A Student Evaluates the Teacher: by Scot Morison

There is a small, narrow seminar room on the fourth floor of the Humanities Building with windows that overlook the North Saskatchewan River Valley, the High Level Bridge and the downtown Edmonton skyline. The view aside, there's nothing really remarkable about the room, but it's my favourite spot on campus. It was here that a gruff, sometimes cranky professor helped an unfocused and indifferent student uncover his true vocation.

I met Rudy Wiebe in the summer of 1979. A zoology major who didn't really want to study science anymore, I had found his introductory creative writing class while flipping through the thick University of Alberta calendar for half-interesting electives to round out my final year. The prerequisites for admission included a portfolio, so I wrote a couple of short stories and slipped them under Wiebe's door in the mostly deserted Humanities Building in late August. When Wiebe summoned me a few days later, he made it quite clear the samples I'd provided were execrable. Then he told me I could go ahead and register because in one of the stories, based on real events, I'd at least tried to write something I had a clue about: being young and stupid.

I was no standout in that first class, but evidently I did well enough to earn entry to Wiebe's intermediate course in the winter term. By its end, I was hooked on the process and challenge of storytelling and had abandoned any remaining thoughts of a career in biology. One way or another, I have made most of my living through writing ever since.

Over the years, Wiebe and I have stayed in touch, our relationship slowly evolving from one of teacher and student to a friendship. It is centred on coffee and conversation every few months in a Second Cup several blocks from Wiebe's home in the Old Strathcona area of Edmonton. Winter or summer, he always walks to our meetings: a man in his 80s still ramrod straight, fiercely engaged with life and arriving with a head full of big ideas to discuss.

We are friends now but he still intimidates me. Part of it is his talent and output. Wiebe is one of the finest writers this country has ever produced. His craggy face, grey-white beard and piercing gaze are well-known to CanLit readers. Beginning with his novel *Peace Shall Destroy Many* in 1962, he has published more than 25 books—including 10 novels and five short story collections—and edited or contributed to many others. His accolades include two Governor General's Awards for English-language fiction.

While Wiebe's themes are many and varied, the principal subjects of his writing are the Mennonite diaspora and the experience of Canada's Aboriginal Peoples under white domination.

Through deeply researched novels he has explored the First Nations perspective on white exploration, commercial expansion, and settlement in Canada with boldness, honesty, complexity and respect. The origins of his interest come from childhood. "I remember when I was a kid growing up and going to school, I was living on a homestead in northern Saskatchewan with reserves on either side of me. We saw Native people driving by with their ragged horses going to Turtle Lake to fish, and sometimes we bought fish from them, but the history we got in school was the Longfellow 19th-century romantic Indian brave and his squaw kind of crap. Completely ludicrous," he says.

Wiebe has also written ambitious historical fiction about the Mennonites in Canada and their experience of leaving Eastern Europe in search of freer, safer lives. His parents were Mennonite immigrants who fled religious persecution under the Stalinist regime in the former Soviet Union in 1930. They homesteaded in the school district of Speedwell, Sask., where Wiebe was born in 1934, before moving to Coaldale, Alberta, in junior high school. His memoir, *Of This Earth: A Mennonite Boyhood in the Boreal Forest*, explores his childhood experiences.

He is grateful for what this country gave his family and, because of that, has little patience for those who are critical of Canada taking in thousands of refugees from countries like Syria, upended by turmoil. "Since so many of us here have come from elsewhere within two or three generations, we, of all people, should be able to understand and accept others in similar situations," he says. "A wealthy middle power like Canada could be doing more."

I confess here I had read none of Wiebe's work when I signed up for that first class with him in 1979, but I slowly caught up and have now read most of his books. Getting through one of his novels requires concentration; he has an idiosyncratic attitude toward punctuation, and his syntax can be a challenge to follow. His entry in the Canadian Encyclopedia says this of his style: "though sometimes ungainly, [it] frequently results in an eloquence that is both appropriate and evocative." To put it another way, he is a writer who expects his readers to do some work, but that work is richly rewarded.

Wiebe could obviously write simpler, more straightforward stories, but he rejects the easy approach to his art. "Writing is hard, so there is no point being half-assed about it," he says.

For me, that uncompromising attitude is evident in his decision in the novel, *A Discovery of Strangers*, to take on a multi-layered story about Sir John Franklin's little-known first expedition overland through the Coppermine River region and his fateful contact with the Dene people. He could have easily, instead, written about the infamous third expedition, in which the explorer and 134 men on two Royal Navy ships disappeared in the Canadian Arctic while searching for the Northwest Passage. A novel about the lost expedition might have attracted more readers but it held no appeal for the author. "I didn't find anything particularly interesting about the idea of a bunch of Englishmen on two ships slowly discovering they are going to die," he says. "We already know the what, but the why is always the more interesting part of a story for me."

Wiebe brought that tough-mindedness about good stories and the storytelling craft to his role as professor. He taught other courses during a 25-year career in the University of Alberta English department, from 1967 to 1992, but spent most of it leading intense and demanding creative writing classes based on the approach he learned as a grad student at the prestigious Iowa Writers' Workshop at the University of Iowa. Wiebe, now professor emeritus in the Department of English and Film Studies, was one of the first teachers in Canada to employ the workshop technique that is, these days, pretty much universally practised in creative writing programs.

Detailed, no-holds-barred vivisection of student work was the main instructional mode in his classes. Perceived laziness on the part of an aspiring writer was something approaching mortal sin. Tom Wharton, author of highly regarded novels such as *Icefields* and *Salamander*, studied with Wiebe and now teaches creative writing at the

University of Alberta, one of Wiebe's successors in the job. Wharton remembers with a rueful laugh that one of the most damning things Wiebe could write in the margins of a draft story submitted to his workshop was a single word, scribbled in response to a sentence or passage he found wanting: "feeble." I remember seeing that cringe-inducing feedback on my work, too.

"Rudy was the kind of teacher you came to appreciate much later," Wharton says, dryly. He remembers retreating to the campus pub more than once with classmates after a workshop "to drink and badmouth" their professor. "But 90 per cent of the time, he was right," Wharton says now.

Suzette Mayr is an associate professor of English at the University of Calgary and the author of several novels including *Moon Honey*, *The Widows*, and *Monoceros*. With Wharton, she was part of Wiebe's final graduate-level writing workshop at the University of Alberta in 1991–92. Mayr says: "He had a really hearty respect for research and for doing your due diligence as a writer." With a laugh, she recalls one session in particular. "Rudy bawled us all out about something Tom had written about the Cretaceous era. He said: 'Do any of you even know what the Cretaceous was?'"

Mayr says she would never undertake the kind of sprawling historical fiction that Wiebe has written but appreciates his view on research: "There is a library of books to read before you start your own book." As a writer who teaches, she also admires his dedication to maintaining a writing practice. "Rudy once told me that he actually took a decrease in pay and course load to keep writing."

Aritha van Herk, professor of English at the University of Calgary and author of five novels and several books of non-fiction, was also a student. "Rudy could be impatient and difficult, and he didn't suffer fools gladly," she remembers. "At the same time, he was generous with his attention and, as a teacher, mostly interested in the quality of the writing. Although he had strong opinions, he didn't indulge in the ego trips of some writing instructors who expect students to be their clones or sycophants."

Van Herk battled with Wiebe many times, particularly as a master's student working under his supervision on her first novel, *Judith*, yet she holds a high regard for the man, his work and his teaching. "Rudy's strengths as a teacher were his attention to detail and his awareness that we should be writing our own stories about Alberta, based on our experience and the world we know."

While Wharton, van Herk, and others worked quite successfully with Wiebe, being his student was not a positive experience for everyone, even in hindsight. One former student who has since gone on to publish a couple of well-reviewed novels responded to my request for an interview in a terse email message: "I don't think I'm the right person to talk to."

Wiebe knows he was famously hard to please and admits to some regrets. "At a certain point, you have to become a kind of judge, you know. And maybe I shouldn't have been as judgmental as I was, but that was my way of approaching things. This is good, this is poor, this is just plain shit. But sometimes," he concedes, "you may miss some really good stuff."

PHOTOGRAPH OF RUDY WIEBE AND MARGARET ATWOOD
BY JOHN ULAN

On the occasion of the 10th annual Kreisel Lecture that took place on April 7, 2016 at the Winspear Centre in Edmonton, Margaret Atwood presented a lecture titled, "The Burgess Shale: The Canadian Writing Landscape of the 1960s." Rudy Wiebe and fellow writer Margaret Atwood reconnect in April, 2016, at the 10th Annual Kreisel Lecture presented by the University of Alberta's Canadian Literature Centre. The two became friends in the late 1960s, when Atwood lived in Edmonton.

Wiebe acknowledges he is not an easy man to get close to, but those who have earned his trust discover a very loyal friend. His best friend in the literary world was the late novelist and poet Robert Kroetsch, whose death in 2011 at age 83 after a car accident was a body blow to Wiebe. He is a tough man but I saw him in tears the afternoon he delivered a eulogy at Kroetsch's funeral. "They were night and day as personalities, but they had a real shared interest in the West and in literature," van Herk says of the writers' close bond.

Another important, if very different, literary friendship is with Yvonne Johnson, the woman with whom Wiebe co-wrote *Stolen Life: The Journey of a Cree Woman*. Johnson, the great-great-granddaughter of Big Bear, read Wiebe's richly layered novel, *The Temptations of Big Bear*, about the Plains Cree chief unjustly implicated in the 1885 Frog Lake Massacre, when she was in Kingston Penitentiary serving a life sentence for murder. (She, who had suffered years of physical and sexual abuse as a child, was part of a drunken group convicted of the beating death in Wetaskiwin, Alta., of a man they believed to be a child molester.) Johnson wrote a letter to Wiebe asking him how he knew so much about her famous ancestor, and they began to correspond. Eventually, they met at the prison and Wiebe helped Johnson tell her poignant and harrowing life story in the book. He also testified on her behalf at parole hearings over the years. Now out of prison and living in southern Alberta, Johnson says: "I love Rudy to pieces. He has always been very respectful, kind and gentle with me."

I was given a glimpse of how seriously Wiebe takes the responsibility of friendship while working on this profile. Late last fall, he got word that Gil Cardinal, the writer and director with whom he collaborated on the screenplay for *Big Bear*, the 1998 CBC television miniseries adapted from *The Temptations of Big Bear*, was in an Edmonton hospital. Though the two men hadn't spoken in quite some time, Wiebe immediately went to visit Cardinal in hopes of buoying his spirits. He got as much out of the visit as Cardinal did. "Gil had the same sharp wit I remembered, even though his body was completely ruined," Wiebe said. A few weeks later, shortly before Cardinal succumbed to his illness, I joined Wiebe at a luncheon where members of the Alberta film and television community honoured the Métis filmmaker with the 2015 David Billington Award for his impressive life's work. Cardinal was by then too sick to attend, but for Wiebe it was important to go and pay tribute. Throughout the afternoon, I watched as he sought out many of Cardinal's other friends in the room to share a story or a memory about the man.

In contrast to his legendary ferocity as writer, teacher and activist, the personal Rudy Wiebe is quiet and private. He and his wife, Tena, who have been married for 58 years, spend much time with their two children, four grandchildren and their church community. But family life has also been a source of great pain for Wiebe. His last novel, *Come Back*, was published in the fall of 2014, around the time of the author's 80th birthday. A long time surfacing, it is the story of a retired professor's attempt to understand his son's decision to take his own life years earlier.

The novel was inspired by the loss of Wiebe's eldest son, Michael, to suicide in 1985. He was 24. When I asked Wiebe about writing the most difficult book of his career, he began to answer by telling me he'd once heard American novelist John Irving declare that he always writes the last sentence of his books first so he knows where he's going. "I did not know where this novel could go, but I knew where it began," Wiebe said. "For a long time, I had never thought of writing a story like that. But at a certain point, when you get a certain distance from it, it tends to grow." He knew the subject matter was not his exclusively, however. "I talked it over with my family. They said, 'Are you sure you want to do this?' but they didn't hesitate at all."

Julienne Isaacs wrote of the novel in the *Globe and Mail*: "There is no cure for the pain of premature loss. Longing for the missing loved one will tug at the heart, call that command in perpetuity. Wiebe makes us attend to the beauty of the call." Possibly even more important to Wiebe than the formal reviews, however, are the informal ones received from others who have endured a similar loss. "It's not a particularly easy book to read, in one sense, because it tries to grapple with that sense of not feeling adequate, or 'What's wrong with me?'" Wiebe said. "But many, many people have thanked me for writing it."

Writing *Come Back* was an act of bravery. Necessary, and hopefully healing, for Wiebe, but brave. In writing the novel, Wiebe exposed himself in ways that he has never been comfortable doing. Then again, Wiebe has never lacked for courage, especially the courage of his convictions. He has written complex books—difficult to write, challenging to read—because that's the way he believes those stories had to be told. He chose being a demanding teacher over a popular one because he felt that doing otherwise would not be doing his job. And through his activism, he has stood up for individuals in trouble when others have abandoned them, like Yvonne Johnson, because of his belief that everyone deserves a chance to reclaim their lives.

One sunny afternoon last September, Wiebe and I took a walk around North Campus. "Look at all the bright young faces," Wiebe said, watching nervous-looking undergrads rush past on the way to class. He pointed to St. Stephen's College, his first residence when he arrived here as a 19-year-old in the early '50s. Later, as we passed the Old Arts Building, he told me a story about legendary writer W.O. Mitchell, who sometimes came up from Calgary to cover Wiebe's workshop. Mitchell used to collect and read student work aloud in class instead of having the students read and analyze it for themselves beforehand. Wiebe wasn't a fan of this approach. "Mitchell was such a good reader—he was an actor, really—that he could make anything sound good, including stuff that probably wasn't," Wiebe recalled with a laugh.

Entering HUB Mall, we passed the coffee stop formerly known as Java Jive. My turn to remember: midway through Wiebe's three-hour workshops, many of us came here to refuel with caffeine, not infrequently nursing the wounds of a stinging critique. Not that it always hurt; Wiebe's stern countenance belies an offbeat sense of humour and I remember plenty of laughter in his workshop, too.

Eventually, Wiebe and I arrived at the last stop of our tour, making our way up to 4–59, the creative writing seminar room in the Humanities Building. Neither of us had been back for a long time. We spent a few moments just absorbing that breathtaking view of the river valley. We both noticed, with a mix of amusement and nostalgia, that although the furniture in the room had been replaced, the same framed print of Alex Colville's painting, *Dog, Boy, and St. John River*, still hung on one wall.

After assuming his usual spot at the head of the long table, Wiebe grew reflective. "We were the first class in here and I was the first teacher. The building had just been built and a room had to be assigned to the writing class, so I asked and they gave me this beautiful space," he said. "It's a very moving experience to sit here now and think of all the people who've worked in here. A lot of students, a lot of stories."

Looking across the table at Wiebe, I contemplated my own experience up here in a handful of undergraduate and graduate classes with him between 1979 and 1984 (a sweaty-palmed, heart-pounding experience whenever it was my turn to present a new piece to the workshop). He was not the warmest or most encouraging prof I had at the University of Alberta, but somehow it was his teaching that had the most profound impact upon me. I have yet to achieve half of what I aspired to as a writer, but Wiebe made me want to reach for something more than mediocrity.

He still does. Now at an age when others might say that's enough and be content to sit back and rest (on the couch if not on their laurels), Wiebe continues to spend part of most days at his desk working. He recently finished the footnotes for a book of his collected essays, *Where the Truth Lies*, to be published in fall 2016 by NeWest Press. And he is definitely writing something else, though he refused to say whether it's a new novel. "You know I never talk about what I'm writing," he scolded.

As a final question, I asked Wiebe what advice he might offer the next generation of writers, in an age dominated by 140-character tweets and other wafer-thin social media, of dying newspapers and magazines and what feels like the near-extinction of independent bookstores. But Wiebe is not worried about the future of literature or those who create it. He believes that for writers, the real ones, this is a calling, not a job, and they will find ways to keep writing—whatever form that takes.

"It seems to me that storytelling is a uniquely human gift that allows us to put visions in each other's heads, and that's not going to stop," Wiebe concludes.

[*A slightly different version of this profile was originally published as "The Annotated Rudy Wiebe" in the Autumn 2016 issue of* New Trail, *the University of Alberta's alumni magazine.*]

Interview: A Conversation With Rudy Wiebe

Hugh Cook

Introduction: Hugh Cook's interview with Rudy Wiebe, first published in *Image*, a quarterly literary journal, issue 90, in the Fall 2016, was conducted after the publication of Wiebe's latest novel, *Come Back*. The interview is an in-depth discussion of Wiebe's academic achievements, his fiction and nonfiction, his devotion to his Mennonite community, and his philosophy on writing and life. A slightly revised version is reprinted in this collection.

Hugh Cook for Image: You've said that early in your writing career you discovered that it was as legitimate to write about a kid growing up in the Canadian bush as on the streets of New York. From the beginning, western Canada has been the locus of all your fiction; what is it about this region that resonates with you and drives your writing?

Rudy Wiebe: All writers face this question, "Where are your stories?" My family came to Canada as refugees from the USSR in 1930. They were homesteading, clearing land never before used for agriculture, in an isolated northern Saskatchewan community of immigrant Mennonites like themselves when I, their last child, was born. I read everything our one-room school had to offer—not much for an omnivorous reader—but even in my teens when I got to the Lethbridge Public Library (paradise!) I realized I was never finding any stories about my world, the particular place and people among whom I was living. Even in our grade-school readers, the Canadian stories were all about eastern Canada, never the West or the North—and by North I don't mean Sudbury, I mean Arctic-Polar North. So, while reading and then trying to write, I gradually began to understand more and more clearly: here is where my stories are, the places and the people of my particular life in western and northern Canada.

Image: I grew up in a Dutch Reformed community in Canada, and my father read from the children's Bible every evening at supper, so I was raised with the Old Testament, powerful stories which contain the same enchantment and bloodthirstiness and undercurrent of sexuality as fairy tales. Was this your experience as well? How did you first experience the power of narrative, of story?

RW: Yes, what mountain ranges of story, the Bible! It was read a great deal in our home, and sometimes aloud, but not at the table as a regular practice; nor can I remember it regularly at bedtime. We worked hard on our homestead, and in bed one fell instantly asleep. I never read in bed; I was too tired, and coal-oil lamps don't work well beside a bed, especially when you share that bed with a much older, very large brother, as I did.

Did your father read the Bible stories to you in Dutch? That was a key matter for me as a child, because my father and mother could read the Bible only in German and that bound all its stories to the faith and the "absolute truth" that was taught at church. I have a battered copy of the book my mother read to us (though oddly, I have no concrete memory of hearing it): *Biblische Geschichten für Schulen und Familien* (Bible Stories for Schools and Families) published by D.W. Friesen & Sons of Altona, Manitoba, in 1937. That book is evocative enough for a whole essay at least, so I'll just mention two Genesis details that have never left me: First, the Fall and the Flood in German are *Sündenfall* and *Sündflut*—both named "sin" before anything else. Second, the engraving of the *Sündflut:* the rain streaks down, darkening a tiny ark on the far horizon, but the clear foreground is a writhing mound of desperate children, birds, women, men, and animals clawing at trees and at each other to stay on a cliff above the heaving water thick with corpses all around them. As I explain in various incidents in *Of This Earth, Sünde* was for me the heaviest, most powerful word—but true!

The readings I felt differently about were the stories I found in the readers at school. They were in English (I don't remember learning to understand or speak it) and simply fascinating: in *Highroads to Reading, Book Two* there was everything from Aesop's "The Lion and the Mouse" to the Grimm Brothers' "The Fisherman and His Wife"; *Book Three* ranged from "The Ugly Duckling" to Brother Fox and Brother Rabbit in "The Tar Baby," not to mention "The Owl and the Pussycat." Then I found a small blue book of Greek myths in the Speedwell School three-shelf library: the marvels of Procrustes's deadly bed, the eagle and Prometheus, Theseus with his thread and labyrinth and Minotaur. I wouldn't have understood what Zeus was doing, raping Europa and Leda, so I have no memory of those bestialities, but Athena springing fully armed from the head of Zeus and Aphrodite born in the sea foam were perfectly delightful. And then there was *The Adventures of Ulysses* by Charles Lamb, in the Highways and Byways of English Literature series published by Blackie & Son of London and Glasgow. Incredibly, I have here on my desk the Speedwell #4860 Reference Library copy of this green-cloth book, the school seal impressed into the first page. I remember finding it in the rubble of the school cellar in August, 1971. I was researching places where Big Bear had lived in the nineteenth century and made a detour to see what, if anything, was left of the place where I was born, and inside the log ruins of my school I found a torn, muddy book I had read in grade five. To its last word of overwhelming vengeance, I read it again.

What I'm saying: my childhood memory of reading has two parallels: German Bible stories read aloud in church and at home devotions, and English stories I read silently to myself. There's a complex interaction here of the sinful (mostly Old Testament, with its often violent God) and the beautiful (mostly New Testament, until the crucifixion); the casual revenge brutality of folk tales and Greek myths and the delightful fun, the obvious right-and-wrong, of fairy tales and fables. By age eleven I was racing through violent Zane Grey; my mother was very concerned about my endless reading, and she would have been horrified if she had known, for example, how similar I found the judges of ancient Israel and Lew Wetzel in *The Spirit of the Border*. When years later I bought and read the Grimms' tales in their original language, read, among so much else (the book contains 210 tales) the song the fisherman sings to the great fish, "My wife, Ilsebill, / she wills not what I will," my experience of reading became even clearer: I was silently speaking in my head, my heart, my spirit, the signs of Homo sapiens' greatest achievement—language—and in so doing was experiencing everything a human being possibly could. So: read.

Image: Your memoir *of this earth: A Mennonite Boyhood in the Boreal Forest* is a beautiful account of your early years in the remote community of Speedwell, Saskatchewan. Since the book was published almost seventy years after the experience, it must have been a challenge to write. *of this earth* uses an epigraph from a Robert Kroetsch poem: "What do you do for a living? I asked. / I remember, she replied." Do you happen to be blessed with a good memory? In the book's acknowledgements you mention other means you used to meet the challenge of recounting such long-ago events. Could you elaborate?

RW: When I told my writer friends that I was writing a memoir about the first twelve years of my life, they laughed with me. "How the heck will you get a whole book out of that?" We laughed some more, and I said, "But just think about it, all you learned about being a person, and how you learned it, loving your mom and dad—or not—and squabbling, playing with your siblings and doing chores and what is death and sex and walking to school in the winter and reading and getting strong enough to fight your buddies and other families' funny habits and church and words, words, all the words there are in English—and for me Low German and High German, too!—and who can run the fastest or piss the farthest and girls and stories and muskeg swamps and girls and ..." and we were all laughing even harder and they said, "Okay, lots, more than enough!"

Some of the work was like the historical research I did for novels. First, places: Speedwell, where I was born and lived my childhood. Not one person lives there now in the entire township. It's the Fairholme Community Pasture with every homestead burned and bulldozed into grass, and the only clearly identifiable spots are the tiny fenced Mennonite Brethren church cemetery with its thirty-two graves in a clump of bush, and two miles north of that the jack pine walls of the one-room Speedwell School where I almost finished grade seven (we left for Alberta in May, 1947). Also Vancouver, where Dad, Mom, Liz, and I briefly lived with my sister Tina's family at 4160 Brant Street.

Second, the calendar: when did something happen? Luckily our family lived at four different homesteads in Speedwell, so most memories could be fixed within a timeline since they hang on a specific place: a barn stall, yard layout, pattern of poplar trees. Also, for five years two of my sisters kept a diary (when Helen died, Liz continued it), and it dated specific events exactly.

Third, documents and conversations: the bits of official records documenting church and school were sparse, and therefore all the more stimulating. There were a few short memoirs, including my brother's wonderful twenty-nine-page, handwritten ramble from Orenburg, Russia, where he was born, to the farm in Alberta, and also *Northern Reflections: History of Glaslyn and the Rural Municipality of Parkdale* (2005), a huge, two-volume assemblage of community information published for the Saskatchewan centennial. More: letters, newspapers, scraps of paper that nudged a memory. Better yet, a few conversations with my brother and my one surviving sister about what we mutually remembered, and how. How and why so much difference could be enfolded in eight decades of the unforgotten.

Last, and best of all, were the hundreds of family and community pictures. Several dozen are included in *of this earth,* and a close study of any one will reveal how evocative in detail and unexpected image one little black-and-white Brownie snapshot can be to the probing imagination.

Beyond the usual research, memoir is character, and here its difference with fiction becomes most clear. Characters in a novel are my creation: I control them completely. On the other hand, since one of the principles of my life is that our Creator has given us free will, when I write memoir I have no license to control my characters' behavior: under God they have made their choices, they have acted in time as they did, and it is my responsibility to reveal that and that action only. To remain true to my convictions and the form in which I am writing, I must dare to discover and reveal what I or they literally did; only out of that can I shape an honest, genuine memoir.

For this understanding I must in particular thank Yvonne Johnson. I could not have written *of this earth* without having worked with her on her story, *Stolen Life: The Journey of a Cree Woman*. In the five years we struggled together to shape that book, she taught me the essentials of memoir as nothing else ever could.

Readers have asked whether I'm going to write about the next twelve years—adolescence to beginning fatherhood and publication of the first novel. As a book it makes sense, but let me tell you: from where I sit, writing childhood is complicated, but it's very easy compared to young manhood. And middle age ... I don't think I've lived long enough yet to dare a memoir about that. For now, fiction will have to do.

Image: In your childhood, your Mennonite community in Saskatchewan lived beside a First Nations community. These two cultures are recurring subjects in your writing. Do you see significant similarities between them?

RW: This is, of course, a book-length question, but I'll just underline one profound similarity. In the Saskatchewan boreal forest, hunting or farming, you are always aware of your total dependence on nature. Therefore, the belief in a loving Creator, as Jesus taught and as First Nations people also believe, who cares for his children by providing all they need, both physical nourishment and spiritual guidance accessible to all through prayer and honorable actions towards your fellow humans—this is fundamental to both. And the longer I live, the more firmly I believe in this profound similarity.

Image: For centuries Mennonites held the ideal of living in communities separate from the world. Today, however, Mennonites live in modern urban societies and occupy positions at the center of government, business, and academia. What does it mean for you to live as a Mennonite today?

RW: I would use the name Anabaptist rather than Mennonite, since there is such an incredible range of groups that call themselves Mennonite, with an extraordinary and often incompatible range of practices.

Historically, there never was a unified Anabaptist or Mennonite movement, as you imply in your question. Anabaptism began among young intellectuals in the city of Zurich and was driven out of that city (often into rural hiding) by both Roman Catholic and Protestant persecution. The movement toward separate Mennonite communities grew out of such persecution. Certain rulers granted religious groups the privilege of settling in their domains if they developed good agriculture and did not proselytize, for example in sixteenth and seventeenth-century Poland and eighteenth and nineteenth-century Russia. Other Dutch Mennonite believers remained in like cities Amsterdam and Haarlem and developed their Golden Age as they call it, especially in the seventeenth century. Every area of business except government was permitted them. They remain in the Dutch cities to this day, active in business, culture, and education.

Today, after five centuries, to be Mennonite is to sometimes be both religious and ethnic, or either, or neither, take your pick. What does it mean to be Mennonite today in Canada? I couldn't say, though I've tried to write novels about bits of that complex question, for example in *Sweeter Than All the World*. We do have the oldest Mennonite communities in Switzerland and France and the Netherlands and Germany and Pennsylvania and Ontario to give us some ideas about what we might do, and what we doubtless should avoid.

Image: Do any of the characters in your novels particularly embody a genuine Mennonite way?

RW: I prefer the word Christian to Mennonite. Every Mennonite novel of mine has characters trying to find genuine Christian ways to live. For example, Thom Wiens and Joseph Dueck in *Peace Shall Destroy Many;* Frieda Friesen and the various Epps and Reimers in *The Blue Mountains of China;* the two Adam Wiebes and others in *Sweeter Than All the World*. All are trying, with certain moments of achieving. Never completely, of course.

Image: When you started publishing in the early 1960s, did you feel somewhat alone as a Canadian Mennonite writing fiction? Today, there's a robust body of Mennonite writing in Canada. What, in your opinion, accounts for this rich output?

RW: In 1955, I wrote a short story (never published) which contained the first strands of character and conflict that grew into *Peace Shall Destroy Many*. At that time I knew of no Canadian who was writing fiction on Mennonite subjects in English. As far as I know, there was no one else until David Waltner-Toews published some poems and stories in the late sixties. The true blossoming began with Patrick Friesen's first poetry collection, *The Lands I Am* (1976), and within a few years Turnstone Press in Winnipeg was publishing Friesen and Di Brandt, Sarah Klassen, Audrey Poetker, Sandra Birdsell, Armin Wiebe, David Bergen, Miriam Toews, and others.

There are many reasons for this extraordinary literary achievement: for Mennonites the shift to higher education, from German to the English language, to supporting the arts in general, especially music; and then for Canada as a whole the 1967 Centennial, which evolved into a celebration of multiculturalism and the promotion of the arts by the Canada Council; and, in particular, Turnstone Press itself. With no direct connection to anything Mennonite, its editors found fine Manitoba writers who happened to be Mennonite and who sold very well, so they published them. It seemed centuries of verbal creativity had been bottled up in the Mennonite psyche, and Canadian freedom released it to the world.

Image: *Peace Shall Destroy Many,* your first novel, created some controversy within the Mennonite community after it appeared in 1962. You've published a good number of novels since. What has been the reaction by Mennonite readers to your novels over the years?

RW: I've written and talked about the reaction to *Peace Shall Destroy Many* numerous times, most recently in an hour-long talk, "Hold your Peace," given at the Mennonite Historical Society of British Columbia. The fact is, in more than half a century of writing fiction, I have had very strong and continuous Mennonite reader support, and this is especially true for such "Mennonite" novels as *Sweeter Than All the World* and *Come Back*. Only one novel since *Peace Shall Destroy Many* has been controversial with Mennonite readers, and that was *My Lovely Enemy*. The novel includes a discussion of the fact that Jesus, as an historical human male, must have had a penis, so, what did he do with it? A number of Mennonite Brethren churches felt such a subject was anathema and that I should be excommunicated. But this did not happen; the Mennonite Brethren have a congregational church structure, and my home church supported me, and with time the matter sank out of collective awareness.

Image: Can you describe your association with Mennonite theologian John Howard Yoder in the sixties, and to what extent his political ideal of pacifism was an influence on your novel *The Blue Mountains of China*?

RW: Yoder was teaching theology at Goshen Seminary when I taught creative writing at Goshen College in Indiana. We were intrigued by each other's writing on how to better live our Christian faith, and the assassination of President Kennedy and the growing intensity of the Cold War as the Vietnam conflict developed during those years drew us deeper into debate about the seemingly endless human need for violence. We became part of a small discussion group that met regularly, and also exchanged notes on problems we struggled with in our ongoing writing, both theology and fiction. During the sixties Yoder was working on the ideas which grew into *The Original Revolution* (1971) and *The Politics of Jesus* (1972), and I read early versions of some of the concepts those brilliant books discussed. Particularly important to me as a novelist was this question: What is the relationship between a Christian's spiritual faith and his political actions as a "free" citizen of a contemporary nation? Did Jesus offer any guidelines on how to live in our century? Yoder sharply focused some new ideas for me; a reader of my first three novels will see how the problems faced by Thom Wiens in *Peace Shall Destroy Many* and Abe Ross in *First and Vital Candle* develop into John Reimer of *The Blue Mountains of China* dragging a cross north along Alberta Highway 2 and offering his "Sermon in the Ditch" to anyone who will listen. He does not offer his teachings from a mountain; what he has to say can only be uttered walking in the mud of everyday roadside existence. But he is on the way.

Image: The word "community" has come up often in this conversation. However one defines it—by religion, ethnicity, geography—how important is it for a writer to be a member of a community? Do you think writers outside of an identifiable community are at a disadvantage?

RW: Writing fiction—I can't speak for poets—is largely a solitary activity. For me, stories are always about human beings doing something in some particular place, and though I might not go quite as far as Thomas King in saying, "The truth about stories is that that's all we are," my imagination can only begin to build on what I have experienced. For that experience, I need to know the lives and places of others. My small life can never be enough. I need others. Those others are my community; that's where I find the bits and pieces, the boulders and plains and rivers and mountains out of which fiction can grow.

As my fiction shows, I have found my community in the past worlds of my ancestors, in the past and present of the Aboriginal people of the place where I live to this day, in the faith community where every week I meet friends I have known for decades, both old and young. For someone who has worked largely alone throughout his life, the loneliness and limited stimulation that come with aging can be especially difficult. I would find it impossible to be a writer without the love of my small, close family, but, above all, impossible without the larger continuing community of interaction, stimulation, visiting, food, and talk which is my church. As a writer, I have many acquaintances and friends throughout Canada and the world, but the ones I meet most regularly and have the most personal contact with are those who gather with me in Edmonton on Sunday morning.

Image: Years ago you said that the role of a Christian novelist is to be "a critic and a witness." Can you say more about what that means, and how you've attempted to embody that in your fiction?

RW: The world has changed so much since I was a child: from the end of World War II to the restricted wars and disasters of this present time, and the emergence of a kind of rationalism which holds that it's impossible to hang onto the old rigidities of faith—unless, like religious fundamentalists, you lock yourself into an immoveable dogma and then lash out at everything.

Given that, one of the guiding thoughts for me as a writer is: Jesus, I believe; help my unbelief. And the second is like unto the first: Lord, have mercy on me, a sinner.

The longer I write, the more I see how little of these great truths I have captured in what I've written. I must trust story; I must trust imagination to bear my writing witness; and it seems to me now that being a witness is more significant than being a critic.

One of the joys of my life is that I was given to write a few of the first published stories of the Aboriginal people of my part of Canada. I no longer need to do that; they have many brilliant storytellers now gaining attention, and will have more. But I did help give some push to starting that witness, and for that I'm grateful.

Image: Some critics raise the question of appropriation of voice, of whether a white person should write about Aboriginal life. Could you speak to that?

RW: Oh, "appropriation of voice," that fancy postcolonial phrase for what is to me a mostly nonsensical way of looking at literature. It emerged in Canada during the late

1980s to early '90s, and I may have contributed to it with my early short story "Where is the Voice Coming From?" about a deadly confrontation between the Cree and the North-West Mounted Police in the 1890s. It's my most popular story, reprinted and translated over sixty times, often in university textbooks. In the late eighties, people asked, how dare a white Canadian write stories about Aboriginal Canadian characters?

Talk about irony. My first novel was set in a Russian Mennonite homestead community similar to the one where I grew up; when it was published, many Mennonite readers were deeply disturbed that I would tell stories about my own people! So, whom can I write about? Whose stories dare I tell?

The answer is obvious: no writer worth her or his salt asks anyone's permission to write on any subject. I know many Aboriginal Canadian writers personally; we read each other's books, we talk, we correspond; not one them has told me what I should not write about. Of course we have talked about voice appropriation, and we have discussed at length how to show proper respect and how to discover and explore the Aboriginal story you're trying to write.

One final point: my Aboriginal stories all come from history; my only major contemporary subject is *Stolen Life: The Journey of a Cree Woman*, a book Yvonne Johnson and I wrote together because she invited me to do so. The largest part of it is given in her own words.

Image: A number of your Mennonite novels are based on historic events as well—as you once put it, they unearth the past. In a conversation with novelist Robert Kroetsch you said that you have a distrust of inherited history, because there is often another side to the official version. Is that part of the role of the novelist for you, to provide that other side?

RW: I wouldn't so much say "the other side" as "the lived, personal experience." In both my major areas of historical interest, western Canadian Aboriginal history and Mennonite history, there has been a huge explosion of research in the last forty or fifty years. More facts, stories, and persons are known about now in areas where, when I began to write, almost nothing imaginative had been done—that is, the work of trying to recreate what daily life was like for individuals, families, and communities. So much was not known, or known only in bits and pieces. To stimulate my imagination, I had to do a lot of what you might call "primary digging." I did not want to write fantasy formula like Fenimore Cooper's Indian tales; I wanted to write fiction that creates, in the reader's mind, a reality that a human being could actually have lived in. I have published essays about that digging, for example, "On the Trail of Big Bear" and "Bear Spirit in a Strange Land" (now collected in *River of Stone* and *Where the Truth Lies*).

Image: Your historical novel *A Discovery of Strangers,* for which you won a second Governor-General's Award, describes the first encounter of the Dene people with members of the first Franklin expedition in what is now the Northwest Territories. It was a disastrous occasion for both the British and the natives. Was it an example of the inevitable tragedy of nineteenth-century British imperialism?

RW: *Discovery* began as a novel of place, but not even tracking the route of the first Franklin expedition over the Arctic tundra by canoe—as my son and I did with four friends in 1988—gave me enough stimulus to write that novel. It came from the Dene people who still live north of Yellowknife, and their ancestral stories, which I discerned in faint strands, almost unnoticeable whiffs, in the laborious *Narrative of a Journey to the Shores of the Polar Sea* Franklin published in 1824. The British courage and suffering is obvious: eleven of the twenty-one expedition members died. It was not as catastrophic as the third expedition twenty-five years later, when all 129 crew members, with Franklin himself, vanished forever, but it was enough. As the *Narrative* makes plain, everyone on the expedition would have died if the Dene had not saved them. That was what shaped the story for me: not the overweening English sense of pride and high purpose brought to nothing by the relentless land, but the beauty of the Dene people who had never seen a white person before. As Dr. John Richardson, the scientist on the expedition, later wrote to his wife:

> [We six] survivors were found by the Indians on Nov. 7 [1821], and these savages (as they have been termed) wept on beholding the deplorable conditions to which we were reduced. They nursed and fed us with the same tenderness they would have bestowed on their own infants, and finally, on December 11, conveyed us to Fort Providence, the nearest post.

Out of such interactive humanity, novels can grow.

Image: In your novel *Sweeter Than All the World*, a history of the Mennonite people from the early days of persecution to eventual settlement in Paraguay and Canada, you describe a number of cruel events: Anabaptist women burned at the stake, the mechanics of the tongue screw, and other acts of violence. These events occurred in the sixteenth century. Has Christianity essentially changed in regard to its use of violence?

RW: Christianity has always and forever been changing. Is any Christian church today like the Jerusalem church of the first century? Like the Gentile Greek church that grew so quickly out of that beginning? Like the churches that developed after the Council of Nicaea declared the charismatic Jewish healer Jesus Christ to be "of the substance of [God] the Father ... consubstantial with the Father"? I see the Protestant Reformation of the sixteenth century as one of many attempts to revitalize and purify our understanding of what living like a follower of Jesus can mean. With all we now understand of human behavior, we cannot be surprised that some of us will always try to stop change with violence, and some try to resist that violence.

The attempts at change on the part of my own Anabaptist-Reformation heritage have always fascinated me. Though Mennonites denounced war, their communal use of the ban could be brutal at times.

In any case, in all my fiction, even where not a single ostensible Christian appears, there lingers the aroma of Thom Wiens's longing at the end of *Peace Shall Destroy Many*: "Christ's teachings...could he but scrape them bare of all their acquired meanings and see them as those first disciples had done, their feet in the dust of Galilee."

That longing remains for me as well.

Image: Your novels are often characterized by dislocations in time and place, shifts in point of view, by the inclusion of historical documents and artifacts, and by what some consider a dense or difficult prose style—all of which might challenge readers. As you're writing a novel are you conscious of the reader at all, or are you wholly focused on telling the story the best way you can?

RW: When I look back over my writing, I think that over the years the personal experience of the characters has become more and more the focus. I seem to have outgrown the omniscient narrator and found the individual central intelligence a more useful point of view (but still in third person). An example of the former would be the short story "The Angel of the Tar Sands"; of the latter, "Finally, the Frozen Ocean." The clearest example of this point-of-view difference is between my first and last novels, *Peace Shall Destroy Many* (1962) and *Come Back* (2014).

Focusing on what is happening in the consciousness of a particular character allows me to shift quickly, as the character's mind does, from one subject to another. I want readers to think about what's going on with those shifts—and in so doing to create the story in their own consciousness. I believe every reader reads a slightly different story, and I want to push that difference as far as I imaginatively can. So, my stories are never a fast trail of connected action to be raced through—not even the manhunt in *The Mad Trapper,* though it comes closest. I want the reader to slow down, to be puzzled, to understand that several complex things are happening at the same time, and to be intrigued enough to want to recognize every one of them. That's really *reading.*

As far as my so-called difficult prose style, to be a bit flippant, my love of the German language may have something to do with that. In German, sentences can be pulled out to almost any length (as the classic German stylists do) because the reader keeps waiting for the dominant verb which must finally, once and for all, appear and nail down the action and meaning and end the sentence. Unfortunately, an English sentence is not structured that way; in English the main verb needs to be close to the main noun, and so the writer must make do with long addendums of phrases and subordinate clauses and commas and semicolons and dashes and brackets. Do I make myself clear?

To sum up, in writing I concentrate on telling the story, but always telling it to a reader. Story and reader should always be I-You, the basic form of all human relationships. (Thank you, Martin Buber.)

Image: You spoke earlier of the three languages spoken in a Mennonite community: Low German for everyday life, High German for church, and English in school. What advantages do you feel are given you—or any writer—by familiarity with a number of languages?

RW: Low German was my first language, what I first babbled as the last baby in our seven-child family. It is what I spoke to my parents all my life. One beauty of Low German was that it was totally oral (I never read it until decades later) and perhaps that is part of why voice is so important to me: the particular voice of a person first impressed me as a child, a voice speaking in words I could never write down, as I could later in English or High German if I wanted to remember them exactly. Low German was sound only, remembered in all the delights of hearing, never visible as written words. This was a strange and profoundly evocative restriction for a writer dealing with his first and most warmly intimate language.

As for knowing several languages, being able to shift from one to the other without a conscious thought, that is a supreme gift for a writer. It teaches you the aural meanings of language, how something can be said in one that is never quite possible in another, how implications, puns, hints are untranslatable. In my English writing, I could try and push the Germanicism of the language, as I did, for example, in *The Blue Mountains of China*, some readers were annoyed, others enlightened. I like intelligent readers.

Image: Your latest novel, *Come Back*, describes the experience of Hal Wiens, an elderly Mennonite man who is painfully brought back to the death of his son by suicide twenty-five years earlier. He struggles with the question every parent in such a situation asks, "Why?" Your novel gives no easy answers.

RW: Homo sapiens are self-aware creatures, and in that sense death is a very simple matter for us: we know death is inevitable. Not one person, no matter how brilliant or disabled, poor or rich, will escape it. But when a person deliberately seizes that inevitability and makes it happen, those who knew and loved that person grieve, grieve deeply, sometimes for the remainder of their own lives. For a beloved to deliberately leave, to choose to be gone forever from what was our mutual life on earth, opens a wound that will not heal. There may come a time when it can be ignored, sometimes for months or years; it may grow less painful, and one feels, well, I can live with this, time heals, I've almost forgotten. But then one day a date will appear on the calendar and before you can skip past it your memory catches: Today was her birthday, she would be forty-seven, and … and …. All the impossible possible "ands" of a lifetime never lived again pour over you.

Image: One epigraph in *Come Back* quotes Jesus's words in Mark 9, "For everyone will be salted with fire." That's a paradoxical image, one that suggests both preservation and purification. Is that how you read Jesus's words? The second epigraph quotes the familiar passage from First Corinthians 13: "For now we look through a mirror into an enigma, but then face to face." Can you comment on how these epigraphs apply to the novel?

RW: The saying of Jesus is found only in Mark, and it has multifaceted, contradictory meanings, as his statements often do. Not only does it imply, as you say, the paradox of preservation and purification: fire can be seen as life-giving—as in cooking food, or providing warmth—but it can also be violently destructive. Which does Jesus mean? In addition, he often used salt as an image for the "good savor" of a Christian life, the grace of God demonstrated by a committed Jesus-follower. So it's a fitting evocation for a novel where, on the final page, the afflicted memories of the protagonist are at last run to ground and he sits motionless, staring into a fire.

The second epigraph builds on the first. What we know of life now, to translate Paul's Greek more literally, is *not* like looking into a mirror at an enigma, but like looking *through* a mirror *into* an enigma. Now, that's an image of life to ponder.

A White Man's View of Big Bear

Myrna Kostash

Book review: Myrna Kostash's "A White Man's View of Big Bear" review of *The Temptations of Big Bear* (1973) is a revised and updated version of the piece first published in *Saturday Night Magazine,* February, 1974, p. 32–33. Myrna's reflection on the original review is as follows:

> In 1973, while I [Myrna] still lived in Toronto (I would return to Alberta in 1975), the editor of *Saturday Night* magazine, Robert Fulford, asked me to write a review of a new novel by Edmonton-based writer and English professor, Rudy Wiebe. The novel was *The Temptations of Big Bear.* I was unfamiliar with Wiebe's work but, by the time I had finished reading *Big Bear* and writing the review, my perspective on the era of the "clearing of the plains" in western Canada had changed utterly. (Kostash, Myrna. Email received by Bianca Lakoseljac 16 February, 2021)

A White Man's View of Big Bear

Someday western Indians[1] will write novels and their voices will tell us, at last, the authentic version of how their nations contracted culture of the reservation after a millennium of running buffalo and dying of old age. These novels may also tell us that the People are reassembling for a retaliatory war, but that is a chapter no white person can write. We can, however, write of the past we shared with them, the inglorious advance of our technology across the bony bleached prairie, while they were pressed back into the corners we did not want for ourselves.

Praise be, this is the way *we* are telling it now; whatever scruples one may have about flagellation as a spiritual exercise, it is possible that, politically, the scourges we fashion for ourselves from the guilt of imperialism and racism help drive out the beast we harboured with the Hudson's Bay Company and the North West Mounted Police. We have been guilty of vicious and venal attacks on the indigenous nations, our vision distorted by the need to spread ourselves over the globe— all potential riches *our* patrimony—and rewrite the history that came before us to cover the tracks of our adversary's dignity and good sense. We may now also be

1. The terminology in use in the 1970s to describe Indigenous lives and identities, while not overtly disrespectful, is no longer acceptable usage. "Indians" collectively are now known as Indigenous peoples, and First Nations." "Reservation" is the American word for the Canadian "reserve." "Imperialism" is now more likely to be called "colonialism." Desperado" by dictionary definition is "bold or reckless criminal," clearly not what I intended, even in 1974.

guilty, in an excess of penitential zeal, of sentimental and mystifying projections, requiring that our POWs manifest the majesty, wisdom and sanctity of preliterates.

Somewhere between the atrocities and the expiation lies Rudy Wiebe's novel, *The Temptations of Big Bear*. Something like a true story, it is social realism raised to the level of the elegy. A gorgeous lamentation for a brother, dead in the prison house of the Philistine, whose life is an archival document as well as a moral fable and a prayer.

Clearly, Wiebe loves the Plains Cree chieftain or, rather, the spirit of the man who was, he says, "at peace with himself, self-contained" even while the flow of his life was stopped up and choked off by the machinery of a hostile civilization. The novel was six years in the making, six years of transcontinental research from library to museum to public archives, picking up the splintered narrative from Frog Lake to Calgary to Ottawa to New York City where, in a museum vault all by himself, Wiebe unwrapped (the first to do so in how many years?) from its layers of ordinary cloth Big Bear's "power bundle": a bear's paw, a twist of tobacco, a twist of sweetgrass. An operation not blithely undertaken. The revelation of the power bundle was to be performed within a sacred circle of warriors, accompanied by sacred chants, so as to contain its powerful *mana*. Excitement, respect and the rumble of the New York subway underground were no substitute.

The desanctified totem of Great Parent Bear. It was effectively exiled by the time Big Bear died in the penitentiary at Stony Mountain, Man., in 1888.[2] Years

---

2. In fact, Big Bear died on Poundmaker Indian Reserve, Cut Knife, Saskatchewan.

before, Big Bear had already ridden on his last buffalo hunt. Years of the last of everything. The last of cohesive community, potent ritual, uninterrupted tradition, free space, plentiful food and good health.

The novel opens in 1876 with a scenario (Wiebe has a wonderful eye not only for the prairie landscape and vegetation but also for cinematic *motion*) of the Plains Cree, under the leadership of Big Bear, refusing settlement on a reservation, refusing the debilitating compromise of other tribes bent by the fear of genocide and the honeyed promises of the Great White Mother's agents as long as there still seemed room enough for everything. Wiebe suggests the sweep of the nomads[3] following in the dust of the herds and, out there, at the periphery of vision, a settler or two, a little town fixed in the prairie grass. The novel ends with Big Bear in a little room, dying with a dream both of the buffalo and the People—just piles of bones—and of the future urban defacement of the land. Between these two events lies the story of Big Bear's temptations: that he could somehow, as none other of the People had, resist this terrible contraction, the *squeezing* of his space into a spiritless acre of poverty, that he could resist it without violence, murder and hate.

Well, we know he lost. Had he never been tempted, we might have received him in our textbooks as a heroic

---

3. It is incorrect to refer to the Plains Cree as "nomads;" they followed the seasonal migration of the bison and made camp on the same hunting grounds year after year; in the winter, they would take shelter in wooded valley areas.

Bad Indian (we can safely eulogize those we "manfully" subdued) slaughtered in some vainglorious massacre or as a shabby Good Indian, docilely leading his people into the corral of our government. All routes ended in the same place. Big Bear's agony was to insist on the one that most closely followed the byways of his nation's righteousness.

The cunning thing about this book is that it speaks from several points of view, not only Big Bear's but also from those of white traders, a missionary, an army volunteer, a Mounted Police inspector (Francis Dickens, son of Charles), a farming instructor and, what I consider a minor *tour de force*, that of Kitty McLean, an adolescent white[4] girl held hostage in Big Bear's camp for two months, her indelicate, energetic and perspicacious female sensibility admiringly and exquisitely rendered.

They all hang together in a single story, chapters towards a definition of the process of imperialism, so that the attitudes and imagination of the whites murdered in the Frog Lake[5] massacre are of as much interest and concern as those of the Indian desperadoes. The switch about of victim/victimizer defies all easy sloganeering. But it is the Peoples point of view, their version of events and their commentary on the experience—perhaps because we have never been instructed in it—which is the single most important accomplishment of the novel.

---

4. Actually, Kitty's mother, Helen Hunter Murray, was Mixed-Blood from northern Saskatchewan, her father a Scotsman with the HBC at Ft Pitt.

5. The events at Frog Lake are now more likely to be referred to as "killings" or "uprising" or "debacle."

It is, first of all, their *language*. I don't suppose Wiebe speaks Cree, but his rendition of the speech, accurate or not, remains a peculiarly impressive variety of English: "But no chief who was there ever walked between him and the fire; they would look at him and go around. And now he has choked out his breath; my son has ridden to the Sand Hills without breath. Without breath, without breath." It is, second, their way of looking at things. For the first time, I began to understand how it *felt* to grow homeless, to face the buffalo across the border of the CPR and know they were dying along with you, to watch Medicine Hat go up on the sacred hills, to live cramped and immobile, told to be a farmer on one, small, designated piece of land. Finally, Wiebe suggests what it was to go down with Big Bear to his surrender, in a ragged, stumbling band, hungry and hopeless, to sit in a wooden chair with leg irons, holding the black ball that weighs the soul down. "I never put a chain on anything," says Big Bear. And, for the first time, my own "heroic" antecedents—the illiterate[6] peasant refugees arriving in the middle of their nowhere and making a go of it—assumed a double edge. I could see the People watching their arrival, sick with their own banishment.

These, then, should be part of the way we see ourselves: Fort Pitt and Fort Carlton, Frog Lake, Turtle Lake and the North Saskatchewan River; the Reverend George McDougall; James McLeod, NWMP Commissioner;

---

6. This was the stereotype of the Galician immigrants which I cheerfully repeated here, while I still lived in Toronto, and before I wrote *All of Baba's Children* (1978).

Edgar Dewdney, Department of Indian Affairs; Fred Middleton, "hero" of Batoche; the American, Howard, with the ubiquitous Gatling Gun. Not, anymore, as catchwords for a concocted glory but as shorthand for our greed and godlessness. And, against them, Big Bear, Lone Man, Root Grubbing Woman, Wandering Spirit and Sits Green On The Earth, as the genealogy of the Chosen, men and women who knew how to live unpossessively, even as they were being dispossessed: "No one can choose only for himself a piece of the Mother Earth. She is. And she is for all that live, alike."

Salted With Fire

Hugh Cook

Book review: Hugh Cook's "Salted With Fire" review of *Come Back* (2014) was first published in *Christian Courier*, (Jan. 7, 2016).

It's a snowy April morning in Edmonton and retired English professor Hal Wiens is enjoying his daily coffee with his Dené friend Owl in a downtown coffee shop. Their attention is drawn outside the shop window by a raven flitting from streetlight to streetlight. Knowing Wiebe's lifelong preoccupation with aboriginal cultures and that ravens, in Native myths, bring messages from the spiritual realm, the reader senses the bird is a harbinger of events about to happen.

Wiebe confirms the omen: "Good sign," Owl says.

"Good for what?" Hal asks.

"Maybe bad," Owl says, "hard to tell sometimes."

"You'll know which when it happens," Hal answers.

"Yeah, for sure," Owl says, "something always happens."

And happen it does. Only moments later Hal's world is rocked when he sees a slender man dressed in an orange down-filled jacket stride past the window. Hal recognizes the jacket, the young man's figure and gait, and is convinced it is his son Gabriel (Gabe). But this is an impossibility: his son committed suicide twenty-five years ago.

"Gabe!" Hal shouts. He rushes out of the coffee shop in pursuit and dashes into the street's heavy traffic, causing a tangle of accidents. He fails to catch up to the young man, returns home before the police can arrest him, and collapses on his kitchen floor.

Thus opens Rudy Wiebe's latest novel, *Come Back*.

Still publishing at 80, Wiebe has been a major figure in Canadian literature since the 1960s. He is a main practitioner of the prairie novel, has written extensively and insightfully about aboriginal peoples, and is the founder of a robust tradition of Mennonite literature in Canada. Wiebe has won the Governor-General's Award for fiction twice, the Charles Taylor Prize for non-fiction, and has been named an Officer of the Order of Canada. *Come Back* is his twenty-fifth book.

Readers of Wiebe's first novel will recognize Hal Wiens, who was an eight-year-old boy in *Peace Shall Destroy Many*. Now 75, Hal is a widower, his beloved wife Yolanda having died only seven months ago. Hal's grief is so deep that he has not disturbed a thing in the house since Yolanda's death, not even so much as "move her last novel or hairbrush on her night table, nor water a plant." Nothing in the house "was left alive." All Hal has is painful memory of Yolanda, and "silent rot."

He has numbed his grief by relying on mundane activities: drinking coffee with Owl, phoning his surviving daughter and son who live in distant cities, suppressing his pain and telling himself "he was fine, just fine." Sighting the young man in the orange down-filled jacket that morning, however, shakes Hal's daily routine and reminds him of September 8, 1985, "that day of irreducible memory" when he was informed of Gabe's suicide at the age of twenty-four. Now his "day is cracked wide open to that remorseless memory always poised to strike."

Realizing he must try to understand what caused his son to take his life, Hal is forced to the basement where Yolanda has filed away Gabe's personal effects and journals in stacks of carefully labeled boxes. "It had to be done," Hal realizes: "face Gabriel's writing."

Two interwoven narrative threads comprise the rest of the novel. The first portrays Hal as he spends the next three days reading through Gabe's writings in the carton boxes and recalls memories of his son. The second thread consists of the jumble of Gabe's writing in the form of diaries, letters, lists, and journals he left behind. The journals describe Gabe's travels across various countries of Europe, finding work at the national Film Theatre after his return home, his response to days spent watching films—and, most significantly, his infatuation with Ailsa, the thirteen-year-old daughter of family friends.

A twenty-four-year-old's obsession with a girl barely "two months a teen" may remind the reader of Nabokov's *Lolita*. Gabe himself describes Ailsa as "an extremely typical very young teenager with childish traits," and his attraction to her as "unimaginably dangerous." Then why the obsession? Gabe admits he has made of her "a legend," suggesting that perhaps Ailsa is for him an ideal of pure and uncomplicated beauty, something he never found in his messy life. In any regard, a twenty-four-year-old young man's fixation on a girl of thirteen may strike readers as deviant, and therefore a questionable aspect of the novel.

Other readers will find that pages and pages of Gabe's tortured, chaotic, and self-absorbed ramblings—at one point 28 pages in a row—make for difficult reading. Gabe himself admits his writing is "mindless dribbly stuff," "the same trivial things over and over in the same childish way." The reader tends to agree, and wonders whether Wiebe should perhaps have exercised more conciseness and selection in the many pages devoted to Gabe's writing.

The journals provide a painful window into Gabe's personal struggles. "All my life," he writes, "I have been alone, even with my family that I love." And later he says, "It's not that I don't want to live, it's that somehow I've lost a means by which to function." He expresses despair for feeling distant from God, and in turn directs anger towards God for his seeming absence: "I would rather burn in hell than go to a 'Father' who just creates and then leaves you on your own." A final possible cause of Gabe's death is depression over his unrequited and impossible love for Ailsa. As he says in frustration, "I need a lover and A is a child."

The reader's sympathies are strongly with Hal, as reading his son's journals re-opens the raw wound of grief and guilt (Hal was out of town when his son's body was discovered). "Why are there so few facts about us," he laments, "you and me being together?" Echoing King David, Hal keens, "O Gabriel my son, O my son, my son Gabriel."

The novel gains poignancy for those readers who know that Rudy Wiebe's own son Michael also committed suicide at the age of 24 in 1985. But it would be prudent to avoid viewing the novel as autobiography.

Wiebe himself warns of this danger. "Fiction is what you make of a fact," he says. "Fiction is an imagined construct which may be triggered by fact. This is what imagination does."

In contrast to Canadian writer Miriam Toews, who has written critically of her Mennonite roots and whose novel *All My Puny Sorrows* also deals with the topic of family suicide, Wiebe shows a more compassionate and gentle tone toward his community. In the throes of grief, Hal, a devout Mennonite, finds spiritual consolation in his upbringing: remembered childhood songs and evening prayers, familiar lines from old hymns, and texts from Scripture. The novel's title, *Come Back*, is therefore not so much a command as a prayer.

After police knock on his door in response to the accidents he caused that snowy morning, Hal escapes to the family cottage at Aspen Creek, waiting for an answer to the agonizing question asked by every parent whose child has committed suicide: "Why?"

In recognition of the painful complexity of the question, Wiebe offers no glib answers. Still, the reader discerns hints of meaning. *Come Back* opens with two epigraphs; the first is Jesus's words recorded in Mark 9:49: "For everyone will be salted with fire," a paradoxical image that suggests both preservation and purification. As the apostle Paul states in Romans 5:3–4, human suffering is a refining fire that leads in turn to perseverance, character, and hope.

The second epigraph consists of the familiar words of I Corinthians 13:12: "For now we look through a mirror into an enigma, but then face to face," which suggests that humans may never understand the tragic loss of a child, but also expresses with steadfast faith that someday all will be revealed. As though he had Paul's words in mind, Wiebe says, "The hope, the faith, the love within human spirituality are the realities that become most powerful in the lives of the novel's characters, though they cannot, of course, experience these realities fully. At least not yet."

Come Back offers honest and eloquent testimony to this profound faith, hope, and love.

A Gift of Understanding

. . . .

Maureen Scott Harris

Book review: Maureen Harris' "A Gift of Understanding" review of *Stolen Life: The Journey of a Cree Woman* (1998) was first published in *Books in Canada*, Vol. 27, No.6, (Sep. 1998). 6.

On November 18th, 1992, the novelist Rudy Wiebe received a letter from Yvonne Johnson. Johnson identified herself as a prisoner in Kingston's Prison for Women (P4W) and a great-great-granddaughter of the legendary Cree leader Big Bear. She wrote because she had read Wiebe's novel *The Temptations of Big Bear*. She asked him:

"Please help me share what it is you know, and how you got it. How is it you came to know as much as you do? Why were you led? What was the force behind you? Who are you? Why did you choose Big Bear to write about? What sparked your interest in this powerful man of long ago?"

What Wiebe did not learn from this letter was that in 1991 Yvonne Johnson had been convicted of first-degree murder and sentenced to life with no eligibility for parole for twenty-five years. She is the only woman in Canada serving this sentence. *Stolen Life* pieces together the complicated story that brought her that dubious distinction. The book is terrible and splendid and absolutely compelling. I read all 444 pages of it almost in a single sitting, and I've hardly been able to stop thinking about it since.

In 1973, *The Temptations of Big Bear* received the Governor General's Award for Fiction. Wiebe's interest in Big Bear began when he was a graduate student, and he speaks of Big Bear's life as "the story that never lets you go." It's not surprising he replied to Johnson's letter and began a collaboration that has lasted six years and produced this remarkable and difficult book. The book's story is not just Johnson's; one of its binding strands is the sense of connection between the two writers and their growing involvement in how to tell the story.

"To begin a story, someone in some way must break a particular silence." This sentence opens the first chapter. It takes courage and work to break silence, and I'm both moved and awed by the courage these writers show in risking this book. Johnson, a Native woman jailed for murder in Canada, might reasonably expect her story to be called a lie or merely predictable (as in a way happened in her trial). She acknowledges herself that she risks completely alienating her mother and others whose support she longs for. Wiebe, by choosing to work with a Native writer and taking on the role of directing and shaping the work, faces complex questions of voice and authority—a minefield he already knows. What did they hope to accomplish? What did they think they were doing? Wiebe explains:

"She has asked me to help her; I have promised her, 'Yes'. And, for these years we have struggled to tell her story so that she, so that I, so that some possible reader will understand. Something.

"Why has she lived such a dreadful life, and why has she been so destructive to herself and those she loves? Why have they been so devastatingly destructive to her? How is it she became entangled in murder? What I already know of her life makes it almost too horrifically representative of what has happened to the Native people of North America; of what her ancestor Big Bear most feared about the ruinous White invasion."

Yvonne Johnson's life has been as full of incomprehensible violence as her ancestor's. One of seven children born in Montana to a Saskatchewan Cree mother and a Norwegian-American working-class father, she grew up poor, surrounded by racist taunts and bullying. Her oldest brother, Earl, was arrested and died in jail, officially a suicide. The family believes he was murdered by police, and Wiebe finds evidence for their belief. With Earl's death, and the Johnsons' inability to get their questions about it answered, something essential in the family dissolved and her parents separated.

How do you write a book with someone who is in jail? Wiebe visited Johnson and talked to her on the phone. In prison she had begun keeping journals, trying to think about her life and what had happened. He urged her to continue and to write down everything she could possibly remember. They exchanged letters and documents. He researched the circumstances of her life, travelling, interviewing family members and people who knew her, as well as lawyers and court officials and police who were involved in the trial. The work was done slowly and painstakingly, piecing together a story full of the gaps and silences that gather around the unspeakable and the denied. Work done "so that she, so that I, so that some possible reader will understand. Something."

Johnson was born with a double cleft palate which was not fully corrected till she was sixteen. As a child she couldn't make herself understood.

"It was like being deaf but still hearing, speaking but speechless—it was there, heaping up inside me. I could not ask questions, just puzzle everything around inside my head, dreaming it, bouncing it back and forth, without any guidance to help me understand. So I learned by instinct, by watching to see and recognize what others don't, to judge myself by taking chances. To depend only on myself. There was no one else .... I think that then, on a deeper level, my spirit already knew and understood how much I was being hurt."

In addition to the racism and violence marking her childhood, Johnson was sexually abused by both strangers and family members. Her cleft palate meant she was silenced; she couldn't tell what was happening to her. At sixteen, following her arrest and conviction for driving a car without the owner's permission, a sympathetic judge sentenced her to corrective surgery at state expense. But the surgery couldn't correct the rest of her life. She was no longer in school and often lived hidden, trying to stay out of her abusers' reach. The experiences of her childhood and adolescence suggest to me it's no surprise she ended up involved in murder. What *is* surprising is that she wasn't killed herself along the way.

Stolen Life is full of mysteries, not mysteries like the ones Nancy Drew solved, but the mysteries of the human heart. Why *did* Yvonne survive? What are the connections that yield an event (the murder) or a work (this book)? One of the most puzzling mysteries this book faces is the ambiguity of family ties. So much power and so much helplessness are braided into these connections. Often love isn't enough to overcome the failures inscribed by poverty and prejudice, or justice turned rancid or violent. Both Wiebe and Johnson understand that families can be helpless to take care of themselves, that love and violence can and do cohabit within individual hearts and the family both.

Yvonne Johnson is now serving her sentence in the Okimaw Ohci Healing Lodge for Native Women in Saskatchewan, transferred there when P4W was closed. While she was still in Kingston she served as door and fire keeper for the sweat lodge and eventually learned she was Medicine Bear Woman, a name she then remembered had been given her ceremonially by her maternal grandmother. This grandmother also had a cleft palate, the mark of the Bear, as does Yvonne's eldest daughter. Finding her spiritual identity and her connection to this grandmother has given her the strength and understanding to begin to live consciously as a medicine person.

"So, could it be that I too, after more than thirty-five years of existence, I can be reborn under the ceremonies?

"My spirit name is Medicine Bear Woman. I ponder this greatly and still endlessly, what is a medicine person? As the Elders tell me, all that you have experienced you must learn from, and the people who live the hardest lives can have the greatest understandings and teachings to give others. So learn well, for the sake of others."

How does a medicine person act? She might write a book. In Johnson's years of journal-keeping and letter-writing, and in her work on this book, she has made herself a writer. Through her writing she extends understanding and teachings beyond the circle of those whom she actually meets. In her first journal (begun in 1991 before she contacted Wiebe), she wrote:

"I wish I could write my life-story book. Maybe then and only then will my life be revealed, and it might help the next abused and hurting person whom the world judges and condemns as already dead. But this dead person, me, is not beyond help. Maybe in death I'll be of some use."

For this white woman reader, it's clear Johnson gives help as well as asks for it. I hope the publisher has sent a copy of this extraordinary life-story book to Tom Wappel, M.P., and I hope he has the gumption to read it. On March 18th, 1991, the Crown Prosecutor J. Barry Hill said in his address to the jury sitting in Yvonne Johnson's trial: "In this case you are exposed to people who are obviously very different from you and me. That's reality. It would be nice if all the Crown witnesses to a murder were bank managers and accountants." While I've been engrossed in this book and writing this review, the Walker trial has been underway in England, and I think it would be nice if we stopped thinking that people in suits never drink wine in the morning and never commit or witness murder. What my mother calls "the best of regulated families" provide prime settings for denial and violence, with their possibility of murderous consequences. We're fools to pretend otherwise, and doubly fools to do it as we drink our morning coffee and read the daily paper. We desperately need the lessons offered by Yvonne Johnson, who has looked hard at her life, trying to see and understand what she has done as well as what has happened to her, and who seeks, from what she has learned, to make amends.

In their collaboration on this book, Yvonne Johnson and Rudy Wiebe show us the importance and the possibility of listening and speaking, of making connections (among people, words, events), and of offering what the connections teach about the difficulty of being human beings. Their hope, which I share, is that such offerings strengthen the human community. The book would not have been written without their collaboration and the feeling of connection beneath it. Take Yvonne Johnson's word on that:

"Nothing just happens, my friend, unless it was meant to be .... If we are guided under the Bear, then even our futures can be changed .... You and I may have been chosen long ago to meet, and our past has given us each a gift of understanding."

—Yvonne Johnson to Rudy Wiebe,

24 December 1992.

A Gentle Eye from Afar

Katherine Govier

Rudy Wiebe was a teacher in the only creative writing class I ever took, in 1970 at The University of Alberta in Edmonton. He was a decade past the publication of *Peace Shall Destroy Many* (1962) and the wounds of being attacked by his own community were still fresh. In fact the year was split between poetry and fiction, with poetry taught by Dorothy Livesay, so I had only about three months of workshop classes with Professor Wiebe, as we called him.

And yet he had a lasting effect on my life and work.

I remember the way he pinched himself, under his lip, not pulling the trim beard hair but the tender cleft, as he looked at us, thinking deeply. He wore his biblical college training proudly, and that was before he enthused about the poetry and stories of the Bible.

I think the class was a struggle for him. We were naïve, and our writing was pretty trivial, as to be expected with twenty-year-olds who have grown up without fear or hunger in a big city surrounded by friends and family. The story I wrote in his class, one of my first, about two friends who got spring fever and walked across Edmonton's High Level Bridge on the exposed train tracks, fully aware that a train could come at any moment to knock them forty-eight meters down into the frozen North

Saskatchewan River. I remember his response; it was that he hoped I had not actually done this!

I had actually done it.

That was my first experience of Rudy as a caring elder.

I took another class from him; the Bible as literature. He got us to read and think about Louis Riel and the Battle of Batoche; we considered Riel's religious writings from jail as inspired utterances. He got us to look in the archives. Rudy had strong views about how, in Western Canada, minorities were despised. Of course he knew something of it. He was solemn, he was serious, he was looking for big moral themes and great dramatic events of our regional history. He was the first to invite us to mistrust the history we read in books. I was ready to listen, after the British history class that I attended at eight o'clock Tuesday and Thursday mornings, which gave the official view of events. His heroes were the Great Russian writers; mine, at the moment, were the newly published Margaret Atwood and Alice Munro.

Only later did I truly digest the facts that he had been born on his parents' barely-sufficient homestead in Northern Saskatchewan. Or that when it failed, he and the Mennonite community had moved to Coaldale, Alberta. Five years after I left Alberta, in Ottawa, I met Joy Kogawa, the other of the two writers who most affected me, and took most interest in me, when I was starting out. Strangely, she and Rudy had attended the same school in Coaldale. Coaldale was a Mennonite town, Joy tells me now. There were two groups, the Mennonite Conference and the Mennonite Brethren, which was the more zealous and fundamentalist. Rudy belonged to the Brethren.

Joy however did not see Rudy as an outsider; she saw him as outstanding, admirable. Maybe that's because she was further outside: hers was among a number of Japanese-Canadian families in the town. They had been rounded up after World War II and sent west, and many had gone to the area to work in the sugar beet fields. Joy hated it. She remembers that her father was very amused to hear her sounding like the Mennonite kids, with low-German habit of using "already" or "already yet" at the end of sentences.

It was 1976 before I saw Rudy again, this time in Toronto where he was working on a play about coal with Theatre Passe Muraille. My friend Scott Lauder, also his former student, then teaching English at Ryerson University, invited him to dinner. Scott felt he had to apologize for being an obnoxious smart ass. Rudy was amazed that Scott could cook. He amused us by saying that he had gone to a supermarket for the first time in his life. He was that otherworldly. He was genuinely curious about how we lived.

I was about to move in with the novelist Matt Cohen, some years my senior and already established. And Rudy warned me about the difficulties of two artists living together. It was good advice. I didn't listen to it though. He asked me if I could cook. It was a salient question. It was if he were trying to reconcile two archetypes. I did not want to be Peggy and Graeme (Atwood/Gibson) or Wilfred and Sheila (Watson) Nor did I want to be Rudy and Teena Wiebe.

He also brought the glad news about my application to the Canada Council to finish the stories that became *Fables of Brunswick Avenue*: he had supported me. After the dinner Scott and I agreed that Rudy was "into goodness". It certainly set him apart.

But over the years Rudy maintained his own bad boy rep. He was almost excommunicated for discussing Jesus' penis and what he did with it in *My Lovely Enemy*. He published some of the first stories of the northern peoples. The Dene saved members of the Franklin Expedition—was it not ok to write about it? He attracted criticism for telling stories about the indigenous peoples, but he had been lambasted for writing about his own. He said that only a fool asked people what he was allowed to write.

Meantime, I too became fascinated with Western Canadian history and was at the same time eager for historical documents and suspicious of the official stories. These attitudes led me to write *Between Men*, and later *Three Sisters Bar & Hotel*.

Rudy and I met again in 1998 at the Senate hearings about Bill C-220, the "Son of Sam" imitation, which sought to have the Crown seize the copyright of any convicted—or accused-felon. I spoke as the President of PEN Canada and he had come to support us in opposing it. As a twice Governor General's Award winner and co-author with Yvonne Johnson of *Stolen Life*, his support was significant. We won the Senate's support and the bill was defeated.

And another time we met for a drink (it can't have been a drink, he didn't drink, it was always grape juice) in the bar of Edmonton's MacDonald Hotel. His son had committed suicide; he was wrestling with this dev-astating event and thought that it had to do with the young man's fascination with an avant-garde film. I re-member being invited to his place in the country, but never getting there. It was dry, nobody drank. Joy was invited and went: she didn't drink either because she was from Mennonite Coaldale.

A gentle voice from afar, a support when needed, an inspiration and a giver of insights into the shape of the world: that is Rudy Wiebe to me. How lucky I was to learn from him. He is a part of my deep roots to Alberta. I remember him telling me, with delight, that when you stand down by the water on the Bow River as it comes into Calgary, the view is entirely unchanged from what it was in 1875 when Fort Calgary was founded—be-cause the skyscrapers disappear into the bushes.

That was some years ago. I wonder if it is true now.

Peace of Mind

John Longhurst

Rudy Wiebe, pictured with Conrad Grebel University College professor Hildi Froese Tiessen after a reading at Conrad Grebel Conference on Mennonite/s Writing where he was a frequent lecturer.

Introduction: On the occasion of receiving a PAX ("Peace") award from Canadian Mennonite University in Winnipeg, Manitoba, Rudy Wiebe was interviewed by *Winnipeg Free Press* religion reporter John Longhurst on a variety of topics related to his career as an author—writing about Mennonites, his books about Indigenous Peoples in

Western Canada, his 1973 novel *The Temptations of Big Bear*, as well as his unwavering faith. It was published March 30, 2019.

Fifty-seven years ago, a young Mennonite author living in Winnipeg published a book that turned the Canadian Mennonite world upside down. That author was Rudy Wiebe, and the book was *Peace Shall Destroy Many*—the first novel about Mennonites in Canada in English. The book, which offered an honest and pointed portrait of Mennonite life on the prairies during World War II, provoked a great deal of anger and pain. "It was hard on them," says Wiebe, 84, of how the book impacted some members of his denomination. "It was a tough story."

In the book, Wiebe, who lives in Edmonton, explored how Mennonites in the fictious community of Wapiti, Saskatchewan opposed the war while, at the same time, their church was divided by conflict and broken relationships. "It was difficult for the older generation to handle," he says of the book, which he once described as a "bombshell" for many Canadian Mennonites. "They didn't speak English, they weren't accustomed to reading fiction, and they didn't share insider problems with the outside world," he shares.

The publication of the book was hard on Wiebe, too. At the time he was the new editor of the Mennonite Brethren *Herald,* the official English-language publication of that denomination. As the criticism mounted Wiebe new he couldn't stay editor of the *Herald.* "I wasn't fired, but I resigned before they would have fired me. There was no question I couldn't continue," Wiebe explains.

That decision led to a distinguished 25-year career as a professor of English at the University of Alberta, and as an award-winning author of 33 books, anthologies and collections of essays about faith, life on the Canadian prairies, and about western Canada's Indigenous peoples. Along the way, Wiebe was a two-time recipient of the Governor General's Award for Fiction; received the Writer's Trust Non-Fiction Prize; and received the Charles Taylor Prize for his memoir of growing up in Saskatchewan. In 2000, he was named an officer in the Order of Canada.

On April 4, Wiebe will return to Winnipeg to receive another honour when he is given the PAX award from Canadian Mennonite University. The award, created to honour people "who lead exemplary lives of service, leadership, and reconciliation in church and society," is being give to Wiebe for how "his works have been critical in exposing societal concerns," and for "the patience and empathy his works awaken," according to CMU president Cheryl Pauls.

For Wiebe, the award from CMU is "particularly welcome" since it is coming from his own faith tradition. "I have received many other awards, but to get an award like this from my own community is really important to me," he says.

Committed to the church

Despite how some Mennonites responded to *Peace Shall Destroy Many,* Wiebe never became angry with the church, or lost his faith. He recently got a letter from an old friend who said "he can't figure out how I stuck with church," Wiebe says.

For Wiebe, "there's no great mystery about it." One reason is growing up as one of seven children in a caring and supportive religious refugee family in Speedwell, in northern Saskatchewan. His early church experience was also positive; there were "hardline" leaders, he says, but he also heard messages about the love and mercy of God.

Another reason is the church he and his wife, Tena, belong to in Edmonton—Lendrum Mennonite. "It's made up of some people that I've known all my life, a few I've just known for some for a few years," he says. "But within a few years you become such close and warm friends."

The church has "been very supportive of me and my writing and the work I've been doing all my life," he notes, adding members of the church have never been "judgemental" about what he has written. The church was also a huge support when his son, Michael, died of suicide in 1985. "When Michael died, it just shortly after there was a very large controversy about what I had written. But they stood with us."

A Christian writer

Although the mainstream writing world is a quite secular place, Wiebe is quite happy to call himself a Christian writer. "That means I'm a believer and a follower of Jesus Christ. I try to look at the world in the way Jesus tried to teach us," he says. That doesn't mean he has faith all figured out, or that he lives perfectly as a Christian. Living faithfully is "sometimes hard to maintain," he says.

His understanding of his faith has also changed over the decades. "We live as Christians in a world that keeps changing," he says. "You just can't go plodding along thinking I know what's right and what we've been taught for the last 500 years or something like that is the only right thing.

"The world changes, and you need an imagination to understand that. You can't just say that certain practices today are out the window because they didn't they didn't exist in the Jesus' time. This is where the imagination and spiritual discernment are important."

As for whether being so open about his faith has ever hurt him as a writer, Wiebe says no. "People kept publishing my books," he says, noting *Peace Shall Destroy Many* has never gone out of print and is still taught in high schools. "There was never any question about what my approach to the story was, and they didn't object my philosophy in life. Nobody objected to me [about my faith] in terms of the publishing world."

Telling the western Canadian Indigenous story

In addition to writing about Mennonites, Wiebe is also well-known for his books about Indigenous people in western Canada. He traces that interest to growing up on the northern prairies, "so close to the land." When his family and other Mennonite refugees from the former Soviet Union showed up in northern Saskatchewan in the 1930s, the land was considered "empty because nobody had farmed it before. But they [Indigenous people] were there the first, using it in a different way."

But he soon realized "there was no question they had lived there for a long time before we refugees showed up. This was intriguing to me."

As a boy, he enjoyed wild saskatoons and strawberries, knowing "these have been eaten by 500 generations of Indigenous people before me. But I enjoyed them just as much as they did." His interest in Indigenous people led him to want to write books about them. "What I basically was trying to do was tell the story of what happened to them, a story that basically had never been talked about in western Canada before," he says.

Of his 1973 book *The Temptations of Big Bear,* he says "I don't think there had been a book from an Indigenous standpoint" until it came out, where the Indigenous character is "the hero of the book." Until then, he says, Indigenous people were "stereotyped basically, either romanticized or portrayed as down and out, poverty stricken addicted people, on the fringes. Certainly never worthy of being the protagonists of a major work of fiction."

He is sensitive to the issue of cultural appropriation, but says Indigenous people have always told him "if you treat us with respect and know what you're writing about go ahead and do it." Besides, he adds, that was a different time; today, there is no need for non-Indigenous people to write about Indigenous people since they have "so many good writers of their own."

Wiebe's experiences with Indigenous people have also influenced how he sees his own faith. "I can't believe that the God who created the world would just give one little vision [of himself] to one small group of people in the

Middle East and keep everything else hidden from everyone or every human being all over the earth," he says. "That's not from the kind of God I understand."

He also believes Mennonites are well-placed to be empathetic towards Indigenous people, due to their own history of being displacement and refugee flight. Noting how many Mennonites, including his own family, were forced off their land in the former Soviet Union in the 20th century, "you start thinking about what it would be like for someone to invade your country, and taking over your home ... these are profoundly the same issues."

Looking back and looking ahead

As for what he is reading now, Wiebe speaks positively about Katherena Vermette, a Manitoba author with Metis and Mennonite roots. "Her first novel is very good," he says of *The Break,* which is set in Winnipeg.

But he's also reading letters he and Tena exchanged in the late 1950s, when she was in Canada and he lived in Germany for ten months. "There are 168 letters," he says. "Boy oh boy, they're really interesting."

He's also thinking about mortality. "I have Parkinsons," he says, noting he needs a cane for walking. "It's uncomfortable and painful in the morning, and it's not going to improve," he says. "It's debilitating, but you don't lose your mind to it. That's the main thing."

Is he worried about losing his mind to something like dementia? "That kind of thing, well, God knows," he says. "I need to take what life brings. It's part of what life is. And we take what it is."

What gives him peace about the future is community—both the larger writing community, and especially his church. "It's lovely the way many older people carry on, especially if they have a community like a church," he says.

For now, his mind is focused on the award he will receive next week. "The award is called PAX—peace," he says, noting that when *Peace Shall Destroy Many* was published "it destroyed peace for many." But because of it, "I have never been able to stop writing, not for the rest of my life." Faith@freepress.mb.ca.

The Other Wiebe: Decoding a Novelist's Nonfiction

George Melnyk

Prologue:

Rudy Wiebe has published many more books of fiction than he has nonfiction. Nonfiction writing by prominent fiction writers seldom attracts literary scholarship, which considers nonfiction a secondary level of achievement. While scholars can delve into the textual strategies and metaphoric universes of fiction, this is not the case with nonfiction. Nonfiction either lacks these fundamental elements completely, or is insufficiently attuned to them to make it worthy of study. As an essayist, nonfiction writer, and literary historian I want to understand the value and meaning of his nonfiction.

To show how any accomplished fiction writer's nonfiction differs from most nonfiction writing I turn to Wiebe's introductory statement in *War in the West: Voices of the 1885 Rebellion* that he compiled and edited with historian Bob Beal in 1985. Beal's style is typical of historical writing. "In the late nineteenth century," Beal states in his introductory essay, "most newspapers published few illustrations. But there were those that specialized in artwork and they were very popular" (*War in the West* 12). In contrast to this prosaic statement Wiebe's writing tends to use metaphor, enigma, and irony. In his introduction titled "Paper Treason" he compares the fate of Gabriel Dumont, an expert marksman, with that of the crucifix-carrying Riel. "But words are more lethal than bullets," Wiebe states emphatically, "and in 1885 Canada's greatest state trial proved that words written on paper are the most deadly of all" (*War in the West* 10). In this simple, yet powerful, sentence we hear the emotional engagement of a novelist, who understands that Riel's concepts were more of a threat to the Canadian state, than Dumont's military prowess. While Dumont was pardoned, Wiebe reminds us in the essay, Riel was hanged. The Christian idea of martyrdom is not far from Wiebe's thoughts about Riel, nor is his Mennonite pacifism. There may be more stylistic flourish in his sentence than one finds in the writing of historians, but that is not my main point. It is the thematic unity that links his fiction with his nonfiction that matters and its source in his personal consciousness. These themes that appear in both his fiction and his nonfiction were first explored by academic critics of his fiction.

Critical Understanding of Wiebe's Fiction and its Bearing on his Nonfiction

Wiebe's fiction has attracted the attention of a number of scholars over five decades, but what interests me the most is their commentary on his historical novels, which relates to his nonfiction work on the same topics. In one of the earlier studies Richard Harrison noted that contemporary prairie novelists like Wiebe were expressing "... skepticism about the given past" in the sense of challenging the dominant white Anglo-Canadian narrative of prairie history (*Unnamed Country*, 184). A quarter century later Herb Wyile termed Wiebe's approach to historical fiction as "fracturing the authoritative version" (Wiebe, "Walking Where" 67). The source of this disruptive approach had been identified earlier by E.D. Blodgett (a colleague of both Harrison's and Wiebe's at the University of Alberta) in Wiebe's literary use of non-Anglo voices like that of the Cree leader Big Bear. Bringing Indigenous voices into his historical novels allows Wiebe to point out the contradictions in late nineteenth century Anglo-Canadian colonialism and its view of the land (*Configuration*, 214). Wiebe used the voice of Big Bear as a proxy for his own ideology and its social and political alienation from the region's dominant "given past." This ideology was rooted in his Mennonite heritage. In his 1974 interview with me he confirmed his identification between the Indigenous viewpoint and his own when he said:

> One very beautiful thing about the Indian people is
> their belief that the Land is given to everyone ...
> This is also a basic Christian belief—that the land
> is a gift of God! (Melnyk, 33)

From what he said and what he wrote I can identify two significant characteristics of his fictional writing in the 1960s and 1970s that carried over into his nonfiction.

The first is its *ethno-religious ideology* (the Mennonite imagination) and secondly its *Indigenophilia* (the pro-Indigenous imagination).[1] According to W.J. Keith, whose 1981 book *A Voice in the Land: Essays by and About Rudy Wiebe* blends critical commentary on Wiebe's fiction with "explanatory" essays by the writer in order to "... provide the information needed as a prerequisite for an intelligent appreciation of his novels" (10). One of Wiebe's essays titled "An Author Speaks About His Novel" defends his characterization of certain Mennonite figures in *Peace Shall Destroy Many* against criticism from the community. The essay presents a clear statement about the nature of his ethno-religious imagination. He makes it clear that Mennonites are not above human nature and that a novelist's honest realism needed to be brought to bear on them (67). In another essay on the same topic he views the novelist's role as that of critic and witness, not teacher or preacher (The Artist).[2] Criticizing and witnessing are key features of these two essays and of others as well.

The "explanatory" or commentary essay is one way of linking his fiction with his nonfiction. Another link

1. For an in-depth discussion of the religious underpinnings of Wiebe's fiction see G.H. Hildrebrand's PhD Dissertation "The Anabaptist Vision of Rudy Wiebe: A Study in Theological Allegories" (McGill 1983).

2. For a discussion of this characterization of the Mennonite novelist see Harry Loewen, "The Mennonite Writer as Critic and Witness" *Journal of Mennonite Studies* Vol. 2 (1984) 113–123. https://jms.uwinnipeg.ca/index.php/jms/issue/view/6. Accessed 29 October 2020.

is the historical research that underpins both his historical writing and historical fiction. W.J. Keith in introducing Wiebe's essay, "On the Trail of Big Bear" describes the essay as documenting "…the considerable research and planning that preceded the writing of the novel [*The Temptations of Big Bear*] … (132). Wiebe states that, "For the facts themselves I go to mostly the same places as historians …" ("On the Trail", 137). Yet he will not let facts dominate narrative the way a historian might. Instead he presents the unwritten stories and undocumented personalities of his main characters in order to give emotional weight to history. As he says in the essay, he will not let facts become "invariable tyrants of story" ("On the Trail", 133).

In his nonfiction writing about the same topic—the life of Big Bear—there is cross-pollination coming from the novelist's fictional imagining and literary style. In "Bear Spirit in a Strange Land" Wiebe's autobiographical account of his experience in New York, where he sees and touches Big Bear's medicine bundle in the vaults of American Museum of Natural History, we find sentences reminiscent of similarly charged ones in his introduction in the Beal/Wiebe book a decade later. For example he writes:

> I am holding in my hands the sacred bundle of Big Bear. In the centre of this bundle is that spirit gift which gave Big Bear his name and his wisdom and his power, which hung around his neck when he rode on a raid or danced his vows to the Thunderbird in the Thirst Dance. ("Bear Spirit", 146)

While the contextual genre is that of the essay, many of the sentences are written with a novelist's spirit.

The American literary scholar Delbert Wylder reviewed Wiebe's second Indigenous-themed novel *The Scorched-Wood People* and concluded that "Wiebe has been able to blend both the earthiness and the spirituality of the Metis way of life into a powerful human document" (238). The concept of human documentation captures both the documentary underpinnings of Wiebe's historical novels and his own emphasis on seeking out the human dimension in historical events. So when Wiebe writes himself into the real-life story of his search for Big Bear's medicine bundle, he is able to blend his own earthiness (Mennonite homesteader origins) and his Mennonite spirituality (Anabaptist Christianity) with the Indigenous earthiness and spirituality of an imagined and recreated Big Bear.

Underlying this unity is Wiebe's distrust of dominant narratives and their biases because he comes from a minority about whom the majority have written pejorative and inaccurate accounts (Neuman, 226). Because of this identification, he feels at home with the land-oriented spirituality of Indigenous people. Since Indigenous accounts of white-recorded and described events are often oral, difficult to access and in many cases undocumented, he enters Indigenous thought through the lens of his own viewpoints. Using his own Anabaptist sentiments to get close to Aboriginal mythologies and ideologies allows him to feel a kinship between Indigenous history and his own settler history. Wiebe's historical fiction and his nonfiction on Indigenous topics are attempts to redress or upend dominant narratives that ignored or sought to erase the valid experiences of silenced subjects. His nonfiction also serves to augment and clarify his fictional representations by discussing his motivation and foregrounding his engaged research approach.

The Importance of the Essay in Wiebe's writing

In the evocatively-titled "Where the Black Rocks Lie in the Old Man's River" published by Wiebe in a book of photographs by Geoffrey James titled *Place: Lethbridge, A City on the Prairie* Wiebe writes about the Oldman River in southern Alberta in a way that expresses the personal interconnectedness of his inherited European mythologies and the ones he attributed to Indigenous cultures.

> Even after ten years in southern Alberta [1950s] I would have no intimation of the mind-expanding world of story contained in the word, Napi-ooch-a-tay-cots in Blackfoot: "the River the Old Man Played Upon," in a playing field that can still be seen in the foothill wilderness beyond the Porcupine Hills. Napi, the Blackfoot creator and trickster, the Old Man known to the Cree farther north as Wi-suk-i-shak, whose stories would eventually become as evocative to me as those of Moses and Odysseus, Shakespeare and Goethe. ("Black Rock", 103)

The evocativeness of stories situated in what he comes to consider his neck of the woods is present in the first volume of Wiebe's essays published in 1989 by NeWest

Press. *Playing Dead: A Contemplation Concerning the Arctic* is composed of essays presented as the Larkin-Stuart Lectures at Trinity College of the University of Toronto in 1987. There were three essays plus a two-page introduction in the original volume and five essays in the expanded and updated 2003 reprint. The geography is different from his earlier western Canadian orientation but the topic continues his Indigenophilia—the exploration of Aboriginal life, this time in northern Canada.

In the first essay he writes about an early Franklin expedition to the Coppermine River and the role of Indigenous peoples in that expedition. In the second essay he writes about Albert Johnson, "The Mad Trapper" of the North, about whom he had published a novel. The third essay he writes about European explorers Frobisher and Stefansson, among others. He is at his best in these essays when he pits the hubris, ignorance, and total misunderstanding of European (especially English) explorers with the subtle and generations-old knowledge of navigating the North found among its Indigenous inhabitants. His essays seek to redress the historical record left behind by the explorers. They carry his personal outrage against Euro-Canadian misunderstanding that his Indigenously-themed novels of the 1970s also contain. In the expanded 2003 edition there are two additional essays from the 1990s. In the first of these latter essays he describes a Dene caribou hunt in which he participates. In it he frees himself from historical research and the facticity of the earlier essays by becoming a participant. In writing about carrying a heavy load using a tumpline he says, "my neck creaked, squashed together by dead weight; in ten steps I felt I had compacted two centimetres" (*Playing Dead*, 5). By placing his body into the landscape he entered into communion with it.

The essays of *Playing Dead* are a dialectic between history and the present, between his own experience and the historical record, between Indigenous understanding and a colonizer's understanding, and between a need to voice criticism and a need to express the voice of the silenced. His second collection of essays is special in that it combines works of nonfiction with short stories. Because of this blending *River of Stone: Fictions and Memories* (1995) becomes an exercise in counterpoint. There are twenty-two separate pieces in the book more or less evenly divided between fiction and nonfiction. They play off each other and offer a perfect study of how the two separate genres combine in the mind of the writer.

The best example of this linkage is "Where is the Voice Coming From", a short story first published in 1971 in *Fourteen Stories High*. It was reprinted in the 1974 collection *Where is the Voice Coming From and Other Stories* and subsequently much anthologized, including this 1995 volume.[3] Wiebe says in the beginning of that story: "The problem is to make the story" (*River of Stone*, 27). In his view the writer's challenge is about "making" or constructing a narrative. The essay then quotes the mystic Catholic philosopher Teilhard de Chardin and the

---

3. The book was an idea proposed by Louise Denny, the publisher of *A Discovery of Strangers* that won a Governor-General's award. She wanted to take advantage of that publicity. Private email correspondence from Rudy Wiebe to the author 18 Nov. 2020.

British historian Arnold Toynbee. Referencing a theological mystic and a renowned historian in the same breath
is his way of holding up a mirror to his own voice, to the
two sides of his storytelling—the creative and the factual. When one begins to read this piece on the death of
Almighty Voice, another figure from nineteenth century
western Canadian Indigenous history, one is drawn immediately into the problem of the historical record.
Wiebe's stance is that the writer is an "element in what is
happening at this very moment [i.e. in the act of writing]
(*River of Stone*, 38). As that element, the writer is embedded in the story and so there can be no pretense of ob-
servational objectivity in his writing or that of anyone
else's writing. It is all personal and constructed to certain ends. For Wiebe *all* writing is highly personal and
its *truth is a construct* reflecting who the author is.

The essay ends with his attempting to give voice to the
nineteenth century figure of Almighty Voice in his final
moments. While this is a stance he would most likely
not adopt today because of the issue of cultural appropriation, it is interesting to see how this half-century old
piece of writing still carries elegance and power. To me
"Where is the Voice Coming From" is an excellent example
of creative nonfiction, a genre that combines the two
genres seamlessly. Of course, in 1971 when it was written
the term had not yet come into use. It was just another
story like the others.

The title story in the collection, "River of Stone" was
published a quarter century later (1994), when the debate over cultural appropriation was beginning. The debate arose out of the demand by racialized minority

writers to have their stories be told by themselves and not by what they considered white appropriators. This historical change made Wiebe's earlier historical novels and his portrayal of Indigenous characters seem suspect, in spite of his respectful treatment.[4] Wiebe addressed this issue directly in his 2004 interview with Herb Wyile, when he reported that he had not been attacked on this issue for his novel on Big Bear ("Walking Where", 70) and that the Indigenous community felt he had done a good thing by writing about this heroic figure.

In the book there are examples where Wiebe avoids the appropriation issue by putting himself front and center of the story. In one story he discusses a canoe trip he and some colleagues take in the Northwest Territories and the preparations for it. The trip parallels that of First Franklin Expedition of 1819–21 that he has already written about in *Playing Dead: A Contemplation Concerning the Arctic*. In the essay he discusses Dene creation myths, wolves, and his desire to walk on water, when the Mackenzie river turns to ice in winter, making it hard as stone. His foregrounding the present moment and featuring himself as the protagonist not only avoids the appropriation debate but also gives the work authenticity, not only as reportage, but also as an expression of his caring for Indigenous realities and traditions.

His final collection of nonfiction is *Where the Truth Lies: Selected Essays* (2016). Published in NeWest's The

---

4. For a recent discussion of this issue see Drew Hayden Taylor, "The write way to include Indigenous characters" 18 Nov. 2020 *Globe and Mail* A15.

Writer as Critic Series, the book has 21 entries covering 60 years of writing, a small number of which are reprints from the early collections. The selection reflects what he considers to be a true mirror of what he thought as a writer "during the particular times when they were composed" (*Where the Truth Lies*, xi). The 300-page volume is a mixture of lectures, talks, magazine articles, and essays in books. The title essay, "Where the Truth Lies: Exploring the Nature of Fact and Fiction" dates from public presentations made in 2007. In it he claims that: "… an imaginative writer wrestles with 'the truth' all the time, whatever he is writing, fiction or (so-called) non-fiction" (*Where the Truth Lies*, 79). He is saying that imagination is crucial to both fact and fiction. Truth is present in both genres and that it is always a struggle to represent it. A text is always imagining because that is what storytelling is. What is claimed to have occurred is rooted in the imaginative construction of that event.

He grounds story-telling of any kind in a person's experiences and how those experiences have shaped that person's view of the world. This is what makes the writer's truth subjective. When that subjectivity meets the objectivity of fact it molds fact to its interpretative liking. Any writing results in a "representation" of facts. Narrative truth is what positions the reader's thoughts in a certain way so as to identify with the characters and their situations in the way the writer wanted. In equating *all writing* with fiction Wiebe is saying that there can be no fiction without some semblance of facts or verisimilitude, and conversely there can be no facts presented without being fictionalized or imagined.

In 2005 Wiebe offered the Margaret Laurence Lecture at the annual meeting of the Writers Union of Canada. He titled his talk "A Writer's Life." In his statement about the nature of writing he says clearly that, "imaginative powers are initiated and nourished for years by our connectedness to the humanity from which and within which we grow" (Margaret Laurence Lecture). Here again he notes that writing for him is grounded in a specific real world or life out of which a particular imagining arises. His narratives require that specific grounding for them to work for. He ends the lecture by listing the two main ideas that underlie his writing as "first encounter" and "the immigrant experience", which are mirrors of each other. First encounter is the Indigenous-European interface that he writes about fictionally and non-fictionally, and the immigrant experience in Canada which is another variant of first encounters, of strangers meeting strangers. In other words, his writing is born from the facticity of his own personal roots, which has been framed by the meeting of cultures and peoples. That is what guides his writing.

One could say that his western Canadian birth to immigrant parents then very new to Saskatchewan provides the horizon for his later discovery of the Indigenous world that flourished in his birth place before colonization, and that as a writer in the settler tradition he has spent much time grappling with how to develop a respectful and just approach to a world whose peoples came so very close to being totally destroyed. His engagement with the topic comes from this point of intersection, of meeting and the ensuing consequences.

The Novelist as Biographer and Memoirist

While the essay is one pillar of his nonfiction writing, the other is his work as a biographer and autobiographer. These latter forms allowed him to approach important topics in his nonfiction writing with a breadth comparable to the novel. Yet it was over 35 years after his first novel appeared that he published his first monograph. The relative lateness of this development indicates that he did not feel any need to express himself by writing a nonfiction book because shorter pieces were all that was required. The appearance of a *Stolen Life: The Journey of a Cree Woman* (1998) was the result of an unexpected intervention. Yvonne Johnson, a Cree woman and the great great-granddaughter of Big Bear, wrote to Wiebe in 1992 from Kingston Penitentiary, where she was serving a life sentence for murder. Their correspondence and acquaintance lead to a collaboration that resulted in Wiebe's first volume of nonfiction, a mix of biography, autobiography, and memoir. The co-authored work won the Hilary Weston Writers' Trust Prize for Nonfiction in 1998.

The process by which the book came "to be written" reflects the kind of due diligence that Wiebe put into his historical novels—intense research, commitment to accuracy, and a writer's goal of creating a readable literary narrative. In his "Prefatory Note" he says its composition was based on his "research", "dialogue", and "interviews" (xi). On Johnson's side there are her "notebooks", "her letters" and his notes of their conversations plus audiotapes that he used to put the text together. He goes on to say that the book is a compilation that "the two authors believe is honest and accurate" (xii). Of course, the end result of this co-authorship involves two levels of writers—the diarist and the novelist. What is important here in terms of Wiebe's nonfiction body of work is that this first of his nonfiction monographs was stimulated by an outside source reaching out to him, rather than he embarking on a project of his own. He answered a call.

The crucial issue of co-authorship is taken up by Julia Emberley, who sees an unequal relationship between "… the writerly power of the professional class that Wiebe embodies and the oral and visual power of Johnson's account of her dispossession …"(219). The book is highly dependent on Wiebe's writing ability and his work in structuring the two voices into a coherent narrative.[5] His engagement with Johnson's story and her written and oral accounts is highly reminiscent of his engagement with the story of Big Bear, except that in Johnson's case there was an abundance of her own documentation and accounts for him to draw on.[6] There were two powerful

---

5. Wiebe describes the issues in the writing process as "the structure, the order, and the amount of content that we should include." He attributes the final result to "the support and brilliant insights" of the book's publisher, Louise Dennys. Private email correspondence from Rudy Wiebe to the author, 18 Nov. 2020.

6. For a crucial and in-depth discussion of the writing of the book and the collaboration itself see Michael Jacklin, "What I Have Done, What was Done to Me': Confessions and Testimony in *Stolen Life: Journey of a Cree Woman*." In *Kunapipi: Journal of Postcolonial Writing and Culture* 29(1) 2007, 19–69. Pages 19–32 are his article. Pages 33–52 constitute his interview with Yvonne Johnston in 2002 about the book and her role, followed by pages 54–68 which are his interview with Rudy Wiebe the day after he interviewed Johnson.

entities at work, but in different ways. Emberley sees Wiebe as the main architect of the book's structure and Johnston as "a phantom storyteller …" whose words are dependent on Wiebe's constructive abilities (222). While she considers his framework to be one of integrity because the text is clear on whose voice it is presenting, I would add that his structuring of the narrative displays his empathy for Johnston's plight and his long time commitment to being both critic and witness.

The reciprocity/collaboration between an inmate and a writer is always problematic because of power imbalances, but in this case the result is closer to equality than is ordinarily the case. The struggle to express equality as storytellers echoes the intensity of Wiebe's commitment to telling an untold story also found in *The Temptations of Big Bear* a quarter century earlier. The Indigenous/settler interface is represented in both books, but in *Stolen Life* it moves to a higher level, both in terms of a greater amount of Indigenous voicing present and controlled by the co-author, Yvonne Johnson, and also in terms of Wiebe's goal of not dominating the text with his own voice. *Stolen Life* represents Yvonne Johnson's soul and Rudy Wiebe's mind.

While autobiographical/memoirist narratives such as *Stolen Life* present themselves as expressions of authenticity, biographical texts are considered to be expressions of interpretative bias or understanding, since the voice is primarily that of the biographer and not the biographed. A decade after *Stolen Life* Wiebe published a biography of Big Bear in a series titled "Extraordinary Canadians" edited by John Ralston Saul. It is a small book of two hundred pages and it came out two years after his memoir, *Of this Earth: A Mennonite Boyhood in the Boreal Forest* that was published to great acclaim and the awarding of the prestigious Charles Taylor Prize for Nonfiction.

Big Bear is a commissioned work. Nevertheless it represents a mature writer's engagement with a topic he had been dealing with for some time, even though its writing style is simplified at times to meet the requirements of the series. In his "Author's Note" he raises the issue of a twenty-first century writer writing about "... a nineteenth century man who lived within the oral, hunting culture of Plains Cree and Saulteaux" and for whose life there is a paucity of documentary evidence (xvi). This paucity leads him to use the technique of the creative nonfiction genre by creating, "... short dramatic scenes that no history before the invention of the motion-picture camera could possibly record ... [using] invented conversations" (xvii). In this way he slips into the role of a novelist.

The *Globe and Mail's* reviewer felt the biography of Big Bear needed "fresh eyes" because Wiebe had become the go-to guy on this subject (Taylor). He meant that Wiebe had been immersed in the topic for so long and had written so much on Big Bear that his singular interpretation had become the dominant one. His re-telling and re-telling of the story had given the narrative a certain repetitiveness that even the fictionalized dialogues could not alleviate. This was not the problem with his own memoir, *Of This Earth*, which opened a door into the inner sanctum of his own life and out of which came mesmerizing and intriguing writing.

Advertised in the paperback edition as a "national bestseller" the book begins with two maps showing the homestead his parents came to farm in 1930's Saskatchewan in an area just north of the Battlefords. The definitiveness of maps sets the parameters for the narrative—its specificity and its realism or as he says in his voice: "The ground of whatever I was or would be, root and spirit" (3). Written in an elegiac tone of both pain and tenderness the narrative covers almost 400 pages illustrated with the few photos he had access to. He categorizes himself as "a bush homestead boy" whose first language was Russian Mennonite Low German attending a small country school (226). He attributes his form of storytelling to "stories heard in your head through your eyes, exactly" (236). The role of memory is fundamental for him, but first it has to be visualized for it to be "truly well written" (236).

At one point he discusses the untimely death of his sister Helen in 1945 and the fictional story he wrote about her death that was published in a Toronto magazine in 1956. Much later he was shown his sister's diary, which included "... the many tiny details in it that collaborated my story ..." (246). This revelation only strengthened his trust in authorial memory because his description of the moment of her dying was written a full decade after it had occurred. He chooses to reproduce the "first fumbled draft" of the published story in full as a kind of memorial to her (250–260). The final result (the nonfiction text about the event and his long lost fictional treatment) is a perfect rendering of how fiction and nonfiction meet in Wiebe's writing world and how they play off each other. They are both streams feeding the deep river of his writing. The memoir ends in 1947 when the Wiebe family moves to Coaldale Alberta to begin the second chapter of their immigrant journey and 13-year-old Rudy begins his journey to becoming one of Alberta's pre-eminent writers. There has not been a sequel.

Decoding Wiebe's Nonfiction

> "Words are the way we try to live in/with our world/reality. Nonfiction or fiction—that's simply a word issue: trying to get a bit of order to the basically unorderable human reality." (Wiebe Email, 18 Nov 2020)

Wiebe is emphasizing two things—language and narrative is our way of grasping the world and its chaos, and the distinction between nonfiction and fiction is a false dichotomy because as he has said previously, they are simply two sides of the same coin—our grasping the world through words.

Wiebe's motivation to write nonfiction has various sources. It can be an issue or experience he feels compelled to comment on (*Playing Dead*), or an invitation to create a memoir (*Stolen Life*), or the need to give an autobiographical narrative the power that infuses his fiction (*Of This Earth*). That he is remembered for his fiction rather than nonfiction is part of the dynamics of literary life and cultural values. Wiebe said in the Margaret Laurence Lecture that he viewed himself as a fiction writer and since his number of fiction books are three times of nonfiction books he is right in terms of his writing profile. Yet the wellsprings of his nonfiction and the topics he covers in them do not diverge dramatically. There is a unity of purpose and engagement that links the genres, not necessarily stylistically, but always in emotional spirit. He wrote in a recent email that he finds "writing a speech like 'Killing our way to peace' or 'Flowers for the Approaching Fire' can be just as artistically and spiritually satisfying [as writing fiction]" (Wiebe email 18 Nov. 2020).

The three characteristics that link Wiebe's fiction and nonfiction—ethno-religious ideology, Indigenophilia, and the constructed nature of truth—create a unified thematic field, encompassing novels like *The Temptations of Big Bear* as well as nonfiction such as *Stolen Life: The Journey of a Cree Woman*. As I have shown Wiebe links his own Mennonite values with Indigenous beliefs when he creates "the truth" of the story. The identification he finds between the two worlds allows him to enter the world of the Other and then deconstruct that otherness to create both human equality and moral similarity. By identifying with his Indigenous characters and historical figures he stands in solidarity with the oppressed and their resistance to historic wrongs. In this he is a witness and a critic.

Using his own words, I have pointed out that he does not make a great distinction between the fact-based narrative in nonfiction, which, for him, always produces an interpretation, and the creative imagining he uses in his historical fiction. What the writer makes of a fact is more powerful than the bald fact itself. Because of this subjectivist view Wiebe's writing displays what I term "cross-pollination." He takes factual/historical material and uses it to the full in his fictional historical narratives, and in turn he uses fictional techniques to enhance his nonfictional narrative. This cross-pollination is based on his personal need to redress what he considers false historical narrative and his desire to give voice to those that earlier narratives treated as outsiders.

While ethno-religious ideology, Indigenophilia, and constructed truth bind the two genres, his nonfiction writing also needs to be assessed on its own terms. For example, how does his biographical voice compare with his autobiographical voice? And what makes some of his nonfiction so engaging? While this essay does not offer an in-depth comparative analysis of his numerous nonfiction essays or his nonfiction books, I would like to point out one major dividing line between his more engaging nonfiction and his less engaging nonfiction. The dividing line is that of personal truth versus historical truth. Whenever Wiebe writes about a personal direct experience his words are captivating. I call this the stance of personal truth. On the other hand, when he makes the subject matter of his nonfiction historical figures they are not as alive to us as his personal narrative. I call these works the stance of historical truth.

The superiority of personal truth in storytelling over historical truth in storytelling is evident in *Stolen Life: A Cree Woman's Journey*, which won the Writers Trust award for nonfiction, while his biography of *Big Bear* was virtually ignored (I found only a few reviews in the

Canadian media of the day). When he puts himself on the page as its subject he generally engages the reader in the ways I have discussed earlier. As for the Indigenophilia that has captivated him for so long, I would characterize it as reflecting the spirit of reconciliation beginning to be practiced in Canada today. He sees the world he grew up in, then learned about through historical research, and finally experienced himself, as one that must be "shared" in the way the treaties intended. His best nonfiction work has contributed to his own and in turn our path to reconciliation with the colonized and dispossessed. It should not be dismissed, forgotten, or relegated to secondary status. His accomplishments as a nonfiction writer need be acknowledged, understood, and applauded.

Works Cited:

Blodgett, E.D. *Configuration: Essays on the Canadian Literatures.* Toronto: ECW Press, 1982.

Emberley, Julia V. *Defamiliarizing the Aboriginal: Cultural Practices and Decolonization in Canada.* Toronto: U of Toronto Press, 2007.

Harrison, Richard. *Unnamed Country: The Struggle for a Canadian Prairie Fiction.* Edmonton: University of Alberta Press, 1977.

Keith, W.J. *A Voice in the Land: Essays by and about Rudy Wiebe.* Edmonton: NeWest Press, 1981.

Melnyk, George. "An Interview with Rudy Wiebe". *The Canadian Fiction Magazine*, No. 12, Winter 1974, pp. 29–34.

Neumann, Shirley. "Unearthing Language: An Interview with Rudy Wiebe and Robert Kroetsch" in W.J. Keith. *A Voice in the Land: Essays by and about Rudy Wiebe*. Edmonton: NeWest Press, 1981. Pp. 226–247.

Taylor, Peter Shawn. "Big Bear: 'A Troublesome fellow' *Globe and Mail* 15 Nov. 2008, D10.

Wiebe, Rudy and Bob Beal, eds. *War in the West: Voices of the 1885 Rebellion.* Toronto: McClelland and Stewart, 1985.

Wiebe, Rudy. "The Artist as a Critic and a Witness" in W.J. Keith, ed. *A Voice in the Land: Essays by and about Rudy Wiebe.* Edmonton: NeWest Press, 1981. Pp.39–48.

----- "An Author Speaks About His Novel" in W.J. Keith, ed. *A Voice in the Land: Essays by and about Rudy Wiebe.* Edmonton: NeWest Press, 1981.pp.64–78.

----- *Big Bear.* Toronto: Penguin Canada, 2008.

----- "Bear Spirit in a Strange Land" W.J. Keith, ed. *A Voice in the Land: Essays by and about Rudy Wiebe.* Edmonton: NeWest Press, 1981.pp.143–149.

----- Private correspondence email to the author. 18 Nov. 2020.

----- *Of This Earth: A Mennonite Boyhood in the Boreal Forest.* Toronto: Random House, 2006.

----- "The Writer's Life" Margaret Laurence Lecture, 2005. Typescript courtesy of the author.

----- "On the Trail of Big Bear" in W.J. Keith, ed. *A Voice in the Land: Essays by and about Rudy Wiebe.* Edmonton: NeWest Press, 1981.pp.132–141.

----- *Playing Dead: A Contemplation Concerning the Arctic.* Edmonton: NeWest Press, 2003.

----- "Walking Where His Feet Can Walk" in Herb Wyile, *Speaking in the Past Tense: Canadian Novelists on Writing Historical Fiction.* Waterloo, Ont. Wilfrid Laurier U Press, 2007. 53–78.

----- "Where Is the Voice Coming From" in Rudy Wiebe, *River of Stone: Fictions and Memoirs*. Toronto: Vintage, 1995. Pp. 27–40.

----- "Where the Black Rocks Lie the Old Man's River" in Geoffrey James and Rudy Wiebe. *Place: Lethbridge, a City on the Prairie*. Vancouver: Douglas and McIntyre, 2002. Pp. 93–126.

----- *Where the Truth Lies: Selected Essays*. Edmonton: NeWest Press, 2016.

Wylder, Delbert E. Review of *The Scorched-Wood People*, by Rudy Wiebe. *Western American Literature*, vol. 14 no. 3, 1979, p. 237–238. *Project MUSE*, doi:10.1353/wal .1979.0081.

Wyile, Herb. "Introduction" in Herb Wyile, *Speaking in the Past Tense: Canadian Novelists on Writing Historical Fiction*. Waterloo, Ont. Wilfrid Laurier U Press, 2007. 1–24.

Rudy Wiebe's "Unearthing" of Big Bear: a Plains Cree Hero of Canada's Past

Bianca Lakoseljac

Abstract: Rudy Wiebe's fourth novel, *The Temptations of Big Bear,* published in 1973, won the author's first Governor General's Award for Fiction. The story is a poignant epic of the tumultuous period in western Canada at the end of the nineteenth century marked by colonization and the takeover of First Nations lands. The novel's protagonist Big Bear (whose Cree name was Mistahimaskwa) is a Plains Cree chief who resisted pressures to cede the rights to the lands his Peoples had lived on for thousands of years. The story follows Big Bear through the last buffalo hunt, the building of the Canadian Pacific Railway, his own imprisonment, and the largest mass hanging in Canadian history. On November 27, 1885, eight First Nations men were hanged. After the publication, the novel stirred much debate, and has since been recognized as one of Wiebe's most highly praised works of fiction. The novel also marked a turning point in the depiction of First Nations Peoples in English Canadian literature. In 1990, based on the script co-written by Wiebe and Métis director Gil Cardinal, the book was made into a CBC television mini-series. Rudy Wiebe's creative biography of Big Bear entitled, *Big Bear,* was published as part of The Extraordinary Canadians Series in 2008, with John Ralston Saul as series editor.

> I [Rudy Wiebe] have always looked at myself more as a storyteller than anything else. ... He [Big Bear] is an ideal novel subject because he is a great and wise man who lives a tragic life. And no one knows much about him. Big Bear is a great hero of our past whom nobody has done much with. Even the Indians don't know much about him. (Keith, Translating Life into Art, *A Voice in the Land* 128)

Rudy Wiebe's view of himself as primarily a storyteller offers a glimpse into his philosophy on writing as well as a window into the complexity of his novel, *The Temptations of Big Bear.* The novel is based on an extensive six-year examination of historical events and issues surrounding the Frog Lake "massacre" of 1885.[1] The research involved travel to "every place that I [Wiebe] had ever heard Big Bear was" (Translating Life into Art, VL 127), a study of historical documents and fictional and biographical accounts, and interviews with a surviving participant, Duncan McLean, and descendants of the Plains Cree band, including Horsechild's wife[2] Mary

---

1. The Frog Lake Massacre (April 2, 1885) was part of the North West Rebellion uprising. https://library.usask.ca/northwest /index/subject/110.html

https://firstpeoplesofcanada.com/fp_metis/fp_metis_frog _lake.html

2. Big Bear's daughter-in-law, the wife of Big Bear's youngest son, Horsechild. Her Christian name was Mary PeeMee, but she

PeeMee, who at the time was still living on Poundmaker Reserve where Big Bear had died. Yet Wiebe does not see *The Temptations* as a historical novel. Wiebe explains that unlike the historical novel, where a fictional character leads the reader to examine historical events, all characters in this novel are based on real-life individuals. He also states that unlike history, where events are depicted impartially, this novel is "my [Wiebe's] way of looking at the world, and that's why I call it a novel and I don't pretend that it's a history which is written impartially" (Where the Voice Comes From, VL 152). Although the focus of this essay is not the historicity of the novel, Wiebe's perspective on writing attests to his insight into the complex treatment of the First Nations historical characters through fiction.

Published in 1973, *The Temptations of Big Bear* examines the tumultuous years of the Canadian West a century before, at the time of the land treaties. The novel explores the Plains Cree chief Big Bear's refusal to sign Land Treaty Number 6 in 1876, his efforts to prevent The Frog Lake Uprising in 1885, and his death in 1888. It addresses the breakdown of the Plains Cree culture and way of life stemming from the takeover of their land rights and human freedoms by one of the largest colonial superpowers. Coral Ann Howells, in her essay, "History from a different Angle: Narrative Strategies in *The Temptations of Big*

---

much preferred to be called by her Indian name, See-ascum-ka-poo, which means "Little Stones on the Prairie." The word, "Indian" is used in a historical context. Also, "Status Indian" is still an accepted term. https://archive.macleans.ca/article/1975/9/1/she-who-knows-the-truth-of-big-bear

Bear," observes that although Wiebe does not attempt to rewrite history, "he argues that it [history] is far from all inclusive, being full of gaps and silences and moments out of sequence which open up world views not contained in official histories" (162).

To gain a better understanding of Wiebe's view of this novel and its characters, it is helpful to consider his inspiration for writing the novel, which arose from his indignation over the Canadian educational system that emphasized British and American history as depicted from the perspective of the White[3] colonizer. Wiebe's disillusion with Canadian history's failure to acknowledge and study the First Peoples[4] culture which, in his words, presents "our past" without which we are, as Wiebe states, "memory ignorant, and the less are we people"

---

3.   https://cssp.org/2020/03/recognizing-race-in-language-why-we-capitalize -black-and-white/In addition to capitalizing Black, Center for the Study of Social Policy (CSSP) has also made the decision to capitalize White. "We [CSSP] will do this when referring to people who are racialized as White in the United States, including those who identify with ethnicities and nationalities that can be traced back to Europe. To not name 'White' as a race is, in fact, an anti-Black act which frames Whiteness as both neutral and the standard."

4.   https://www.ictinc.ca/blog/indigenous-peoples-terminology-guidelines-for-usage or https://www.ictinc.ca/ This essay follows the Indigenous Peoples Terminology Guidelines from Indigenous Corporate Training Inc. at the above website. Terms for Indigenous Peoples have evolved over time and continue to evolve. Please note: the plural possessive for First Nations, First Peoples, Indigenous Peoples, or Aboriginal Peoples does not generally use the apostrophe. For example, the correct way is, First Nations land; not First Nations' land.

(On the Trail, VL 134) fueled his drive to "vindicate the Canadian Indian from the taboos of the cliché[s] of the bloodthirsty savage" (On the Trail, VL 134) depicted in western fiction. Wiebe alludes to Michelangelo's contention that "he [Michelangelo] studied the rock for the shape that was inside it and then used his chisels not to create that shape out of the rock but rather to release the shape from all encumbering rock around it" (On the Trail, VL 133), which Wiebe saw as a model of creation for the art of storymaking as well.

It is evident from Wiebe's reflections on the novel that his primary intention was to portray, "what was it like to live as an Indian during the time of the treaties", thus to "release", or as Wiebe points out, "unearth ... the story of Big Bear ... the greatest chief of the Plains Cree", and to free him from the "tragic-farcical manner and tone" with which he has been treated in historical and fictional accounts (On the Trail, VL 137). However, as Wiebe has chosen the novel form to portray an Indigenous Peoples historical leader, the reader becomes aware of Wiebe's perception of himself as primarily a storyteller and his inclination as such to leave, as Walter Benjamin[5] states, his "handprints", or as

---

5. Walter Benjamin's approach to storytelling and "storymaking" is similar to Wiebe's, for both authors perceive the "story maker" as a craftsman whose role is to adapt the "raw material", be it elements from real-life events, from history, or simply from other forms of fiction, and personalize it, or make it his own. In his essay "The Storyteller", Benjamin states that "[t]he storytelling ... does not aim to convey the pure essence of the thing like information or a report. It sinks the thing into the life of a storyteller, in order to

Wiebe[6] states, "the impression of recognizable life," on his story. Therefore, his depiction of the Plains Cree chief which defines the novel's protagonist, at the same time positions him against the past treatment typical of an Indigenous Peoples character.

In the "Eli Mandel and Rudy Wiebe" 1974 Interview, Mandel proposes that Wiebe's approach in turning historical characters and facts into a fiction may be Wiebe's way of "being experimental, or ... working with a new form (or relatively new form) in Canadian fiction" (Where the Voice, VL 152). It is Wiebe's new form of fiction that this essay is concerned with—a new way of crafting a fictional First Peoples character based on a historical figure. Since the publication of the novel, Big Bear has earned a place among the highly debated characters in English-Canadian literature.

The objective of this essay is to show that Wiebe viewed the historical Big Bear as "a great hero" of First Nations Peoples of this era (Where the Voice, VL 152) and portrayed him that way. A further examination of

---

bring it out of him again. Thus, traces of the storyteller cling to the story the way the handprints of the potter cling to the clay vessel. ... Thus his tracks are frequently evident in his narratives, if not as those of the one who experienced it, then as those of the one who reports it. (*Illuminations* 91–92)

6. Wiebe, in his introduction to *The Storymakers*, states the following: "The maker (storymaker) selects and orders the event pattern in such a way that the impression of recognizable life is felt, an *impression* (not real life itself), that may be more powerful and incisive than if we had actually lived through the event, because the maker is lending his or her eyes out and we see more deeply with these than we do with our own." (XXVII)

the novel will demonstrate that Wiebe wanted the reader to witness what life was like for First Peoples in Canada during the time of the treaties. More specifically, what it was like to live as a Plains Cree leader, and to deal with his Peoples loss of economy, freedom of mobility, family structure—loss of a traditional way of life that had spanned many centuries. Wiebe wanted to take the reader through this drastic change that took place over a short period at the end of the nineteenth century.

One way to contemplate the complexity of Big Bear's character is to examine how he has been viewed by critics and readers over the past few decades. This process, however, will not be a simple or an easy one. Paul Tiessen, in his essay, "The Naming of Rudy Wiebe" explains that,

> Rudy Wiebe is … a serious (and, with few exceptions, "difficult") novelist who exercises a high sense of "purpose" in his art. In his novels, complex in cultural implication and narrative conception, he makes bold assaults on audiences comfortably taken up with otherwise largely unchallenged cultural preconceptions. Creating on a broad canvas filled with histories of Métis or Indian or his own Mennonite people, he instructs his audience by satire and precept, challenges his readers' received versions of history and world-view, subverts secular beliefs about the technological and material world by asserting assumptions based on man's shared spirituality, and defies the demand for contemporary antiheroes by appending his own voice to romantic visionaries who strode the Canadian prairie where

he now lives. In the wide spaces of his novels he
gives his readers, especially through "historical"
characters such as Big Bear ... not just new myths
of the past, but warnings, by strong and often
threatening implication and analogy, about the
future. (*Journal of Mennonite Studies*, 115)

The complexity of Big Bear's character has prompted
many readers and critics to disagree with certain aspects
of his portrayal. It is Wiebe's depiction of Big Bear as
an epic hero of Canada's past—a multi-faceted, complex, sagacious persona, who cannot be slotted into any
of the traditional categories used to depict an Indigenous
character over the centuries—which has sparked numerous debates.

In discussing the internal progression of *The Temptations*,
Coral Ann Howells observes that by engaging a variety
of characters and narrative methods,

> Wiebe deliberately separates the events as lived facts
> from history as recorded facts, and by his frequent
> use of flashbacks and flashes forward he dissolves
> any sense of time progression in a kaleidoscopic
> presentation of a variety of intensely realised
> subjective experience. ... Arguably, dislocation and
> discontinuity are what the novel is about, and we
> might see Wiebe ... making the reader undergo a
> similar experience of chaos to that experienced by
> the characters in the fiction. (164)

Notably, it is Wiebe's use of multiple voices by different narrators which helps the reader to separate events depicted in the novel as fiction from the historical facts derived from research.

To fully appreciate the importance of Wiebe's characterization of Big Bear at this point in Canadian literature, this essay will first step back and briefly examine how Indigenous Peoples have been depicted in English literature over the past centuries. Next, it will consider how Big Bear has been seen by various critics since the publication of the novel. The last part will attest to Wiebe's lifelong commitment to bring the story of Big Bear to Canadian readers and to set the stage for a new way of depicting the Frist Nations Peoples in literary fiction.

The typical portrayal of Indigenous Peoples characters in fiction over the past centuries

Over the centuries, the traditional portrayal of Indigenous Peoples and their cultures has placed them in one of two camps: that of a Wild Man[7], by emphasizing their presumed "backwardness" and lack of "civility;" or more

---

7. The wild man, wild man of the woods, or woodwose/wodewose is a mythical figure that appears in the art and literature of medieval Europe, comparable to the satyr or faun type in classical mythology and to Silvanus, the Roman god of the woodlands. See Kenneth H. Jackson, 'The Wild Man of the Woods', Yorkshire Society for Celtic Studies (1935); R. Bernheimer, *Wild Men in the Middle Ages* (Cambridge, MA, 1952). See Dudley, Edward and Maximillian E. Novak. Ed. *The Wild Man Within: An Image in Western Thought from the Renaissance to Romanticism*. Pittsburgh: U of Pittsburgh P. 1972.

recently, that of a Noble Savage[8] by idolizing their supposed "simplicity" and "purity." Both concepts have been used to dehumanize the so-called, "New World" societies.

As far back as Saint Augustine's *City of God* (A.D. 413–426), images of the Wild Man fascinated European imagination. Saint Augustine devotes an entire chapter to the question of "Whether the descendants of Adam or the sons of Noah produced monstrous races of men" (531–2), which does not question the existence of monstrous races of men, but rather their origins. About a thousand years later, we discover that concepts of the world had not changed much. In the fifteenth and sixteenth century, Europeans were fascinated with stories about distant places and people who were different in customs and way of living. Travel writing became

---

8. The term "Noble Savage" first appeared in English literature in John Dryden's heroic play, *The Conquest of Granada* (1671): "I am as free as nature first made man/Ere the base laws of servitude began/When wild in wood the noble savage ran." The oxymoron implies that primitive human beings are naturally good in their "innocent" or "unlearned" state before they are "corrupted" by the damaging action of civilization, laws, ownership of property, and knowledge. Following the discovery of America, the phrase "savage" for indigenous peoples was used disparagingly to justify colonialism. The concept of the savage gave Europeans the supposed right to establish colonies without considering the possibility of pre-existing, functional societies. Montaigne's essay, "Of Cannibals" (1580) stated the basic concept. Aphra Behn's *Oroonoko: or, The Royal Slave* (1688) portrayed a *noble savage* in chains. The greatest impulse toward the doctrine of natural nobility came from Rousseau's *Emile* (1762): "Everything is well when it comes fresh from the hands of the Maker; everything degenerates in the hands of Man." However, Rousseau never used the term, "Noble Savage," (French *bon sauvage*) (Holman, A Handbook to Literature 319).

popular. To please the readers, writers of travel narratives felt that it was not enough to provide specific geographical locations and accounts of actual events; readers also expected to be entertained. One of the most popular fifteenth-century travel narratives was *The Travels of Sir John Mandeville.* The book was written by an unknown author believed to be an English knight who traveled from about 1322 to 1356, and who embellished his narratives with images of the Wild Man:

> There is a race of great stature, like giants, foul and horrible to look at, they have one eye only, in the middle of their foreheads. ... In another part there are ugly folk without heads, who have eyes in each shoulder; their mouths are round like a horseshoe in the middle of their chest. ... [Another is] a tribe of evil customs, for fathers eat their sons, and sons their fathers ... ... in another, people have feet like horses, and run so swiftly on them that they overtake wild beasts and kill them for their food. ... another isle where people are hermaphrodite, having the parts of each sex, and each has a breast on one side. (Mandeville 137)

The story exerted a strong influence on late-medieval and early-Renaissance society. Since numerous travel books were in circulation at the time *The Travels* was published, one could reason that it is the concepts of the world held in this period that contributed to the popularity of the book. Mandeville's narrative contained factual geographical information, references to classical authors, images from the Old Testament and Saint Augustine's writing, and images from myth and fable mixed with conjuring from the author's imagination, which made it difficult for the Renaissance public with limited scientific knowledge to discern fictitious from real elements. Originally written in French, Mandeville's narrative was translated into most European languages, and for the next two hundred years became popular not only for its entertainment value, but also as a geographical guide for many explorers, including Columbus (Robe 15–20, 42).

Columbus' travels and his contact with "the natives of the New World," combined with Spain's policy of Christianisation, was to have a profound impact on the concept of the Wild Man. Columbus suspected that a group of Indigenous communities he encountered in 1492, in what is now the Bahamas, were members of a "cannibalistic tribe of Caribs" (Columbus 170). These claims provided enough fuel to the European mind, stifled for centuries by religious dogma and societal constraints, to extend its imagination and invent what it could not comprehend (Nash 56–65).

During the European colonization of the Americas in the early sixteenth century, the most notable debate arose between Friar Bartolomé de las Casas, and his adversary, the Spanish Renaissance philosopher and theologian Juan Ginés de Sepúlveda. Las Casas was a Spanish Dominican monk who spent his life raising concerns over the mistreatment of the Indigenous population. He insisted that it was the clergy's responsibility to Christianize and protect the Indigenous Peoples from annihilation through massacres and hard labour inflicted by the Spanish colonizers. Sepúlveda, who was highly influential at the Spanish court, asserted that the best strategy for dealing with the Indigenous societies was to apply Aristotle's theory of natural slavery (Robe 45–51). Up to this point, Portuguese colonizers of Africa systematically enslaved the Indigenous Peoples, for the idea of "natural slaves", found in Aristotle's *The Politics*, was not foreign to European thought. Aristotle states that "... the art of war is a natural art of acquisition ... which we ought to practice against wild beasts, and against men who, though intended by nature to be slaves, will not submit" (*The Politics*, p. 40). Thus the European measure of civilized men seemed to be defined by men's ability to subjugate nature, animal life, or civilizations perceived as weaker or underdeveloped (Antonello Gebri-Buffon 6, Hanke 8, Robe 47–51).

The controversy between Las Casas and Sepúlveda is particularly important, for it addresses the philosophical question of the spiritual state of the Indigenous Peoples of the Americas. The decree by Pope Paul III in 1537 proclaimed that, "Indian was not a Wild Man. Rather, they were 'truly' men, capable of 'understanding the Catholic faith'" (Robe 47). Although this was an important ecclesiastical decision, the mistreatment of the Indigenous Peoples continued. All that was decided is that they were to be Christianized, the term which was to become further abused by the colonizers. If an Indigenous band was accused of practicing cannibalism, the accusation alone could be used to justify the annihilation of the band. Similarly, any form of defence or resistance by the Indigenous bands was an invitation for further oppression by the colonizers. This system was the most effective way of obtaining land for the Spanish and the Portuguese colonizers, as it was for the English in Ireland, and later in Canada (Robe 40–45, Nash 60–61).

Once the Indigenous Peoples were no longer a threat to colonization, the colonists began to accept what they considered the positive aspects of Indigenous culture. Michel de Montaigne's sixteenth-century essay "Of Cannibals" published in his *Essays* expresses regret that the positive aspects of Indigenous cultures have not been recognized earlier and "reincarnated" into the contemporary societies in hopes of proving beneficial to them. This essay had a major influence on the formation of the Noble Savage myth.

> They [the Indigenous Peoples] are still governed by natural laws and very little corrupted by our own. They are in such a state of purity, that it sometimes saddens me to think we did not learn of them earlier, at a time when there were men who were better able to appreciate them than we. (Montaigne, 110)

One of the best-known Noble Savage figures is Aphra Behn's Oroonoko. In Behn's *Oroonoko: or The Royal Slave* (1688), the author depicts Oroonoko as having, "all the civility of a well-bred great man, and nothing of barbarity in his nature, ... real greatness of soul, ... those refined notions of true Honour" (9). Behn depicts Oroonoko's physical appearance as, "his face was not of that brown, rusty black which most of that nation are, but of perfect ebony ...... his nose was rising and Roman, instead of African and flat" (10). Oroonoko is set apart from the "rest of his nation", which reveals Behn's clear dislike for the African appearance and behaviour, and reflects an inability to escape her prejudice. She also makes Oroonoko an object of idolization, for it is the qualities of a White European Behn esteems and assigns to her Noble Savage.

Although many early eighteenth-century writers continued to depict the Aboriginal population as "inhuman," some historians, such as Robert Beverley in *The History and Present State of Virginia*, published in 1705, showed an appreciation for the Aboriginal communities with which he became well acquainted. In "Book III: the Native Indians, their Religion, Laws, and Customs in War and Peace," Beverley depicts Aboriginal men as "perfect in their outward frame," and women as "beautiful, possessing an uncommon delicacy of shape and features" (89). James Adair, in *The History of the American Indians*, published in 1775, carries forward this depiction and marvels at the Aboriginal Peoples physical appearance and peaceful, orderly way of life (5). The admiration of the physical appearance and the culture of the Aboriginal communities was significant to the formation of the Noble Savage myth. (Novak 185–90).

The Europeans' encounter with numerous Aboriginal communities on the North American continent, combined with the favourable depiction of their societies by various eighteenth century writers, particularly by the Jesuits, led to a dramatic change in the image of the "North American native." The portrayal of a "native," first shaped by the Wild Man myth, transformed into the Noble Savage figure, against whom European cultural values were to be judged. Scientists and thinkers became aware of the valuable elements of other cultures, which they saw as lacking in their own. They developed an interest in earlier societies and studied their social and cultural systems in hopes of applying this knowledge to the betterment of their own, contemporary society. Jean-Jacques Rousseau is considered to be one of the first social thinkers, "to place the figure of Noble Savage within a scheme of historical development, [and] to locate him in the dimension of time" (Symcox, "The Wild Man's Return" 233; also, Hazard 435–437, 446).

In the philosophical treatises, *A Discourse on the Origins of Inequality,* first published in 1755, Rousseau asserts that in this Natural state, "where man's self-preservation is the least prejudicial to self-preservation of others" (35), men are likely to live in peace. He sees the "North American Indian" way of life at the point of European contact as the most desirable stage in human development, and refers to it as,

> A golden mean between the indolence of a primitive state and the petulant activity of our amour-propre, [which] ... must have been the happiest and most durable epoch. The more one thinks about it, the more one finds that this state was the least subject to revolutions, the best for man, and that he must have come out of it only by some fatal accident, which for the common utility ought never to have happened. The example of Savages, who have almost all been found at this point, seems to confirm that

> the human Race was made to remain in it always;
> that this state is the veritable youth of the World;
> and that all subsequent progress has been in
> appearance so many steps toward the perfection of
> the individual, and in fact toward the decrepitude
> of the species. (*Discourse*, 48–49)

Rousseau's idealization of the simple life and the physical and moral state of "the man in a state of Nature" parallels his depiction of the Indigenous Peoples of the Americas who, as Rousseau states, are self-dependent and live "in rustic huts, make their clothing and utensils from animal skins and bones, paint their bodies, and use feathers and shells as ornaments" (*Discourse,* 49). Although Rousseau did not use the term, "Noble Savage," this depiction of the Indigenous inhabitants contributed to the establishment of the late eighteenth-century movement that emphasized the domination of feeling over reason and the rejection of European societal standards in favour of a life close to nature. In this state, man would be able to live in a freedom and allow his innate goodness to lead him (Symcox, 223).

The characterization of Big Bear: in *The Temptations of Big Bear*

Similar to other parts of the Americas, the First Peoples culture in Canada began to decline soon after the encounter with the Europeans: the introduction of European viruses led to widespread death among the First Nations; European tools and weapons meant that wars were fought at a technological advantage for the colonizers; alcohol was used to undermine First Peoples. Together, these and other factors led to a deterioration of First Peoples culture. In *The Temptations*, Wiebe depicts the Plains Cree life at this point in history, and how it was ravaged by Canada's policy of expansion westwards. He explores the crisis arising from the Indian Land Treaties and the building of the Canadian Pacific Railway which led to the decimation of the buffalo herds and the destruction of First Peoples lands that contributed to their inability to sustain their independence. Wiebe portrays colonial occupation as eroding the First Peoples way of life that proved devastating to Big Bear and his Cree society.

In *The Art of Rudy Wiebe*, Keith observes that in the early 1970s, Wiebe's quest to "set the Indian in his rightful place within Canadian literature ... [became] ... something of a cultural crusade" (63). Keith cites Wiebe's essay, "Western Canadian Fiction: Past and Future," published in 1971, in which Wiebe reasons that, "The Indian ... must become our central, not our fringe figure ... he must become the centre of serious fiction as other groups have" (29). The challenge Wiebe faced was whether Canadians were ready to confront the facts of their colonial history.

In her essay "Indian Heroes," published in 1981 in *A Native Heritage: Images of the Indian in English Canadian Literature*, Leslie Gordon Monkman observes that "the role of an Indian" in contemporary Canadian literature has recently become that of "the mediator between red and white worlds whom the white man tragically failed to acknowledge and to understand in the past but who now is a guide to potential new harmonies between man and man and man and nature" (114). Monkman cites Wiebe's depiction of Big Bear as an example:

> In *The Temptations of Big Bear*, Rudy Wiebe bridges these cultures through his introduction of a Cree leader rarely seen in heroic terms by whites. Old and wrinkled, Wiebe's Big Bear is physically unprepossessing in comparison with his nineteenth-century predecessors; yet, what *The Temptations of Big Bear* documents is the tragic defeat of 'the head and soul' of the Plains Indians. What Big Bear lacks in physique he gains through association with the sun, the focus of all life within Cree culture. Thus, in his first confrontation with whites, he appears in dramatic silhouette, 'huge against the sun.' (115)

Monkman conveys three noteworthy points. First, she recognizes Wiebe's departure from the traditional portrayal of a First Nations character at the time of the novel's publication in 1973 and identifies it as a new step in English-Canadian literature—as Eli Mandel proposed in 1974. Second, she refers to Big Bear as "the mediator" who bridges the two cultures. And third, she offers an intriguing view on Big Bear's association with the sun.

To address Monkman's view of Big Bear's supposed bridging of the cultures, it is helpful to examine Carla Visser's essay, "Historicity in Historical Fiction: *Burning Water* and *The Temptations of Big Bear*," published in 1987. Visser fittingly sees *The Temptations* as, "An effort to come to terms with a clash between two cultures and to remedy the one-sidedness of the account ... in Canadian historiography" (95). Visser points to Lieutenant-Governor Morris' treaty negotiations, where Morris explains that the Queen is not in the West to trade, to buy land, or to wage war: "All we [the colonizers] want is to protect you [the Cree Peoples] and your lands from the white settlers that are coming, who'll build houses in the places you want to live yourselves" (*The Temptations* 28). Wiebe makes it clear to the reader that Big Bear's refusal to succumb to this deception led to him being labeled a troublemaker. Big Bear's attempts to negotiate between the Cree Peoples and the Whites and prevent the 1885 uprising was unsuccessful. The unrest that began with the "massacre" at Frog Lake eventually ended in Big Bear's imprisonment. It also resulted in the largest mass hanging in Canadian history. On November 27, 1885, eight First Nations men were hanged: Kah-Paypamahchukways (Wandering Spirit), Pah Pah-Me-Kee-Sick (Round the Sky), Manchoose (Bad Arrow), Nahpase (Iron Body), A-Pis-Chas-Koos (Little Bear), Kit-Ahwah-Ke-Ni (Miserable Man), Itka (Crooked Leg), and Waywahnitch (Man Without Blood). Their bodies were placed in a mass grave near the fort in the Town of Battleford.

Wiebe depicts the clash between the Cree and the Whites extending beyond land rights and encompassing all aspects of life, particularly the culture and the language. Big Bear questions how the land the Cree had lived on freely for centuries, and perhaps millennia, suddenly belongs to the Queen of England. At his trial, Big

Bear questions how the Whites can find him guilty of "stealing Queen Victoria's hat"—as "her [the Queen's] crown and dignity" is translated into Cree. Big Bear explains that he had never seen the Grandmother [the Queen]: "How could I [Big Bear] do that?" (387). Wiebe's adept storytelling makes it clear that the sympathy of the novel is with the First Nations, and especially with Big Bear.

Furthermore, the Cree Peoples loss of land leads to the erosion of cultural values, as evident from Big Bear's statement, "I was the greatest chief of the First People. But now they laugh at me" (267). Big Bear is caught in this period of change, for his leadership was on the decline even among the Cree population, as shown in his conflict with his sons, and with other First Peoples leaders. Thus, Monkman's view that "Rudy Wiebe bridges these cultures through his introduction of a Cree leader rarely seen in heroic terms by whites" (116) can be only partially sustained. While Wiebe does launch a new way of portraying a Cree leader, it is not the bridging of the gap, but the conflict between the two cultures, as Visser affirms, that he depicts.

Monkman's third point, Wiebe's association of Big Bear with elements of nature, notably the sun and the rock (115), is of particular interest. She fittingly sees Wiebe's connection of Big Bear with the sun as a storytelling device, dramatizing the scenes and evoking symbolism as a way of engaging the reader and setting the stage for the narrative.

In her essay, "History from a Different Angle," Coral Ann Howells offers additional insight:

> In the clash between white and Indian cultures one
> of the fundamental differences is their perception
> of time: where the white men consult watches and
> diaries, the Indians consult the sun and the seasons
> and so have a concept of duration rather than of the
> significance of any specific moment. (164)

In *The Temptations*, the conflict between the White and the Indigenous cultures extends to all aspects of their existence. To understand Wiebe's writing, one must recognize these differences rather than fall into the trap of centuries-old depictions where the First Peoples everyday actions were defined and misjudged through the White people's perception of life and customs.

Wiebe also links Big Bear with the concept of "silence" which has a special place in his writing. In his essay "The Words of Silence: Past and Present," Wiebe lists seven words of silence. He invites the readers to examine various sources such as fables, Biblical references or literary ones, and develop their own connotations of the word. He lists "stone" as the sixth word of silence and explains its meaning through the story of a man who wishes for immortality and is turned into a rock, which in the novel Big Bear recounts to Kitty McLean at Loon Lake.

Notably, the story told by Big Bear also evokes the story of Jesus, "... when the Pharisees tell Jesus to order his followers to be silent. Jesus looked at them for a moment and then said: Truly I tell you, if these were silent, the very stones would cry out" (Luke 19:39–40). Moreover, Wiebe's rhetorical question "Do stones ever, have stones ever broken their silence?" (*The Words of*

Silence, 18), can be linked to Big Bear's association with a rock, seen as a symbol of steadfastness and strength. The Cree leader who must speak for his Peoples is depicted as a figure who transcends spatial and temporal realms. Similar to Jesus, in his death, Big Bear becomes immortal. He, like the man who asks for immortality and is turned into a rock, also becomes "everlasting, unchanging, rock" (*The Temptations*, 415). In the story Big Bear tells, he becomes, "the grandfather of all, the first of all being as well as the last" (The Words of Silence 18).

At the moment of Big Bear's death, the scene that presents itself to him is, "the red shoulder of Sun at the rim of Earth" (*The Temptations*, 415). Instead of cessation, he becomes part of the earth. Howells proposes that in death, Big Bear achieves "the prophetic vision which sees beyond the limits of the present and the logic of circumstances to a cosmic harmony resting in the Only Great spirit" (168). Howells reasons that this moment of transcendence is what Wiebe refers to as "The apprehension of a perfection." In a conversation with Robert Kroetsch, recorded by Shirley Newman in 1980, Wiebe states, "I think [a human being] is an animal capable of the apprehension of perfection" (*A Voice in the Land*, 234).

In my interview with Wiebe published in this anthology, Wiebe explains "the apprehension of a perfection" as follows: "We humans can both understand and grasp a vision of perfection, but at the same time we are anxious, fearful about it. Forty years after that talk with Bob [Robert Kroetsch], this "apprehension" (noun) is still with me; perfection is possible; dare I face it? I long for, and face that possibility every day of my life" (Wiebe,

Rudy. Email received by Bianca Lakoseljac 12 December, 2020). Has Wiebe faced this perfection in his quest to understand the Big Bear's character? I believe he has, and if my understanding is correct, so does Howells.

A further examination of Wiebe's storymaking approaches and his emphasis on "voice" reveals additional qualities Big Bear embodies. Keith refers to the possibility of Wiebe's "total sympathetic identification" (*Epic Fiction: The Art of Rudy Wiebe*, 77) with the historical Big Bear. Wiebe's genuine admiration for the First Peoples culture, as discussed earlier in this essay, is also evident during Wiebe's examination of Big Bear's power-bundle in a New York museum. When Wiebe held the power-bundle, in spite of its simple content, or perhaps because of it, he experienced a sense of "religious appreciation" and reports the following:

> As I touch it [Big Bear's power-bundle] I should feel something ... Something for my own apprehension for wanting to see this, to somehow *have* this, like any white who never has enough of anything, as if it were even possible to actually have enough of anything except within yourself; something of a prayer to the great Spirit who Big Bear, and I also, believe shaped the universe as He did for no other reason than that apparently He wanted to. (Bear Spirit in a Strange Land, VL 148)

Keith points to Wiebe's experience of complete transcendence when he identifies with Big Bear and sees the Great Spirit as the creator of the universe, a view which

Wiebe shares with the Cree leader (EFARW, 77). The offer of a prayer, where Wiebe equates Big Bear's Creator with his own, leads to the conclusion that Wiebe perceives Big Bear as taking on the role of a prophet. It also supports Paul Tiessen's conviction that Wiebe asserts "assumptions based on man's shared spirituality." The reader concludes that it is the new form of characterization, as Eli Mandell proposes, that best describes Wiebe's depiction of Big Bear.

Wiebe does not craft single-dimensional characters which slot easily into categories. Instead, as Penny van Toorn reasons in *Rudy Wiebe and the Historicity of the Word*, characters are shaped through dialogic tension and depiction of ceremonies and rituals characteristic of the historical context that defines the story and gives it meaning (99–101). Van Toorn explains that,

> Five varieties of dialogue warrant close attention in *The Temptations of Big Bear*: compositionally marked dialogues between the characters, the implicit dialogues between narratorial voices, the dialogue between the text and the readers, the dialogue between the author and the narrating characters, and the novel's dialogue with the other texts and discourses sounding in the wider Canadian cultural arena. (99–100)

The complexity of Wiebe's text leads the reader to examine Wiebe's characters' words and actions with a keen eye on the voice. Van Toorn reasons that, in addition to being a historic figure, Big Bear also "functions as a rhetorical device whereby Wiebe exposes the artificiality of certain axioms which dominate thinking about the land and the social order in twentieth-century Canada" (RWHW 104).

To explore Big Bear's role as a rhetorical device, it is helpful to examine Wiebe's depiction of Big Bear's perception of himself and his society, or the microcosm-macrocosm concept, which is related to the process Hayden White refers to as "the technique of ostensive self-definition by negation" (152). In his *Tropics of Discourse: Essays in Cultural Criticism*, published in 1978, Hayden White reasons that throughout centuries, the so-called civilized man has been using the method of defining his civility by juxtaposing himself to this other, unruly, uncivilized man, for one certain way of defining what civility is, is by stating what it is not.

> In times of sociocultural stress, when the need for positive self-definition asserts itself ... it is possible to ... point to something ... that is manifestly different from oneself. ... It appears as a kind of reflex action in conflicts between nations, classes and political parties. ... If we do not know what we think 'civilization' is, we can always find an example of what it is not. (151–152)

Thus, one man's civility is defined as the opposite of the other man's lack of it.

Wiebe employs similar method of reversal—an intriguing storytelling technique. He shows Big Bear using the colonizers' way of life to define what he and his

Peoples are not, in order to recapture, during the rapid changes of his society's way of life, what his Peoples are. He examines the past way of life of the Cree population, his wars with past enemies, such as the Sioux, Siksikawa, Bloods, and Crows, some of whom had become his allies, and states that "everyone needs good enemies to become a good man" (98). When he recalls past conflicts with other First Nations, he feels admiration for his enemies. He even sees the conflicts as positive elements which help to improve the human race. However, he sees "Whiteskins" as that "other", not Indigenous, for while past conflicts were fought between technological equals who used their physical strength, which led to an improvement in the agility and health of the First Nations society as a whole, he realizes that the occupation by the White man implies annihilation of a life the First Nations value.

> But now with the end of everything we have
> ever lived standing at the end of it, pray our Only
> One *give me back those days*. But I see now they
> will not come. Never. I see that. Unless we [the
> First Peoples] all together make a life circle with
> our hands and face the Whiteskins as one.
> (*The Temptations*, 99)

As Van Toorn reasons, Big Bear does function as a rhetorical device. Furthermore, through the first-person narrative, Big Bear also follows Hayden White's process of "ostensive self-definition through negation." When faced with the threat of losing the culture which defines his existence, the Cree chief envisions other bands uniting against the "Whiteskins." It is clear to Big Bear who he is not, and that the real enemy is the White man. The First Peoples, perceived by the colonizers as "savages," in fact see the White man as the destroyer of the First Nations culture: "everything we [the First Peoples] have ever lived." Therefore the "savage" is no other but the White man. As Van Toorn points out, Wiebe does expose the falseness of dominant thinking about the land and the social order in colonial Canada. Also, as Paul Tiessen reasons in "The Naming of Rudy Wiebe," Wiebe questions his readers' "received version of history and world view" (115).

If one has a difficulty understanding who Big Bear is, one certainly has a clear sense of who he is not: he is certainly not a White man, not in appearance nor in his thought or his perception of himself. Big Bear is not handsome by the colonizers' standards. He does not desire to acquire any traits of the "Whiteskins" and certainly not of their nobility. Furthermore, he is portrayed as the moral opposite to his sons Imasees, known as Little Bad Man, and a Cree war chief Kah—Paypamahchukways, known as Wandering Spirit. Wiebe does not identify the Cree characters by the colonizers' standards nor solely by their Indigenous attributes. He does not depict them as all negative or all positive figures, and thus does not portray the Indigenous Peoples world in stereotypical terms. Wiebe's Indigenous Peoples characters are neither idealized nor vilified. Rather, they are depicted in general, human terms, where within a society there exist the morally strong and the morally weak.

Wiebe's themes of division run throughout the novel. This conflict is seen in disputes among the various bands, as well as within bands. The last is memorably dramatized in the juxtaposition of Big Bear and his rebellious sons. Furthermore, Big Bear's depiction as, "head held high ... his eyes gleaming bright obsidian pierced in the unpainted folds of his face," takes the reader into another temporal and spatial realm, into the world of an epic hero. Big Bear is similar to a prophet, with Christ-like powers as Keith observes in *Epic Fiction* (77).

Big Bear is praying throughout *The Temptations,* and just before his death reference is made to "the long prayer to The Only One that was his life" (414). Power in this context is not the might-is-right ethic of the White man. Instead, power lies in Big Bear's inner strength, the quality he derives from The Only One through his power-bundle. Like Christ, Big Bear withstands his temptations; like Christ, Big Bear suffers for his people. "You will carry it all on your back," James Simpson tells Big Bear after the killings at Frog Lake (267), and this proves as prophetic as Big Bear's own vision of hanged Cree warriors (77).

Eli Mandel has also observed that Big Bear's first-person narrative sometimes echoes Biblical speech (VL 152). Wiebe does not deny that the depiction of his characters might be influenced by his Christian beliefs. In his discussion of the novel, Wiebe states the following: "I am a Christian so I write from that viewpoint ... I write as a Christian, just as Camus writes as an existentialist. ...To write the kind of stuff that I do you have to write out of yourself, genuinely (A Voice in the Land 127).

If simplicity and naturalness attributed to Big Bear can be linked to Christian virtues, then Lieutenant-Governors Dewdney and Morris, and the colonizers who are parading in the Queen's uniform, can be seen as objects of Wiebe's criticism. In contrast to Big Bear's shrewd logic, Lieutenant-Governor Morris points to his uniform as a symbol of position and power: "I am the representative of the Queen. As my blue coat shows . . ." (21). Wiebe's tone leads the reader to mistrust the colonial government and law, for it is explained through a "childish voice," using superficialities such as a uniform rather than justifiable reason. The hypocrisy of the colonial system is further emphasized by contrasting it to Big Bear's profound reasoning, thus reaffirming Wiebe's sincere admiration for the First Peoples culture.

In the novel, Wiebe depicts Big Bear as the rightful inhabitant of land given to him and his Peoples by The Only One. He projects a heroic image of Big Bear as a weapon to undermine colonial rule, particularly the colonial acquisition of land, and to expose the duplicity of the colonizers. In Paul Tiessen's words, Wiebe "instructs his audience by satire and precept" (115).

In addition, Penny van Toorn points out that "Through Big Bear, Wiebe shows that all questions of land rights depend on a prior question: who controls the social process whereby truth and value come into being?" (RWHW 104).

> No one can choose for only himself a piece of the Mother Earth. She is. And she is for all that live, alike. . . . I have always lived on the earth with my people, I have always moved as far as I wished to see. We take what the earth gives us when we need anything, and we leave the rest for those who follow us. (*The Temptations*, 28, 29)

Van Toorn reasons that Big Bear does not argue against the number of acres. Instead, he opposes the concept of land as acreage which could be privately owned and used for commercial development: "Big Bear surrenders neither physical territory nor ideological ground" (RWHW 104). Rather, through the juxtaposition of the logical justifications that each nation bases its land claims on, Big Bear provides a philosophical reasoning rooted in the full comprehension of himself and his place in the world.

Big Bear's traits are revealed to the reader not only through his actions and words, but also through responses of various other characters from the novel. Some of these responses include comments such as:

> "He [Big Bear] is a complete untouched pagan";
> "... if Indians followed any logic discernable to us, they should elect him [Big Bear] 'prime minister'...";
> "... [Big Bear] is a man who seemingly contains so complete an assurance of and confidence in his own self-ness ... that he cannot be moved by any mere white words ..."; "... an old heathen on plains ..." (117, 121, 122 Dewdney); "Big Bear is an agitator ..." (210 Major Read)

These remarks by Edgar Dewdney and Major Reed are based on the actual letters to Ottawa Wiebe consulted in his research. They exemplify Wiebe's skill as a storyteller who depicts Big Bear as a complex figure, fully aware of his responsibilities to his Cree Peoples, and unwilling to obey Ottawa's demands and sign the treaty as all other

"Indian chiefs" had done. This refusal is seen by Ottawa as a demonstration of Big Bear's rebelliousness, for he is viewed as causing much inconvenience to government officials by disobeying the Queen.

Penny van Toorn refers to Wiebe's method of deriving meaning as "dialogical ... through negotiation between voices speaking with one another in the evolving context of human history" (RWHW 100). Wiebe depicts Dewdney as unable to hide his admiration and respect for Big Bear's self-confidence and wisdom. The reader sees this method of storytelling as Wiebe's way of conveying his own regard for the historical Big Bear's strength and his refusal to sign the treaty.

In *The Temptations*, Wiebe makes it clear that the dissatisfaction of the First Peoples bands who had accepted the reserves but discovered that the government promises were not being fulfilled, combined with rumours of Big Bear's collaboration with Louis Riel and the possibility of an uprising, caused the Lieutenant-Governor to become extremely agitated and anxious for Big Bear to accept the treaty.

> All that summer, 1884, telegraph wires of the North West Territories sang daily with information for Lieutenant-Governor and Indian Commissioner Dewdney. ... Nothing that summer would make the Governor change his opinion. Rae wrote him and to the Prime Minister: 'The Indians who are *very* badly off must either be treated rationally, if not generously, or as I said before, we must be prepared to fight them.' ... It does not seem to me

> reasonable to expect a lot of pure savages to settle
> down and become steady farmers all at once ...
> Big Bear is an agitator ... only too glad to have an
> opportunity of inciting the Indians to make fresh
> and exorbitant demands ... Government policy
> should be, as it has been in the past, one of
> conciliation. There is only one other, and that is to
> fight them. (209, 210)

The controversy of how to treat the "rebellious Big Bear and his Indians," echoes the larger one colonizing powers have faced over the centuries. This debate questions whether the Indigenous inhabitants should be treated in a humane manner, or through military force which, given the technological advantages of the colonists, meant their certain destruction. This question is reminiscent of the sixteenth-century Las Casas and Sepúlveda debate during the colonization of the North American Continent.

In the late fifteenth and the early sixteenth century, as the Spanish colonizers entered the various parts of the "New World," the Indigenous communities were decimated through massacres, enslavement, disease and forced labour. The atrocities inflicted by the Spanish conquerors are referred to as the *black legend* and remain a controversy which persists in Spanish history (some apologists for Spain's treatment of the Indigenous Peoples are still engaged in ongoing debates). Spain's colonizing strategies, supported by Pope Alexander VI, were rationalized through the assertion that Christianisation was Spain's primary goal. For Spain, the question which arose was whether the Indigenous populations were capable and worthy of Christianity—in other words, were they rational, and did they possess a human soul? As bizarre as these questions seem to a contemporary reader, these were serious questions for the Renaissance Europeans. Dewdney's reference to Big Bear and his "Indians" as "pure savages" resonates with these misconceptions.

The deliberation on the treatment of Big Bear and his band, as evident from Dewdney's letters, leads one to conclude that the dispute over "Indian treatment" at the end of the nineteenth century in Canada remained a reality, demonstrating that questions from a few centuries earlier which dealt with "the treatment of Indians in the conquered territories" seem to be perpetuated with a simple change of temporal and spatial factors.

Wiebe's indignation over the treatment of the First Nations by the colonizers and its questionable representation in colonial history, his attempt to, as Keith proposes, bring the First Nations culture and society into the mainstream Canadian literature (63), combined with his Christian upbringing, has led him to depict Big Bear as a material loser who emerges as a moral winner, spiritually superior to his conquerors. This depiction supports Wiebe's assertion that to understand human relations between the colonizers and the First Peoples, one must grasp the concepts of human rights and freedoms which define each society's culture and understanding of life— as they are fundamentally different between the two societies (*Where the Truth Lies* 114–139, 64–76).

In *The Temptations*, it is this form of rightful inheritance Big Bear professes for his Cree Peoples in his attempt to preserve the way of life given to them by, "The Only

One." This method of storytelling is also Wiebe's way of establishing Big Bear and his Peoples as the rightful inhabitants of the land they are about to lose.

> I am fed by Mother Earth. The only water I will be touched by comes from above, the rain from The Only One who makes the grass grow and the rivers run and the buffalo feed there and drink so that I and my children live. That we have life. (23)

In Wiebe's terms, Big Bear is the Cree Messiah defending his Peoples human rights and freedoms. Furthermore, using the first-person narrative, "I [Big Bear] was free, and the smallest Person in my band was as free as I because the Master of Life had given us our place on the earth and that was enough for us" (398), Wiebe emphasizes the difference between the First Peoples philosophy on life which defines their culture, as opposite of the White man's.[9]

The Colonial Law, on the other hand, which does not recognize the First Peoples philosophy on life and land tenure is professed by the judge. Through his statement, "This land never belonged to you. The land was and is the Queen's" (399), the judge negates not only Big Bear's and his Peoples rightful inheritance, but he also negates all concepts of their, and their predecessors' existence. The Cree perception of who they are as people

---

9. For further study, see T.W. Smyth's Ph.D. Thesis, *Rudy Wiebe: Witness and Critic Without Apology*, p. 72–77. University of Toronto. file:///C:/Users/bianc/Downloads/NQ28061%20(2).pdf

is inextricably linked to their land which, as Big Bear states, provides all the necessities of life; in Wiebe's terms, it also grants their sense of freedom which is equated to their perception of themselves as men. Since Big Bear had not become a part of the "social contract" as a "free agent," but was forced through famine resulting from the White man's destruction of First Nations land, the judge's law has no bearing on Big Bear and his Cree band. The judge's application of his White law upon Big Bear is an act of colonial law, void of philosophical substance.

In addition, Big Bear's plea for aid, "But you [the colonizers] have taken our inheritance and our strength. *You have done this.* And there is nothing left now but that you must help us" (398), echoes Las Casas' appeal to colonizing powers to treat the Indigenous communities with "Christian" mercy, for it is the colonizers who have intruded upon the Indigenous Peoples way of life. Hence, Big Bear cannot be seen as "innocent" or "uninformed" —in other words, "naïve"—idealized character, blindly trusting in the colonizers to improve the life for him and his Cree Peoples. Instead, he is fully aware of the trickery and dangers facing him and searches for ways to postpone the signing of the treaty which would forever alter the Cree Peoples way of life. Big Bear's profound understanding of his and his Peoples position within the colonial law elevates him above his conquerors. Therefore, the Cree chief and his Peoples cannot be ruled by the colonial law. Wiebe invites the reader to observe a new, sincere, way of depicting a First Peoples hero from Canada's past with all his human strengths and weaknesses as he stands up for his Peoples rights and freedoms.

Extraordinary Canadians: *Big Bear,*
by Rudy Wiebe—a biography

"There was once a baby boy born at Jackfish Lake [in 1825], near present-day North Battleford, Saskatchewan, who would grow up to receive the Cree name Mistahimaskwa, Big Bear" (1), thus begins Rudy Wiebe's creative biography, *Big Bear.* The biography of Big Bear was published as part of The Extraordinary Canadians Series in 2008, with John Ralston Saul as series editor.

Wiebe wrote the Cree chief's biography over fifty years after he first read William Cameron's *The War Trail of Big Bear* (written in 1927), and over three decades after the publication of his novel, *The Temptations of Big Bear* in 1973. It is evident that Wiebe's "trailing" of Big Bear's biography, studying the controversial and often contradictory accounts of the historical period, and unearthing of Big Bear's story, first suitable to fiction and later to a biographical account, have been an extensive and lifelong venture. It was Wiebe's journey to "find that spiritual place where land and friendship offer us the optic power of the audible heart" (*Big Bear* Xvii). In his essay, "On the Trail of Big Bear," Wiebe sheds light into his drive to bring the story of Big Bear to Canadian readers:

> I first realized that the bush homestead where I
> was born in northern Saskatchewan probably
> was traversed in June 1885 by Big Bear and his
> diminishing band as among the poplars they easily
> evaded the bush-clumsy military columns ... that I
> first realized the white sand beaches of Turtle Lake,

> where Speedwell School [where Wiebe attended
> grade school] held its annual sports day ... right
> there where that brown girl had once beaten me in
> the grade four sprints ... perhaps on that very
> beach Big Bear had once stood looking at the
> clouds trundle up from the north. (WTTL, 65)

Wiebe ends his biography of Big Bear with,

> Big Bear died at Poundmaker reserve, Saskatchewan
> Territory, on January 17, 1888. He was buried on
> the snow-covered bluffs overlooking the Battle
> River. In August 1972, Elder John Tootoosis led me
> to the place. He said an Elder had shown him the
> grave in 1905 when he was six years old, and told
> him to remember. (212)

John Ralston Saul, in his Introduction to Rudy Wiebe's,
Big Bear, a biography, reasons that Canadian perception
of our country through European Traditions and our
attempt to disregard the Aboriginal experience, "is a be-
trayal of our own past." He points out that "Rudy Wiebe
tells Big Bear's story in that great, dramatic tradition"
(Xiii). Saul observes that,

> For much of Canada, the latter part of the nineteenth
> century saw unbridled land hunger and political
> ambition tear the country apart. From that confusion
> Big Bear emerges—calm, ironic, coolly angry, always
> ready to explain—as one who can show us the way,
> thanks to his actions and to his words. (Xiii)

Big Bear's heroic struggle to preserve his and his Peoples way of life was a story Wiebe pursued for most of his life. It was a story Wiebe saw as his own, part of his own history, part of who he is as a man and as a Canadian.

Conclusion:

In the introduction to *The Story Makers*, Wiebe notes that a "story worth pondering is story doubly enjoyed." *The Temptations of Big Bear* is not only a story "worth pondering," but a multilayered story irresistible to endless pondering. Using a variety of narrative devices from various perspectives, Wiebe expertly reveals the story of Big Bear who emerges as an enigmatic figure, and for the reader arouses a multiplicity of images, and even a sense of indignation with the Canadian history, similar to that conveyed by Wiebe.

It is important to remember that the First Nations culture during colonization relied primarily on oral tradition. In the last chapter of *The Temptations*, after the judge rejects Big Bear's spoken words as evidence and sentences him to prison, Big Bear is at last permitted to speak: "I [Big Bear] ask the court to print my words and scatter them among white people" (399). Big Bear, who has total mistrust for written words, uses the colonizers' way to communicate the truth for he is fully cognizant that the colonizers will never understand the First Peoples ways. Carla Visser observes that "In a sense, he [Wiebe] has printed Big Bear's words and scattered them among White people" (118).

In her 1974 review of *The Temptations*, Myrna Kostash points out that, "Someday western Indians will write novels and their voices will tell us, at last, the authentic version of how their nations contracted culture of the reservation after a millennium of running buffalo and dying of old age" (A White Man's View of Big Bear, 32). True to Kostash's words, we are now privileged to read a wide spectrum of Canadian literature by some of the most profound First Nations authors.

Tomson Highway, in his highly acclaimed anthology, *From Oral to Written: A Celebration of Indigenous Literature in Canada, 1980–2010*, published in 2017, cites a sampling of 176 works by 119 Indigenous Canadian writers. In Highway's words, these authors are "the first wave of Indigenous Canadian writers" (365). Back in the 1970s, it was Wiebe who opened a window into a sincere way of depicting a First Peoples character in Canadian literary fiction.

I would like to leave the reader with John Ralston Saul's image of the Cree leader Big Bear as, "an illustration of what is best in our civilization. An ethical leader who suffers tragedy and defeat will often become a model for those who follow" (*Big Bear* Xiii). Through his depiction of Big Bear's *temptations*, both through fiction and creative nonfiction, Wiebe has taken Canadian recollection of history and myth, and deconstructed it with ethics, morals, and an insight into land rights based on human rights and freedoms, until we are gifted with a new understanding of how we became a nation and who we are today. Through his masterful story-making techniques, Wiebe has transformed Big Bear into a blend of an epic, prophetic figure, whose attributes are expertly transcended through a First Peoples hero of Canadian past—the wise and heroic Plains Cree chief Big Bear in Wiebe's "story of beginnings that reveals a basic way of seeing the world [in which] divinity is man with super human knowledge and powers" (The Story Makers XXI).

Works Consulted:

Behn, Aphra. *Oronooko, or, The Royal Slave: A Critical Edition*. Ed. Adelaide P. Amore. New York: U of America P. 1987.

Benjamin, Walter. "The Storyteller" in *Illuminations*. Ed. Hannah Arendt. New York: Harcourt Brace. 1955.

Cameron, Donald. *Conversations with Canadian Novelists*. Toronto: Macmillan of Canada. 1973.

Columbus, Christopher. *The Voyage of Christopher Columbus: Columbus' Own Journal of Discovery Newly Restored and Translated*. Ed. And Trans. John Cummins. New York: St. Martin's P. 1992.

Cro, Stelio. *The Noble Savage: Allegory of Freedom*. Waterloo: Wilfrid Laurier. 1936.

De Las Casas, Bartholome. *A Short Account of the Destruction of the Indies*. Ed. And Trans. Nigel Griffin. Toronto: Penguin. 1992.

De Montaigne, Michel. *Essays*. Trans. Cohen, J. M. London: Penguin Books, 1958.

Dudley, Edward and Maximillian E. Novak. Ed. *The Wild Man Within: An Image in Western Thought from the Renaissance to Romanticism*. Pittsburgh: U of Pittsburgh P. 1972.

Gebri, Antonello. *The Dispute of the New World: The History of a Polemic, 1750–1900*. Trans. Jeremy Moyle. Pittsburgh: U of Pittsburgh P. 1973.

Goldie, Terry. *Fear and Temptation: The Image of the Indigene in Canadian, Australian, and New Zealand Literature.* London: McGill-Queen's UP. 1989.

Grace, Sherill E. "Structuring Violence: 'The Ethics of Linguistics' in *The Temptations of Big Bear*," in *Canadian Literature*, No. 104, Spring 1985, pp.7–22. https://www.enotes.com/topics/rudy-wiebe/in-depth

Grauer, Lalage. *In the Camp of Big Bear: Narrative Representations of the Frog lake Uprising.* Thesis, PHD. U of Toronto, 1991.

Guptara, Prabhu. "'Clutching a Feather in a Maelstorm': Rudy Wiebe's Critique of the Contemporary West," in *Journal of Commonwealth Literature*, Vol. XVII, No. 1, 1982, pp. 146–52. https://www.enotes.com/topics/rudy-wiebe/in-depth.

Hanke, Lewis. *Aristotle and The American Indians: A Study in Race Prejudice in the Modern World.* Chicago: Henry Regnery Co. 1959.

Hazard, Paul. *The European Mind.* New York: The World P C, 1963.

Highway, Tomson. *From Oral to Written: A Celebration of Indigenous Literature in Canada, 1980–2010.* Vancouver: Talonbooks, 2017.

Holman C. Hugh, and William Harmon. *A Handbook to Literature.* 6th edition. Toronto: Macmillan Publishing, 1992.

Howells, Coral Ann. "History from a Different Angle: Narrative Strategies in *The Temptations of Big Bear*," in *Journal of Commonwealth Literature*, Vol. XVII, No. 1, 1982, pp. 161–71. https://www.enotes.com/topics/rudy-wiebe/in-depth

Keith, W. J. Ed. *A Voice in the Land: Essays by and About Rudy Wiebe.* Edmonton: NeWest press. 1981.

Keith, W. J. *Epic Fiction: The Art of Rudy Wiebe*. Edmonton:
U of Alberta P. 1981.

Mandeville. *The Travels of Sir John Mandeville*. Trans.
Moseley, C. W. R. D. Markham: Penguin. 1983.

Monkman, Leslie. *A Native Heritage: Images of the Indian in
English Canadian Literature*. Toronto: U of Toronto P. 1981.

Rousseau, Jean-Jacques. *Discourse of the Origin of Inequality
(Second Discourse), Polemics, and Political Economy*. Trans.
Bush, Judith R., Roger D. Masters, Christopher Kelly, and
Terence Marshall. Ed. Masters Roger D. And Christopher
Kelly. London: UP of New England. 1992.

Saint Augustine. *The City of God*. Trans. Marcus Dods, D.
D. New York: The Modern Library, 1950.

Smyth, T. W. *Rudy Wiebe as Novelist: Witness and Critic
Without Apology*. 1997. University of Toronto. Ph.D. dissertation, National Library of Canada. file:///C:/Users
/bianc/Downloads/NQ28061%20(2).pdf

*The Roanoke Voyages: 1584–1590: Documents to Illustrate the
English Voyages to North America Under the Patent Granted
to Walter Raleigh in 1584*. Ed. David Beers Quinn.
Volume I. Germany: Kraus Reprint. 1955.

Tiessen, Paul. "The Naming of Rudy Wiebe." *Journal of
Mennonite Studies* Vol 7 (1989): 115–122.

Travel and Works of Captain John Smith. Ed. A. G. Bradley.
Volume I and II. Edinburgh: John Grant. 1910.

Van Toorn, Penny. *Rudy Wiebe and the Historicity of the
Word*. Edmonton: The University of Alberta Press. 1995.

Visser, Carla. "Historicity in Historical Fiction: *Burning Water*
and *The Temptations of Big Bear*," in *Studies in Canadian
Literature*, Vol. 12, No. 1, 1987, pp. 90–111. https://
www.enotes.com/topics/rudy-wiebe/in-depth

Whaley, Susan. *Rudy Wiebe and His Works*. Toronto: ECW Press. 1987.

White, Hayden. *Tropics of Discourse: Essays in Cultural Criticism*. Baltimore: John Hopkins University Press. 1978.

Wiebe, Rudy. *A Discovery of Strangers*. Toronto: Alfred A. Knopf. 1994.

-----. *Big Bear*. (Extraordinary Canadians) Toronto: Penguin Canada. 2008.

-----. *Come Back*. Toronto: Alfred A. Knopf. 2014.

-----. *First and Vital Candle*. Toronto: McClelland and Stewart, and Grand Rapids, Michigan, Eerdmans. 1966.

-----. *My Lovely Enemy*. Toronto: McClelland and Stewart. 1983.

-----. *of this earth: A Mennonite Boyhood in the Boreal Forest*. Toronto: Vintage Canada. 2007.

-----. *Peace Shall Destroy Many*. Toronto: McClelland and Stewart. 1962.

-----. *Sweeter Than All the World*. Toronto: Alfred A. Knopf. 2001.

-----. *The Blue Mountains of China*. Toronto: McClelland and Stewart and Grand Rapids, Michigan, Eerdmans. 1970.

-----. *The Mad Trapper*. Toronto: McClelland and Stewart. 1977.

-----. *The Scorched-Wood People*. Toronto: McClelland and Stewart. 1977.

-----. *The Temptations of Big Bear*. Toronto: McClelland & Stewart. 1973.

-----. *The Storymakers*. Toronto: MacMillan of Canada. 1970.

-----. "The Words of Silence: Past and Present" in *Silence, the Word and the Sacred*. Eds. Blodget, E. D. and H. G. Coward. Waterloo: Wilfrid Aurier U. P. 1989.

-----. "Western Canadian Fiction: Past and Present," *Western American Literature*, 6 (Spring 1971), 29.

-----. *Where the Truth Lies*. Edmonton: NeWest Press. 2016.

Bibliography:
Through the Eyes of Rudy Wiebe

Bianca Lakoseljac

Preface: Through the Eyes of Rudy Wiebe

There is power in the words of a good storyteller, and a good story will outlast the facts even if they are real—if they actually happened in real life. A good story will outlive the details even if they are recorded, and it is the images and thoughts and emotions it evokes, which will be remembered. Rudy Wiebe's stories depict a mosaic of diverse voices, events, and places in which western Canadian life is presented and recorded in all its complexity, multiplicity, and resonance. It is no wonder that Wiebe's bibliographical range encompasses a whole spectrum of genres that include novels, short stories, biographical accounts, histories, children's books, plays, many essays and lectures, and most recently—poems. The titles in this bibliography have been compiled over the last few decades of following Wiebe's writing and the works by other authors relating to it, in addition to sourcing material at a number of research facilities. I would like to express my gratitude to various libraries for providing access to library materials, services, and research assistance. These include: York University Libraries and the Archives, especially Scott Library; University of Toronto

Libraries, especially Robarts Library; Toronto Metropolitan University (Ryerson University) Library; Toronto Public Library and Archives, especially the Toronto Reference Library, among others. I am grateful for the notable research found at Athabasca University's English Canadian Writers' website as updated by Student & Academic Services. In addition, the Goshen College Mennonite Writing in Canada website edited by Ervin Beck, Professor Emeritus of English, Goshen College, Goshen, Indiana, provided detailed study. Updated in August 2016, the bibliography was originally assembled by Hildi Froese Tiessen of Conrad Grebel University College, Waterloo, Canada, funded by the Social Science and Humanities Council of Canada. https://www.goshen.edu/academics /english/ervinb/canada/ In addition, the website, https:// biography.jrank.org/pages/4832/Wiebe-Rudy-Henry .html edited by Penny van Toorn (deceased) and updated by Marta Krogh was very helpful. I would especially like to thank the authors and scholars who have contributed their essays, interviews, reviews, and commentaries to *Rudy Wiebe: Essays on His Works*. Their careful studies and astute observations offer additional insights into Wiebe's writing and enrich the varied and expansive collection of works about Wiebe's fiction and nonfiction.

For *Essays*, I set out to compile a comprehensive Bibliography of works by and about Wiebe's writing. The first part, Bibliography of Works by Rudy Wiebe consists of: (1) Wiebe's ten novels, (2) six collections of short stories, (3) a play, (4) two children's books, (5) six nonfiction books, (6) four poems, (7) and eight books edited and co-edited by Wiebe. The second part, Bibliography of Works about Rudy Wiebe consists of two parts: (1) Books about Rudy Wiebe and (2) a section titled as Other: Essays by and about Rudy Wiebe, published elsewhere such as in anthologies, literary journals, and magazines. In total, I assembled just over 270 titles, as the body of writing by Wiebe and about his fiction and nonfiction is extensive, nationally and internationally. For certain essay collections, under the book title, I also listed the essay titles to make it easier for researchers and scholars to locate them. I trust our readers will find the information useful.

I. Bibliography Of Works By Rudy Wiebe

Novels:

Peace Shall Destroy Many. Toronto: McClelland & Stewart, 1962. Vintage Canada, 2001.

First and Vital Candle. Markham, Ont.: Fitzhenry & Whiteside, 2006; 1966.

The Blue Mountains of China. Toronto: McClelland and Stewart, 1970.

The Temptations of Big Bear. Swallow Press/Ohio University Press ed. Athens, Ohio: Swallow Press/Ohio University Press, 2000; 1973.

The Scorched-Wood People : A Novel. Toronto: McClelland and Stewart, 1977.

The Mad Trapper : A Novel. Toronto: McClelland and Stewart, 1980.

My Lovely Enemy : A Novel. Toronto: McClelland and Stewart, 1983.

A Discovery of Strangers. Toronto: A.A. Knopf Canada, 1994.
Sweeter than all the World. Toronto: Vintage Canada, 2001.
Come Back: Toronto: Random House, 2014.

Collections of Short Stories:

Where is the Voice Coming from?. Toronto: McClelland and
   Stewart, 1974.
Another Place, Not Here. Toronto: Knopf Canada, 1996.
Wiebe, Rudy, Harry Savage, and Tom Radford. *Alberta, a
   Celebration.* Edmonton: Hurtig Publishers, 1979.
The Angel of the Tar Sands and Other Stories. Toronto:
   McClelland and Stewart, 1982.
River of Stone: Fictions and Memories. Vintage Books Canada
   ed. Toronto: Vintage Books, 1995.
Collected Stories. Edmonton: University of Alberta Press. 2010.

Play:

Wiebe, Rudy, and Theatre Passe Muraille. *Far as the Eye can
   See: A Play.* Edmonton, AB: NeWest, 1977.

Children's Literature:

Chinook Christmas. David Moore. Red Deer, AB: Red Deer
   College Press. 1993.
Wiebe, Rudy Henry, and Michael Lonechild. *Hidden
   Buffalo.* Calgary: Red Deer Press, 2003.

Non-Fiction Books:

Wiebe, Rudy, and Bob Beal. *War in the West: Voices of the 1885 Rebellion.* Toronto, ON: McClelland and Stewart, 1985.

Playing Dead: A Contemplation Concerning the Arctic. 1st ed. Edmonton: NeWest, 1989. NOTE: The three essays in this collection were originally presented under the title, "The Arctic: The Landscape of the Spirit," as a series of lectures at the University of Toronto. The essays are titled: "Exercising Reflection," "On Being Motionless," and "In Your Own Head."

Wiebe, Rudy, and Yvonne Johnson. *Stolen Life: The Journey of a Cree Woman.* 1 Vintage Canada ed. Toronto: Alfred A. Knopf Canada, 1999; 1998.

of this earth: A Mennonite Boyhood in the Boreal Forest. Vintage Canada ed. Toronto: Vintage Canada, 2007.

Extraordinary Canadians: Big Bear. Toronto: Penguin Group Canada, 2008.

Where the Truth Lies: Selected Essays. Edmonton: NeWest Press, 2016. NOTE: *Where the Truth Lies*, published in 2016, is Wiebe's latest essay collection, written as well as compiled by Wiebe. It comprises a selection of essays and presentations produced in about sixty years of writing, editing, and teaching. Below is the list of essays reprinted in this collection, with the sources of their original publications. The essays are listed in the order they appear in Wiebe, Rudy. *Where the Truth Lies: Selected Essays.* Edmonton: NeWest Press, 2016.

—. "Terminal Disease." *Writers Guild of Alberta Newsletter,* 1991. Rep. *Where the Truth Lies: Selected Essays.* Edmonton: NeWest Press, 2016. 3–5.

—. "A Frontier Visit." University of Alberta's 75th Anniversary Celebrations; published in University of Alberta's *Folio*, 23 December, 1982. Rep. *Where the Truth Lies: Selected Essays*.7–13.

—. "With the Flow." *Rhubarb* (Spring 2009). Rep. *Where the Truth Lies: Selected Essays*.15–19.

—. "Documenting a Writer's Life." *Prairie Fire*, Spring 2002. Rep. *Where the Truth Lies: Selected Essays*.21–44.

—. "Hold Your Peace." B.C. Mennonite Historical Society, Abbotsford, 2012. Rep. *Where the Truth Lies: Selected Essays*.45–62.

—. "On the Trail of Big Bear." Western Canadian Studies Conference, University of Calgary, March 1974. Journal of Canadian Fiction, 3. 2 (1974). Rep. *Where the Truth Lies: Selected Essays*.63–76.

—. "Where the Truth Lies: Exploring the Nature of Fact and Fiction." Various versions presented at several Canadian and American universities, 2007. Rep. *Where the Truth Lies: Selected Essays*.77–101.

—. "In the West." *Globe and Mail*, March 25, 1978. Rep. *Where the Truth Lies: Selected Essays*.105–8.

—. "On the Civil Right to Destroy Canada." *Edmonton Journal*, November 8, 1995. Rep. *Where the Truth Lies: Selected Essays*.109–12.

—. "Land, Language, and Law." The Shumiatcher Lecture, University of Saskatchewan, February, 1999. *Saskatchewan Law Review*, 63, 1 (2000). Rep. *Where the Truth Lies: Selected Essays*.113–40.

—. "The Elusive Meaning of 'North'." *Canadian Geographic* (January-February 1996). Rep. *Where the Truth Lies: Selected Essays*.141–46.

—. "The Wind and the Caribou." Edmonton Journal, September 24, 1995. Rep. *Where the Truth Lies: Selected Essays.* 147–54.

—. "On Being on the Top of the World." *Brick,* 64. Spring 2000. Rep. *Where the Truth Lies: Selected Essays.*155–74.

—. "Acceptance Speech, Governor General's Award." Award Ceremonies, Montreal, November 15, 1994. Rep. *Where the Truth Lies: Selected Essays.*175–6.

—. "Where the Black Rocks Lie in the Old Man's River." *Place: Lethbridge, A City on the Prairie,* Rudy Wiebe (author) and Geoffrey James (photographer). Vancouver: Douglas and McInture, 2002. Rep. *Where the Truth Lies: Selected Essays.*179–208.

—. "The Sweet Fiction of Owning Land." *Collection Canada* 2004. Ottawa: Canada Post, 2004. Rep. *Where the Truth Lies: Selected Essays.*209–21.

—. "On Death and Writing." American Association of Canadian Studies, Bangor, Maine, September 1983; Canadian Literature, 100. Spring 1984. Rep. *Where the Truth Lies: Selected Essays.*223–32.

—. "Killing our Way to Peace." The Thomas Merton Celebration, Vancouver, February, 2003. Rep. *Where the Truth Lies: Selected Essays.*233–62.

—. "The Body Knows as Much as the Soul." Samuel Yodel Lecture, Goshen College, Indiana, March 1995. Mennonite Quarterly Review (April 1997). Rep. *Where the Truth Lies: Selected Essays.*263–80.

—. "Flowers for Approaching the Fire." Edmonton Mennonite Centre for Newcomers Benefit, March 1998. *Conrad Grebel Review,* Spring 1998. Rep. *Where the Truth Lies: Selected Essays.*281–98.

—. "Look to the Rock." Thanksgiving Worship Service, 200th Anniversary of the Founding of the Molotschna Mennonite Colony, Tokmak, Ukraine, October 2004. Rep. *Where the Truth Lies: Selected Essays.*299–305.

Poems by Rudy Wiebe in Magazines, Journals, and Anthologies

"Departure Level." *Brick 108*, winter, 2022. https://brickmag .com/product/brick-108/. Rep. in *Rudy Wiebe: Essays on His Works*. Ed. Bianca Lakoseljac. Hamilton: Guernica Editions, 2023. Essential Writers Series #56.

"Everything." *Rudy Wiebe: Essays on His Works*. Ed. Bianca Lakoseljac. Hamilton: Guernica Editions, 2023. Essential Writers Series #56.

"Hands in Time of Pandemic." *Alberta Views*, August 1, 2020. https://albertaviews.ca/life-in-upheaval/ Rep. in *Rudy Wiebe: Essays on His Works*. Ed. Bianca Lakoseljac. Hamilton: Guernica Editions, 2023. Essential Writers Series #56.

"The Question." *Rudy Wiebe: Essays on His Works*. Ed. Bianca Lakoseljac. Hamilton: Guernica Editions, 2023. Essential Writers Series #56.

Books Edited and Co-Edited by Rudy Wiebe:

Editor, *The Story-Makers: A Selection of Modern Short Stories.* Toronto, Macmillan, 1970.

Editor, *Stories from Western Canada: A Selection.* Toronto, Macmillan, 1972.

Editor, with Andreas Schroeder, *Stories from Pacific and Arctic Canada: A Selection.* Toronto, Macmillan, 1974.

Editor, *Double Vision: An Anthology of Twentieth-Century Stories in English*. Toronto, Macmillan, 1976.

Editor, *Getting Here: Stories*. Edmonton, Alberta, NeWest Press, 1977.

Editor, with Aritha van Herk, *More Stories from Western Canada*. Toronto, Macmillan, 1980.

Editor, with Aritha van Herk and Leah Flater, *West of Fiction*. Edmonton, Alberton, NeWest Press, 1982.

Editor, with Bob Beal, *War in the West: Voices of the 1885 Rebellion*. Toronto, McClelland and Stewart, 1985.

Ii. Bibliography Of Works About Rudy Wiebe

Books About Rudy Wiebe:

Blodgett, E.D. et al. *Silence, the Word and the Sacred*. Waterloo: Wilfred Laurier University Press. 1989.

Harrison, Dick. *Unnamed Country: The Struggle for a Canadian Prairie Fiction*. Edmonton: University of Alberta Press, 1977.

Keith, W.J. *Epic Fiction: The Art of Rudy Wiebe*. Edmonton: University of Alberta Press, 1981.

—. "Peace Shall Destroy Many." 14–27.

—. "First and Vital Candle." 28–41.

—. "The Blue Mountains of China." 42–61.

—. "The Temptations of Big Bear." 62–81.

—. "The Scorched-Wood People." 82–104.

Keith, W.J. Ed. *A Voice in the Land: Essays by and About Rudy Wiebe*. Edmonton: NeWest Press, 1981.

—. Rudy Wiebe, "Tombstone Community," 16–24.

—. Rudy Wiebe, "For the Mennonite Churches: A Last Chance," 25–31.

—. Rudy Wiebe, "The Meaning of Being Mennonite Brethren," 32–39.

—. Rudy Wiebe, "The Artist as a Critic and a Witness," 39–49.

—. Herbert Giesbrecht, "O Life, How Naked and How Hard When Known!" 50–63.

—. Rudy Wiebe, "An Author Speaks About His Novel," 64–68.

—. Elmer F. Suderman, "Universal Values in Rudy Wiebe's *Peace Shall Destroy Many*," 69–79.

—. Rudy Wiebe, "Moros and Mennonites in the Chaco of Paraguay," 80–87.

—. Ina Ferris, "Religious Vision and Fictional Form: Rudy Wiebe's *The Blue Mountains of China*," 88–96.

—. Magdalene Falk Redekop, "Translated into the Past: Language in *The Blue Mountains of China*," 97–125.

—. Margaret Reimer and Sue Steiner, "Translating Life into Art: A Conversation with Rudy Wiebe," 126–31.

—. Rudy Wiebe, "On the Trail of Big Bear," 132–42.

— Rudy Wiebe, "Bear Spirit in a Strange Land" ("All That's Left of Big Bear"), 143–49.

—. Eli Mandel and Rudy Wiebe, "Where the Voice Comes From," 150–57.

—. Rudy Wiebe, "Riel: A Possible Film Treatment," 158–62.

—. Brian Bergman, "Rudy Wiebe: Storymaker of the Prairies," 163–70.

—. R.P. Bilan and Sam Solecki: Two Reviews of *The Scorched-Wood People*," 171–78.

—. David Jeffrey, "A Search for Peace: Prophecy and Parable in the Fiction of Rudy Wiebe," 179–203.

—. George Melnyk, "The Western Canadian Imagination: An Interview with Rudy Wiebe," 204–08.

—. Rudy Wiebe, "In the West, Sir John A. is a Bastard and Riel a Saint. Ever Ask Why?" 209–11.

—. Rudy Wiebe, "A Novelist's Personal Notes on Frederick Philip Grove," 212–25.

—. Shirley Neuman, "Unearthing Language: An Interview with Rudy Wiebe and Robert Kroetsch," 226–48.

Lakoseljac, Bianca. Ed. *Rudy Wiebe: Essays on His Works.* Hamilton: Guernica Editions, 2023. Essential Writers Series #56.

Morley, Patricia. *The Comedians: Hugh Hood and Rudy Wiebe.* Toronto: Clarke Irwin, 1977.

Redekop, Magdalene. *Rudy Wiebe: Profiles in Canadian Literature.* Toronto: Dundurn Press, 1981.

Tiessen, Hildegard Froese. *Rudy Wiebe: A Tribute.* Kitchener: Sand Hill Books & Pinch Penny Press. 2002.

Van Toorn, Penelope. *Rudy Wiebe and the Historicity of the World.* Edmonton: University of Alberta Press. 1995.

—. "The Politics of Narrative Practice," 1–17.

—. "*Peace Shall Destroy Many*: Breaking Open the Capsule," 17–34.

—. "*First and Vital Candle*: Beyond Polyphony," 35–65.

—. "*The Blue Mountains of China*: History as Inadvertent Confession," 67–98.

—. "*The Temptations of Big Bear*: Redeeming Canada's Past," 99–138.

—. "*The Scorched-Wood People*: Freed into Certain Bondage," 139–164.

—. "*My Lovely Enemy*: The Beloved Familiar and the Beloved New," 165–194.

—. "Where is Your Voice Coming From, Rudy Wiebe?" 195–203.

—. "The Early History and the Doctrines of the Mennonite Church," 205–212.

Whaley, Susan. *Rudy Wiebe and His Works.* Toronto: ECW Press. 1986.

Wylie, Herb. *Speaking in the Past Tense: Canadian Novelists on Writing Historical Fiction.* Waterloo: Wilfred Laurier University Press. 2007.

Other: Including Essays About and by Rudy Wiebe

Antor, Heinz. "The Mennonite Experiences in the Novels of Rudy Wiebe." *Refractions of Germany in Canadian Literature and Culture.* Ed. Heinz Antor, et al. Berlin: deGruyter, 2003.

Atwood, Margaret. "Teaching Rudy to Dance ... all true events," a cartoon. *"Rudy Wiebe: A Tribute.* Kitchener, ON: Sand Hills Books, 2002. Rep. *Rudy Wiebe: Essays on His Works.* Ed. Bianca Lakoseljac. Hamilton: Guernica Editions, 2023. Essential Writers Series #56.

Bailey, Nancy. "Imaginative and Historical Truth in Wiebe's *The Mad Trapper.*" *Journal of Canadian Studies/Revues* 20:2 (Summer 1985): 70–79.

Beck, Ervin. "The Politics of Rudy Wiebe in *The Blue Mountain of China.*" *Mennonite Quarterly Review* 73:4 (Oct. 1999): 723–51.

—. "Postcolonial Complexity in the Writings of Rudy Wiebe." *Modern Fiction Studies* 47.4 (Winter 2001): 855–86.

—. "Rudy Wiebe and W.B. Yeats: Sailing to Danzig and Byzantium." *Ariel* 32:4 (Oct. 2001): 7–19.

Bergman, Brian. "Pacifist and Doomed." *Maclean's*, Oct. 22, 2001, 68–71.

Bilan, R. P. "Wiebe and Religious Struggle." *Canadian Literature* 77 (Summer 1978): 50–63.

Blanc, Marie. "Tales of a Nation: Interpretive Legal Battles in Rudy Wiebe's The Scorched-Wood People." *Canadian Literature* 117 (Summer 2003): 34–54.

Bossanne, Brigitte. "A Canadian Voice within the Text: Rudy Wiebe's *The Temptations of Big Bear.*" *Etudes Canadiennes /Canadian Studies* 7:10 (June 1981): 223–34.

Bowen, Deborah. "Squaring the Circle: The Problem of Translation in *The Temptations of Big Bear.*" *Canadian Literature* 117 (Summer 1988): 62–70.

Bowering, George. "Wiebe and [Murray] Bail: Re Making the Story." *SPAN* 36 (Oct. 1993): 668–75.

Brandsma, Nicole. "'They will never let me die in their country': Aborigine Hospitality and Surviving in the North in Rudy Wiebe's *A Discovery of Strangers* and Joseph Boyden's *Three Day Road.*" In Sue Matheson and John Butler, eds. *The Fictional North: Ten Discussions of Stereotypes and Icons above the 53rd Parallel.* Newcastle upon Tyne: Cambridge Scholars, 2012. Pp. 121–29.

Braz, Albert. "The Omnipresent Voice: Authorial Intrusion in Rudy Wiebe's 'Games for Queen Victoria.'" *Studies in Canadian Literature* 26:2 (2001): 91–106.

Brydon, Diana. "Troppo Agitato: Writing and Reading Cultures." *Ariel* (Calgary) 19:1 (Jan. 1988): 13–32.

Brydon, Diana & Tiffin, Helen. *Decolonising Fictions.* Sydney: Dangaroo, 1993.

Cameron, David. "Rudy Wiebe: The Moving Stream is Perfectly at Rest" (interview). *In Conversations with Canadian Novelists*, Part 2. Toronto: Macmillan, 1973. 146–60.

Cameron, William Bleasdell. *The War Trail of Big Bear.* Boston: Small Maynard & Co., 1927.

Clunie, Barnaby W. "A Revolutionary Failure Resurrected: Dialogical Appropriation in Rudy Wiebe's *The Scorched-Wood People." University of Toronto Quarterly* 74.3 (Summer 2005): 845–65.

Cook, Hugh. "Interview: A Conversation with Rudy Wiebe." *Image Journal*, Issue 90. (2014). https://imagejournal.org/issue/issue-90/ Rep. *Rudy Wiebe: Essays on His Works*. Ed. Bianca Lakoseljac. Hamilton: Guernica Editions, 2023. Essential Writers Series #56.

—. "Salted With Fire." Rev. of *Come Back,* by Rudy Wiebe. *Christian Courier,* (Jan. 7, 2016). https://www.christiancourier.ca/salted-with-fire/ Rep. *Rudy Wiebe: Essays on His Works*. Ed. Bianca Lakoseljac. Hamilton: Guernica Editions, 2023. Essential Writers Series #56.

Coupal, Michel. "Rudy Wiebe and the Mennonites: Forty Years On." *The Conrad Grebel Review* Special Issue: 22:2 (Spring 2004).

—. "Voix et construction narrative dans *The Temptations of Big Bear* de Rudy Wiebe." *Annales due Centre de Rechercher sur l'Amerique Anglophone* 19 (1994): 25–33, 209–10.

Craig, Terrence. "Religious Images of the Non-Whites in English-Canadian Literature: Charles Gordon and Rudy Wiebe." In *The Native in Literature.* Ed. Thomas King, Cheryll Calves, Helen Hoy. Oakville, ON: ECW, 1987. 94–114.

Darnell, Regna. "The Primacy of Writing and the Persistence of the Primitive." In *Papers of the Thirty-First Algonquian Conference.* Ed. John D. Nichols. Winnipeg: U. of Manitoba, 2000. 54–67.

Davidson, Arnold E. "The Provenance of Story in Rudy Wiebe's 'Where Is the Voice Coming From?'" *Studies in Short Fiction* 22:2 (Spring 1985): 189–93.

Deringer, Ludwig. "Kulturelle Identitat in zeitgenossischen anglokanadischen Drama." Ed. Hans Hunfield.*Wozu Wissenschaft haute? Ringvorlesung Zw Ehren von Roland Hagenbuchle.* Tubingen: Nair, 1997. 39–53: "As Far as the Eye Can See."

—. "Old Worlds, New Worlds: Migration, Multilingualism and Cultural Memory in Rudy Wiebe's *Sweeter Than All the World.*" In *Literature and Lebenskunst,* Ed. Eva Oppermann. Kassel, Germany: Kassel University Press, 2006. 270–40.

Dill, Vicki Schreiber. "The Idea of Wilderness in the Mennonite Novels of Rudy Wiebe." Diss., U. of Notre Dame, 1983.

—. "Land Relatedness in the Mennonite Novels of Rudy Wiebe." *Mennonite Quarterly Review* 58 (1984): 50–69.

Doerkson, Victor G. "From Jung Stilling to Rudy Wiebe." *Mennonite Images: Historical, Cultural and Literary Essays Dealing with Mennonite Issues.* Ed. Harry Loewen. Winnipeg: Hyperion Press, 1980.

Dueck, Allan. "Rudy Wiebe as Story-teller: Vision and Art in Wiebe's Fiction." M.A. thesis, U. of Alberta, 1974.

—. "Rudy Wiebe's Approach to Historical Fiction: A Study of *The Temptations of Big Bear* and *The Scorched-Wood People.*" *The Canadian Novel Here and Now.* Ed. John Moss. Toronto: N.C. Press, 1978. 182–99.

Dueck, Jonathan. "From Whom Is the Voice Coming? Mennonites, First Nations People and Appropriation of Voice." *Journal of Mennonite Studies* 19 (2001): 144–55.

Duffy, Dennis. "Wiebe's Real Riel? The Scorched-Wood People and Its Audience." *In Rough Justice: Essays on Crime in Literature.* Ed. M. L. Friedland. Toronto: U. of Toronto Press, 1991. 200–13.

Dyck, E. F. "Thom Wiens to Yvonne Johnson: Rudy Wiebe's Appropriate Voice." *Rhubarb* 1:1 (Fall 1998): 29–33.

Egan, Susanna. "Telling Trauma: Generic Dissonance in the Production of *Stolen Life*," *Canadian Literature* 167 (2000): 10–29.

Engler, Bernd. "'Spiritual Dislocations': Stratagein des Neuverortung des Spirituellen in Rudy Wiebes A D*iscovery of Strangers*. In *Spiritualitat and Transzendenz in der modernen englischsprachen Literature*. Ed. Suzann Bach. Paderborn, Germany: Schoningh, 2001. 245–58.

Ferris, Ina. "Religious Vision and Fictional Form: Rudy Wiebe's *The Blue Mountains of China*." *Mosaic* 11 (Spring 1978): 79–85.

Fisher, John J. "Byzantium North: Some Contextual Notes for Rudy Wiebe's *Collected Stories*. *MQR* (2013): 89–94.

Froese, Edna. "'Adam, who are you?' The Genealogy of Rudy Wiebe's Mennonite Protagonists." *Conrad Grebel Review* 22:2 (Spring 2004): 14–24.

—. "Voices of Faith in *Blue Mountains of China* and *A Community of Memory*." *Mennonite Quarterly Review* (Oct. 1998): 127–34.

—. "Why We All Waited for Rudy Wiebe's New Mennonite Novel." *Christian Living* June 2002, 6–9.

Fruwald, Maria. "A Discovery of Strange Things in Rudy Wiebe's *A Discovery of Strangers*." In *New Worlds: Discovering and Constructing the Unknown in Anglophone Literature*. Ed. Martin Kuester, et al. Munich: Vogel, 2000. 133–47.

—. *"The problem is to make the story": Rudy Wiebes historische Romane in Kontext der nordamerikanischenModerne*. Bochum: Brockmeyer, 1995.

Goldie, Terry. "Comparative Views of an Aboriginal Past: Rudy Wiebe and Patrick White." *World Literature Written in English* 23:2 (Spring 1984): 429–39.

—. "Rudy Wiebe and Patrick White. *Fear and Temptation: The Image of the Indigene in Canadian, Australian, and New Zealand Literatures*. Montreal: McGill-Queen's University Press, 1989. 191–214.

Gove, Joan Marie Frame. "Making Stories: Strategies of Narrative Communication in the Novels of Rudy Wiebe." Diss., 1990.

Govier, Katherine. "A Gentle Eye from Afar." *Rudy Wiebe: Essays on His Works*. Ed. Bianca Lakoseljac. Hamilton: Guernica Editions, 2023. Essential Writers Series #56.

Grace, Sherrill E. "Structuring Violence: 'The Ethics of Linguistics' in *The Temptations of Big Bear*." *Canadian Literature* 104 (Spring 1985): 7–23.

—. "Western Myth and Northern History: The Plains Indians of Berger and Wiebe." *Great Plains Quarterly* 3:3 (Summer 1983): 146–56.

Guptara, Prabhu. "'Clutching a Feather in a Maelstrom': Rudy Wiebe's Critique of the Contemporary West." *Journal of Commonwealth Literature* 17:1 (1982): 146–60.

Gurr, Andrew. "'Blue Mountains and Strange Forms.'" *Journal of Commonwealth Literature* 17:1 (1982): 153–60.

Hancock, Maxine. "Wiebe: A Voice Crying in the Wilderness." *Christianity Today* 16 Feb. 1979, 30–31.

Harris, Maureen Scott. "A Gift of Understanding." *Books in Canada*, Vol. 27, No.6, (Sep. 1998). 6. Rep. *Rudy Wiebe: Essays on His Works*. Ed. Bianca Lakoseljac. Hamilton: Guernica Editions, 2023. Essential Writers Series #56.

Healy, J.J. "Literature, Power and the Refusals of Big Bear: Reflections on the Treatment of the Indian and of the Aborigine." *Australian/Canadian Literature in English: Comparative Perspectives*. Ed. R. McDougall and G. Whitlock. Sydney: Methuen, 1907. 68–93.

Higginson, Catherine. "The Raced Female Body and the Discourse of Peoplement in Rudy Wiebe's *The Temptations of Big Bear* and *The Scorched-Wood People*." *Essays on Canadian Writing* 72 (Winter 2000): 172–90.

Hildebrand, George H. "The Anabaptist Vision of Rudy Wiebe: A Study in Theological Allegories." Diss., McGill U., 1982.

Hochbruck, Wolfgang. "Rudy Wiebe's Reconstruction(s) of the Indian Voice." *Recherches Anglaises et Nord-Americaines* 22 (1989): 135–42.

Hoeppner, Kenneth. "Politics and Religion in Rudy Wiebe's *The Scorched-Wood People*." *English Studies in Canada* 12:4 (Dec. 1986): 440–50.

—. "The Spirit of the Arctic, or Translating the Untranslatable in Rudy Wiebe's *A Discovery of Strangers*," in *Echoing Silence: Essays on Arctic Narrative*, Ed. John Moss. Reappraisals, Canadian Writers, Vol. 20. Ed. Gerald Lynch. Ottawa: University of Ottawa Press, 1997.

Holland, Patrick. "'Great Black Steel Lines of Fiction': Culture, History and Myth in the Novels of Rudy Wiebe." Paper read at the ACLALS conference, Suva, January 1980.

Hostetler, Sheri. "The Mennonite Religious Imagination: A Thesis." M.A. thesis, Episcopal Divinity School, 1990.

Howells, Coral Ann. "History from a Different Angle: Narrative Strategies in *The Temptations of Big Bear*." *Journal of Commonwealth Literature* 17:1 (1982): 161–73.

—. "'If I Had a Reliable Interpreter Who Would Make a Reliable Interpretation': Language, Screams and Silences in Rudy Wiebe's 'Where Is The Voice Coming From?'" *Recherches Anglaises et Americaines* 16 (1983): 95–104.

—. "Re-Visions of Prairie Indian History in Rudy Wiebe's *The Temptations of Big Bear* and *My Lovely Enemy*." In

Colonisations: Rencontres Australie-Canada. Ed. X. Pons and M. Rocard. Toulouse: Universite de Toulouse-Le Merail, 1985. 149+. Also in *Revisions of Canadian Literature*, Ed. Shirley Chew. Leeds: U. of Leeds, Institute of Bibliography and Textual Criticism, 1984. 61–70.

—. "Rudy Wiebe's *The Temptations of Big Bear* and Salman Rushdie's *Midnight's Children.*" *The Literary Criterion* (Bangalore) 20:1 (1985): 191–203.

—. "Silence in Rudy Wiebe's *The Mad Trapper.*" *World Literature Written in English* 24:2 (Autumn 1984): 304–12.

—. "Storm Glass: The Preservation and Transformation of History in *The Diviners, Obasan, My Lovely Enemy.*" *Kunapipi* 16 (1994): 471–78.

Howells, Robin. "Esch-sca(r)-tology: Rudy Wiebe's 'An Indication of Burning.'" *The Journal of Commonwealth Literature* 27 (Aug. 1992): 87–95.

Hunter, Catherine. "Style and Theme in Rudy Wiebe's *My Lovely Enemy:* Love, Language, and 'the big trouble with Jesus.'" *Journal of Mennonite Studies* 4 (1986): 46–52.

Jacklin, Michael. "Interview with Rudy Wiebe," *Kunapipi* 29.1 (2007): 54–69.

James, William Closson. "'A Land Beyond Words': Rudy Wiebe's *A Discovery of Strangers."* In *Mapping the Sacred: Religion, Geography and Postcolonial Literature.* Ed. Jamie S. Scott and Paul Simpson-Housley. Amsterdam: Rodopi, 2001. 71–89.

Janzen, Jean, John Ruth and Rudy Wiebe. "Literature, Place, Language and Faith: A Conversation led by Julia Kasdorf." *Conrad Grebel Review* 26.1 (Winter 2008): 72–90.

Jantzen, Maryann. "'Believing is seeing': 'Re-storying' the Self in Rudy Wiebe's *Sweeter Than All the World.*" *Conrad Grebel Review* 22:2 (Spring 2004), 55–68.

Jeffrey, David L. "Biblical Hermeneutic and Family History in Contemporary Canadian Fiction: Wiebe and Laurence." *Mosaic* 11:3 (Spring 1978): 87–106.

—. "Post-War Canadian Fiction." *Mosaic.* 11:3 (Spring 1978).

Jones, Manina. "*Stolen Life*? Reading through Two I's in Postcolonial Collaborative Autobiography." In *Is Canada Postcolonial? Unsettling Canadian Literature*, Ed. Laura Moss. Waterloo, ON: Wilfred Laurier University Press, 2003. 207–22.

Juneja, Om P., M.F. Salat and Chandra Mohan. "Looking at Our Particular World: An Interview with Rudy Wiebe." *World Literature Written in English* 31:2 (1991): 1–18.

Kaličanin, Milena. "Fact vs. Fiction in Rudy Wiebe's *Where is the Voice Coming From.*" *Springer Nature, Neohelicon*: Volume 44, Issue 1, June, 2017. 169–176. Rep. in *Rudy Wiebe: Essays on His Works*. Ed. Bianca Lakoseljac. Hamilton: Guernica Editions, 2023. Essential Writers Series #56.

Kaltembach, Michele. "Explorations into History: Rudy Wiebe's *A Discovery of Strangers.*" *Etudes Canadiennes/ Canadian Studies* 44 (1998): 77–87.

Kasdorf, Julia Spicher, et al. "Literature, Place, Language, and Faith: A Conversation between Jean Janzen, John Ruth, and Rudy Wiebe." *CGR* (2008): 72–90.

—. "Tribute to Jean Janzen and Rudy Wiebe." *JCMW* (2015). Online.

Keith, W.J. *Canadian Literature in English*. New York: Longman, 1985. 165–67 ff.

—. "From Document to Art: Wiebe's Historical Short Stories and Their Sources." *Studies in Canadian Literature* 4:2 (1979): 106–19.

—. "Riel's Great Vision." *The Canadian Forum* 57 (Dec.-Jan 1977–78): 34.

Kertzer, J.M. "Biocritical Essay." *The Rudy Wiebe Papers First Accession.* Ed. Jean F. Tener & Appollonia Steele. Calgary: U. of Calgary Press, 1986. ix-xxvi.

Killam, G.D. "Wiebe, Rudy." *Encyclopedia of Post-Colonial Literatures in English*, Vol. 2. Ed. Eugene Benson and L.W. Conolly. London: Routledge, 1994. 1653–54.

Klooss, Wolfgang. "Narrative Modes and Forms of Literary Perception in Rudy Wiebe's *The Scorched-Wood People.* *"Gaining Ground: European Critics on Canadian Literature.* Ed. Robert Kroetsch and Reingard M. Nischik. Edmonton: NeWest, 1985. 205–21.

Korkka, Janne. "Engaging the Other in Rudy Wiebe's Early Writing ..." In *Canada: Images of a Post/National Society.* Ed. Gunilla Florby, et al. Brussels: Peter Lang, 2009. Pp. 151–64.

—. *Ethical Encounters: Spaces and Selves in the Writings of Rudy Wiebe.* Amsterdam: Rodopi, 2013.

—. "Facing Indigenous Alterity in Rudy Wiebe's Early Writing." In *Seeking the Self: Encountering the Other ...* Ed. Tuomas Huttunen, et al. Newcastle-on-Tyne: Cambridge Scholars 2008.

—. "'It almost always begins with these kinds of living stories': An Interview with Rudy Wiebe." *Conrad Grebel Review* 22:2 (Spring 2004): 83–89.

—. "Making a Story that Could Not Be Found: Rudy Wiebe's Multiple Canadas." In *Tales of Two Cities: Essays on New Anglophone Literature*, Ed. John Skinner. Turku, Finland: University of Turku, 2000. Pp. 21–35.

—. "Representation of Aboriginal Peoples in Rudy Wiebe's Fiction ..." In *Walking a Tightrope ...* Ed. Ute Lischke and David T. McNab. Waterloo, ON: Wilfred Laurier UP, 2005. Pp. 351–76.

—. "Robert Kroetsch and Rudy Wiebe: From Prairie Communities to Communities of Enlightened Readers." In Roger D. Sell, Ed. *Literary Community-Making: The Dialogicality of English Texts from the Seventeenth Century to the Present.* Amsterdam: Benjamins, 2012. Pp. 219–37.

—. "Where Is the Text Coming From: An Interview with Rudy Wiebe." *World Literature Written in English* 38.1 (1999): 69–85.

Kroetsch, Robert. "Afterword." In Wiebe, *Playing Dead: A contemplation Concerning the Arctic.* Edmonton: NeWest, 2003. Pp. 143–45.

—. "An Archeology of (My) Canadian Postmodern." *International Postmodernism: Theory and Literary Practice.* Ed. Hans Bertens and Donnell Folskema. Amsterdam: Benjamins, 1997. 307–11. On "Playing Dead: A Contemplation."

—. "Representing an Unknowable Spade: Movement and Knowing in Rudy Wiebe's Northern Writing." In Sue Matheson and John Butler, eds. *The Fictional North: Ten Discussions of Stereotypes and Icons above the 53rd Parallel.* Newcastle upon Tyne: Cambridge Scholars, 2012. Pp. 94–107.

—. "Unhiding the Hidden: Recent Canadian Fiction." *Journal of Canadian Fiction* 3:3 (1974): 43–45.

Kostash, Myrna. "A White Man's View of Big Bear." *Saturday Night Magazine,* (February, 1974). 32–33. Rep. in *Rudy Wiebe: Essays on His Works.* Ed. Bianca Lakoseljac. Hamilton: Guernica Editions, 2023. Essential Writers Series #56.

Kramer-Hamstra, Agnes. "At Home in Stories: Indigenous and Settler Writers Counter Exile in Canadian Narratives." Diss., McMaster U., 2010.

Lakoseljac, Bianca. "Interview with Aritha van Herk: Rudy Wiebe, a Mentor and a Critic." *Rudy Wiebe: Essays on His Works*. Ed. Bianca Lakoseljac. Hamilton: Guernica Editions, 2023. Essential Writers Series #56.

—. "Interview with Rudy Wiebe: Can Lit in Time of COVID-19." *Rudy Wiebe: Essays on His Works*. Ed. Bianca Lakoseljac. Hamilton: Guernica Editions, 2023. Essential Writers Series #56.

—. "Rudy Wiebe's 'Unearthing' of Big Bear: a Plains Cree Hero of Canada's Past." *Rudy Wiebe: Essays on His Works*. Ed. Bianca Lakoseljac. Hamilton: Guernica Editions, 2023. Essential Writers Series #56.

—. "Rudy Wiebe's Works and Academic Life: Changing Times in English Canadian Literature." *Rudy Wiebe: Essays on His Works*. Ed. Bianca Lakoseljac. Hamilton: Guernica Editions, 2023. Essential Writers Series #56.

—. "Bibliography: Through the Eyes of Rudy Wiebe." *Rudy Wiebe: Essays on His Works*. Ed. Bianca Lakoseljac. Hamilton. Guernica Editions, 2023. Essential Writers Series #56.

Larden, Stephanie Anne. "The History of the Editorial Process of Rudy Wiebe's *Peace Shall Destroy Many.*" MA thesis, University of Alberta, 1989.

Lecker, R. "'Trusting the Quintuplet Senses': Time and Form in *The Temptations of Big Bear*." *English Studies in Canada* 8:3 (1982): 333–48.

Longhurst, John. "Peace of Mind." *Winnipeg Free Press*, (Mar. 30, 2019). Rep. in *Rudy Wiebe: Essays on His Works*. Ed. Bianca Lakoseljac. Hamilton: Guernica Editions, 2023. Essential Writers Series #56.

Mansbridge, Francis. "Wiebe's Sense of Community." *Canadian Literature* 77 (Summer 1978): 42–49.

McGoogan, Ken. "Fighting Words: Wiebe versus Kinsella Battle Raises Questions about Racism and Censorship in Literature." *Calgary Herald*, Feb. 10, 1990, C1.

Meeter, Glenn. "Rudy Wiebe's Spatial Form and Christianity in *The Blue Mountains of China* and *The Temptations of Big Bear*." *Essays in Canadian Writing* 22 (Summer 1981): 42–61.

Melnyk, George. "Literary Genealogy: Exploring the Legacy of F. M. Salter." *Alberta Views*, April 1, 1998. Rep. in *Rudy Wiebe: Essays on His Works*. Ed. Bianca Lakoseljac. Hamilton: Guernica Editions, 2023. Essential Writers Series #56.

—. "The Other Wiebe: Deconstructing a Novelist's Nonfiction." *Rudy Wiebe: Essays on His Works*. Ed. Bianca Lakoseljac. Hamilton: Guernica Editions, 2023. Essential Writers Series #56.

Mierau, Maurice. "Why Rudy Wiebe Is Not the Last Mennonite Writer." *Conrad Grebel Review* 22:2 (Spring 2004): 69–82.

Mininger, J.D. "Mennonites in Crisis: Figures of Paradox in *Peace Shall Destroy Many*." *Conrad Grebel Review* 22:2 (Spring 2004): 25–37.

Monkman, Leslie. *A Native Heritage: Images of the Indian in English Canadian Literature*. Toronto U of Toronto Press, 1981.

Morley, Patricia. A. *The Comedians: Hugh Hood and Rudy Wiebe*. Toronto: Clark, Irwin, 1977.

Morison, Scot. "The 'Rudy Wiebe Room.'" Originally published as, "The Annotated Rudy Wiebe," *New Trail*, (Autumn 2016) University of Alberta's alumni magazine. Rep. in *Rudy Wiebe: Essays on His Works*. Ed. Bianca Lakoseljac.

Hamilton: Guernica Editions, 2023. Essential Writers Series #56.

Moss, John. *Sex and Violence in the Canadian Novel.* Toronto: McClelland and Stewart, 1997.

Omhovere, Claire. "The Authorization of Story in Rudy Wiebe and Yvonne Johnson's *Stolen Life: The Journey of a Cree Woman* (1998)." *International Journal of Canadian Studies* 29 (2004): 141–59.

—. "The North in Rudy Wiebe's *A Discovery of Strangers:* A Land Beyond Words." *Commonwealth Essays and Studies* 24:2 (Spring 2002): 79–91.

—. "Rudy Wiebe and Yvonne Johnson's Stolen Life ... A Peregrination through Gender and Genre." *Commonwealth Essays and Studies* 26:1 (Autumn 2003): 99–111.

Nickel, James W. "A Conversation with Rudy Wiebe." *The Scepter.* Hillsboro, Kan.: Tabor College, 1964. 24–30.

Pell, Barbara. "Christian Theology in Modern Canadian Fiction," *CRUX* 36:2 (June 2000): 10–19.

Pollock, Zailig. "*The Blue Mountains of China:* A Selective Annotated Genealogy." *Essays on Canadian Writing* 26 (Summer 1983): 70–73.

Rhodes, Shane. "Robert Kroetsch: A Tribute." *Brick* 88 (Winter 2012): 146–53.

Ricketts, Alan. "Packaged Struggle." *Essays on Canadian Writing* 12 (1978): 251–56.

Robb, Kenneth. "Getting Lost in Rudy Wiebe's 'The Naming of Albert Johnson.'" *Notes on Contemporary Literature* 20:5 (Nov. 1990): 7–9.

Robertson, Heather. "Lust, Murder and 'Long Pig.'" *The Canadian Forum* 73 (April 1995): 20–25.

Robinett, Jane Hostetler. "Listening All the Way Home: Theme and Structure in Rudy Wiebe's *Sweeter Than All the World." Conrad Grebel Review* 22:2 (Spring 2004): 38–54.

Rocard, Marcienne. "Les schèmes de la circularité dans *The Temptations of Big Bear.*" Paper read at conference, "Rencontres Australie-Canada," U. of Toulouse, March 1994.

Rymhs, Deena. "Auto/Biographical Jurisdictions: Collaboration, Self-Representation, and the Law in *Stolen Life: The Journey of a Cree Woman.* In *Auto/Biography in Canada: Critical Directions.* Ed. Julie Rak. Waterloo, ON: Wilfred Laurier University Press, 2005. 89–108.

Schafer, Jurgen. "A Farewell to Europe: Rudy Wiebe's *The Temptations of Big Bear* and Robert Kroetsch's *Gone Indian." Gaining Ground: European Critics on Canadian Literature.* Ed. Robert Kroetsch and Reingard M. Nischik. Edmonton: NeWest, 1985. 79–89.

—. Schafer, Jurgen. "Anglo-Kanadische Romanciers der Gegenwart." *Die Neuren Sprachen* 83:4 (Aug. 1984): 422–36.

Schowalter, Lutz. "Church of Peace? An Insider's Perspective on Mennonite Literature and Theology in Canada and Germany: Personal Essay." In *Schriften der Universitatsbibliotek Marburg* 118. Ed. Andrea Wolff-Wolk. Marburg, Germany: Universitatsbibliotek Marburg, 2004. 50–64.

Scobie, Stephan. "Rudy Wiebe: Where the Voice Is Coming From." *Books in Canada* 9 (Feb. 1980): 3–5.

Sheremata, Davis. "White Man's Burden: With *Stolen Life,* Co-author Rudy Wiebe Consolidates His Status as Canada's Apologist for the Indians." *Alberta Report* 20 July 1998), 28–31.

Sheriff, John. "History, Memory, Novel: On Rudy Wiebe's *Sweeter than All the World*." *Mennonite Life* 58:4 (Dec. 2003). On-line.

Sigvardson, Malin. *The Constitution of Movement in Rudy Wiebe's Fiction: A Phenomenological Study of Three Mennonite Novels*. Stockholm: Stockholm University, 2006.

—. "Regenerative Knitting: Works and Hope in Rudy Wiebe's Mennonite Triptych." *Mennonite Quarterly Review*, January 2008.

Singh, Satya Brat. "Rudy Wiebe, Paul Scott and Salman Rushdie: Historians Distanced from History." *The Commonwealth Review* (New Delhi) 1:2 (1990): 146–56.

Skidmore, James. "The Discovery of Franklin: A Contemporary Literacy Exploration." *Ahorblatter: Marburger Beitrage Zur Kanada-Forschung*. Ed. Andrea Wolff-Wolk. Marburg: Universitatbibliotek, 2001. 29–43.

Smyth, Thomas William. "*My Lovely Enemy* Revisited." *Essays on Canadian Writing* 63 (Spring 1998): 113–33.

—. "Rudy Wiebe as Novelist: Witness and Critic without Apology." Diss., U. of Toronto, Centre for the Study of Religion, 1997.

Soleckei, Sam. "Giant Fictions and Large Meanings: The Novels of Rudy Wiebe." *Canadian Forum* 60 (Mar. 1981): 5–8,13.

Spriet, Pierre. "Structure and Meaning in Rudy Wiebe's *My Lovely Enemy*." *Gaining Ground: European Critics on Canadian Literature*. Eds. Robert Kroetsch & Reingard M. Nischik. Edmonton: NeWest Press, 1985.

—. "Rudy Wiebe's *The Blue Mountains of China*: The Polyphony of a People or the Lonely Voice of the Fringe?"

In Multiple Voices: Recent Canadian Fiction. Ed. Jeanne Delbaere. Sydney: Dangaroo, 1990. 59–68.

—. "Les formes du refus dans les nouvelles de Rudy Wiebe." *Recherches Anglaises et Americaines* 16 (1983): 105–119.

—. "Structure and Meaning in Rudy Wiebe's *My Lovely Enemy.* "*Gaining Ground: European Critics on Canadian Literature.* Ed. Robert Kroetsch and Reingard M. Nischik. Edmonton: NeWest, 1985. 53–63.

Stein, Olga. "The 'Wistful, Windy Madness of a Gift': Rudy Wiebe's Books for Young Readers." *Rudy Wiebe: Essays on His Works.* Ed. Bianca Lakoseljac. Hamilton: Guernica Editions, 2023. Essential Writers Series #56.

Sturzebecher, Monika. *Der Heimatbegriff in der Literatur der Russichen Mennoniten.* M.A. Thesis, McMaster University, 1987.

Suderman, Elmer. "Universal Values in Rudy Wiebe's *Peace Shall Destroy Many.*" *Mennonite Life* 24 (Oct. 1969): 172–76.

Taylor, Lauralyn. "*The Temptations of Big Bear*: A Filmic Novel?" *Essays on Canadian Writing* 9 (Winter 1977–78): 134–38.

Tefs, Wayne A. "Rudy Wiebe: Mystery and Reality." *Mosaic* 11:4 (1978): 155–58.

Thieme, John. "Scheherazade as Historian: Rudy Wiebe's 'Where Is the Voice Coming From?'" *Journal of Commonwealth Literature* 17:1 (1982): 172–81.

Tiessen, Hildi Froese. "Between Memory and Longing: Rudy Wiebe's *Sweeter Than All the World.*" *Mennonite Quarterly Review* 77:4 (Oct. 2003), 619–36. Rep. *Rudy Wiebe: Essays on His Works.* Ed. Bianca Lakoseljac. Hamilton: Guernica Editions, 2023. Essential Writers Series #56.

—. "Critical Thought and Mennonite Literature: Mennonite Studies Engages the Mennonite Literary Voice." *Journal of Mennonite Studies* 22 (2004), 237–46.

—. "A Mighty Inner River: 'Peace' in the Early Fiction of Rudy Wiebe." *The Canadian Novel Here and Now.* Ed. John Moss. Toronto: N.C. Press, 1978. 169–81.

—. "'There was nothing to be read about Mennonites': Rudy Wiebe and the Impulse to Make Story." *Conrad Grebel Review* 22:2 (Spring 2004): 5–13.

—. "Tribute to Rudy Wiebe." *Mennonite Quarterly Review* 77:4 (Oct. 2003): 690–92.

— *Rudy Wiebe: A Tribute.* Ed. Hildi Froese Tiessen. Kitchener, ON: Sand Hills Books, 2002.

Tiessen, J. "Canadian Mennonite Literature," *Canadian Literature* 51 (1972).

Tiessen, Paul. "Double Identity: Covering the *Peace Shall Destroy Many* Project." In Robert Zacharias, Ed., *After Identity: Mennonite Writing in North America.* University Park, PA: Pennsylvania State U Press, 2015.

—. "Geoffrey James and Rudy Wiebe. *Place: Lethbridge, a City on the Prairie.*" *Conrad Grebel Review* 22:2 (Spring 2004): 90–93.

—. "Memoir and the Re-Reading of Fiction: Rudy Wiebe's *Of This Earth* and *Peace Shall Destroy Many.*" *Text Matters: A Journal of Literature, Theory, and Culture* 1 (2011): 201–15. Rep. *Rudy Wiebe: Essays on His Works.* Ed. Bianca Lakoseljac. Hamilton: Guernica Editions, 2023. Essential Writers Series #56.

—. "The Naming of Rudy Wiebe." *Journal of Mennonite Studies* 7 (1989): 115–22. Also in *Short Fiction in the*

New Literatures in English. Nice: Faculté des lettres and sciences humaines, 1989. 133–39.

—. "Plotting the City: Winnipeg in Selected Fiction by David Bergen, Sandra Birdsell, Miriam Toews, Armin Wiebe, and Rudy Wiebe." *JMS* (2010): 13–31.

—. "Re-framing the Reaction to *Peace Shall Destroy Many*: Rudy Wiebe, Delbert Wiens, and the Mennonite Brethren," *The Mennonite Quarterly Review* 90.1 (January 2016): 73–102.

—. "Rudy Wiebe and the 1960s Mennonite Brethren: An Archival Study." *Mennonite Historian* 42.2 (June 2016): 8–9.

Toews, Miriam. "Peace Shall Destroy Many." *Granta Magazine* 137. Nov. 23, 2016. Rep. *Rudy Wiebe: Essays on His Works*. Ed. Bianca Lakoseljac. Hamilton: Guernica Editions, 2023. Essential Writers Series #56.

Tomić, Uroš. "Is Grief Rational? Loss and Pain in Rudy Wiebe's *Come Back*." *Rudy Wiebe: Essays on His Works*. Ed. Bianca Lakoseljac. Hamilton: Guernica Editions, 2023. Essential Writers Series #56.

Tremblay, Tony. "Piracy, Penance, and Other Penal Codes: A Morphology of Postcolonial Revision in Three Recent Texts by Rudy Wiebe, John Stiffler, and Joan Clark." *English Studies in Canada* 23:2 (June 1997): 159–73.

University of Calgary Libraries. *The Rudy Wiebe Papers, First Accession*. Calgary: U. of Calgary Press, 1986.

University of Calgary Library, Special Collections, "Wiebe, Rudy, 1934–," Rudy Wiebe fonds. 1953–1992. 15.4 m. of textual records—2 videocassettes. Ucalgary.ca/library/SpecColl/wieber.htm.

van Toorn, Penelope. "Bakhtin and the Novel as Empire: Textual Politics in Robert Drewe's 'The Savage Crows' and Rudy Wiebe's *The Temptations of Big Bear*." *The Journal of Commonwealth Literature* 27 (Aug. 1992): 96–110.

—. "Creating the Realities We Live By: An Interview with Rudy Wiebe." *New Literatures Review* 23 (Summer 1992): 7–15.

—. "Dialogizing the Scriptures: A Bakhtinian Reading of the Novels of Rudy Wiebe." *Literature and Theology: An International Journal of Theory, Criticism and Culture* 9:4 (Dec. 1995): 439–48.

—. "Mastering Ceremonies: The Politics of Ritual and Ceremony in Eleanor Dark, Rudy Wiebe and Mudrooroo." *ANZSC* 12 (Dec. 1994): 73–89.

—. *Rudy Wiebe and the Historicity of the Word*. Edmonton: University. of Alberta Press, 1995.

Vautier, Marie. "Fiction, Historiography, and Myth: Jacques Godbout's *Les Tetes a Papineau* and Rudy Wiebe's *The Scorched-Wood People*." *Canadian Literature* 110 (Fall 1986): 61–78.

—. *New World Myth: Postmodernism and Postcolonialism in Canadian Fiction*. Buffalo: McGill-Queen's University Press, 1998.

Venema, Kathleen. "Shifting Rhetorics of Space in English-Canadian Exploration Literature." In *The Rhetoric of Canadian Writing*. Ed. Conny Steenman-Marcusse. Amsterdam: Rodopi, 2002. 137–60.

Visser, Carla. "Historicity and Historical Fiction: *Burning Water* and *The Temptations of Big Bear*." *Studies in Canadian Literature* 12:1 (1987): 90–111.

Walters, T.L., Ed. *Early Voices: Greg Hollingshead, Carol Shields, Aritha van Herk, Rudy Wiebe.* Edmonton: Juvenilia, 2001.

Weaver, Laura. "Mennonites' Minority Vision and the Outsider: Rudy Wiebe's *Peace Shall Destroy Many* and *The Blue Mountains of China.*" *MELUS* 13 (Fall-Winter 1986): 15–26.

Weisman, Adam Paul. "Reading Multiculturalism in the United States and Canada: The Anthological vs. the Cognitive." *U. of Toronto Quarterly* 69.3 (June 2000): 689–715.

Whaley, Susan. "Narrative Voices in *The Temptations of Big Bear.*" *Essays in Canadian Writing* 20 (Winter 1980–81): 134–48.

—. "Rudy Wiebe." *In Essays in Canadian Literature's Biographical Guide to Canadian Novelists.* Toronto: ECW, 1993. 210–14.

—. *Rudy Wiebe and His Works.* Toronto: ECW Press, 1983.

Wiebe, Rudy. "The Death and Life of Albert Johnson: Collected Notes on a Possible Legend," *Figures in a Ground.* Diane Bessai & David Jackel. Saskatoon: Western Producer Prairie Books, 1978.

—. "Western Fiction, Past and Future," *Western American Literature,* 6 (1971).

—. "Climbing Mountains That Do Not Exist: The Fiction Writer at Work." *Conrad Grebel Review* 22:2 (Spring 2004) 94–113.

—. "Interview by Linda Hutcheon." *Other Solitudes: Canadian Multicultural Fictions.* Ed. Linda Hutcheon and Marion Richmond. Toronto: Oxford U. Press, 1990. 80–86.

—. "Living on the iceberg: 'The Artist as Critic and Witness' 36 Years Later." *Conrad Grebel Review* 18.2 (Spring 2000): 85–91.

—. "A Novelist's Personal Notes on Frederick Phillip Grove." *University of Toronto Quarterly: A Canadian Journal of the Humanities* 47 (1978): 189–99.

—. "Seven Words of Silence." *Conrad Grebel Review* 31:2 (Spring 2013): 148–55.

"Wiebe, Rudy." *Contemporary Authors* 43 (new rev.). Ed. Susan M. Trosky. Detroit: Gale, 1994.

"Wiebe's Fables." *Alberta Report* 19 Sept. 1980, 44ff.

Woodcock, George. "Prairie Writers and the Metis: Rudy Wiebe and Margaret Laurence." *Canadian Ethnic Studies* 14:1 (1982): 9–22.

—. "Riel and Dumont." *Canadian Literature* 77 (Summer 1978): 98–100.

Zacharias, Robert, ed., *After Identity: Mennonite Writing in North America.* University Park, PA: Pennsylvania State U. Press, 2015.

Zimmerman, Jutta. "The Recreation of History on the Prairies: Rudy Wiebe." *Historiographic Metafiction in Modern American and Canadian Literature.* Ed. Bernd Engler and Kurt Muller. Paderborn: Ferdinand Schoningh, 1994. 383–97.

Zirker, Hubert. "Selected Essays in English Literature: British and Canadian." Trierer Studies zur Literatur No. 38. Frankfurt: Peter Lang, 2002.

Contributor Notes

MARGARET ATWOOD, whose work has been published in more than 45 countries, is the author of more than 50 books of fiction, poetry, critical essays, and graphic novels. *Burning Questions,* a collection of essays from 2004–2021 was published in March 2022. *Dearly,* her first collection of poetry in over a decade, was published November 2020. Her latest novel, *The Testaments,* is a co-winner of the 2019 Booker Prize. It is the long-awaited sequel to *The Handmaid's Tale*, now an award-winning TV series. Her other works of fiction include *Cat's Eye,* finalist for the 1989 Booker Prize; *Alias Grace*, which won the Giller Prize in Canada and the Premio Mondello in Italy; *The Blind Assassin*, winner of the 2000 Booker Prize; The MaddAddam Trilogy; and *Hag-Seed.* She is the recipient of numerous awards, including the Peace Prize of the German Book Trade, the Franz Kafka International Literary Prize, the PEN Center USA Lifetime Achievement Award, and the *Los Angeles Times* Innovator's Award. She lives in Toronto.

HUGH COOK holds an M.A. in Canadian Literature from Simon Fraser University and an M.F.A. in fiction writing from the Writers' Workshop at the University of Iowa. In addition to essays published in various journals, Hugh has published four books of fiction with Mosaic Press of Oakville: *Cracked Wheat and Other Stories*; a novel titled

The Homecoming Man; a book of linked stories titled *Home in Alfalfa*; and *Heron River*, a novel. Hugh is retired from teaching at Redeemer University in Hamilton, where he and his wife live. See his website at hugh-cook.ca.

HILDI FROESE TIESSEN is a Professor Emerita at the Conrad Grebel University College at the University of Waterloo—English & Peace and Conflict Studies. Tiessen's interest in Mennonite/s writing began when she was a graduate student at the University of Alberta, where she co-directed a play with Rudy Wiebe and published an article on his early Mennonite texts. Later, at Conrad Grebel University College, University of Waterloo, she taught courses and hosted readings and lectures focused on Mennonite/s writing. Rudy Wiebe was a frequent guest. Her anthology of Mennonite short stories *Liars and Rascals* appeared in 1989; in 1990 she curated the first of eight international conferences on Mennonite/s Writing. Her publications on Mennonite/s writing include guest-editing special issues for *New Quarterly*, *Prairie Fire*, *Journal of Mennonite Studies*, *Conrad Grebel Review*, and *Rhubarb*—most recently *Rhubarb #42: 11 Encounters with Mennonite Fiction* (2017).

KATHERINE GOVIER is the author of 13 works of fiction. Her most recent novel is *The Three Sisters Bar & Hotel*. Her previous novel, *The Ghost Brush,* was published in Japan and worldwide and *Creation* was a New York Times Notable Book of the Year. Winner of the Toronto Book Award and Canada's Findley-Engel Award for a mid-career writer, she has also been honoured for Excellence in the Arts by the Canadian Civil Liberties Association. In 2019 she was made a Member of the Order of Canada. Katherine founded, directed and is Board Chair of The Shoe Project, a national writing and public speaking workshop for immigrant and refugee women.

ARITHA VAN HERK is a professor in the department of English at the University of Calgary, where she teaches Canadian Literature and Creative Writing. She is the author of five novels, *Judith*, *The Tent Peg*, *No Fixed Address*, *Places Far From Ellesmere*, and *Restlessness*. Her irreverent but relevant history, *Mavericks: An Incorrigible History of Alberta*, framed a major exhibition on southern Alberta at the Glenbow Museum in Calgary. With George Webber she has published *In This Place: Calgary 2004–2011* and *Prairie Gothic* (Photographs by George Webber, Words by Aritha van Herk), both books that develop the idea of geographical and historical temperament as tonal accompaniment to landscape. Her work negotiates multiple genres and areas of exploration, with a focus on the west, on women's voices, and on place. Most recently, she published *Stampede and the Westness of West* (2016), prose-poetry which subverts the mythology of the carnivalesque stampede. She has published hundreds of stories, articles, reviews, and essays. She is a Member of the Order of Canada, a member of the Alberta Order of Excellence, a Fellow of the Glenbow Museum, and a Fellow of the Royal Society of Canada. She is the recipient of the Royal Society's Lorne Pierce Medal (awarded to recognize achievement in imaginative or critical literature in Canada), and of the Lt. Governor of Alberta Arts Award. She was awarded a Killam Annual Professorship in 2020.

MILENA KALIČANIAN, PhD, is Associate Professor at the English Department, Faculty of Philosophy, at the University of Niš, Serbia. She is the author of the books *The Faustian Motif in the Tragedies by Christopher Marlowe* (2013), *Political vs. Personal in Shakespeare's History Plays* (2017), *Uncovering Caledonia: An Introduction to Scottish Studies* (2018) and *English Renaissance Literature Textbook* (2020, with Sanja Ignjatović). She is also the co-editor (with Soňa Šnircová) of the book *Growing Up a Woman: The Public/Private Divide in the Narratives of Female Development* (2015). Her academic interests include Renaissance English Literature, Canadian Studies and British (especially Scottish) Studies.

MYRNA KOSTASH is a fulltime writer, author of the classic *All of Baba's Children*, and of *The Frog lake Reader, Prodigal Daughter: A Journey to Byzantium* and *Seven Oaks Reader*. Her essays, articles, and creative nonfiction have been widely anthologized. She is a recipient of the WGA's Golden Pen Award and the Writers' Trust Matt Cohen award for a Life of Writing. Her current project is *The Ghost Notebooks,* about her grandparents.

BIANCA LAKOSELJAC is a novelist, short story writer, poet, and essayist. She is the author of two novels, *Stone Woman* and *Summer of the Dancing Bear*; a collection of stories, *Bridge in the Rain*; and a collection of poetry, *Memoirs of a Praying Mantis*. She holds an MA in English Literature from York University, and has taught communications at Humber College and Toronto Metropolitan University.

She is a recipient of the Matthew Ahern Memorial Prize from York University for essay writing and the Book Excellence Award for fiction. Bianca is past president of the Canadian Authors Association, Toronto branch, where she coordinated an anthology, *Gathered Streams*, featuring the branch members. Her work has been anthologized nationally and internationally, including in *50 + Poems for Gordon Lightfoot*, published by the Stephen Leacock Museum. She lives in Woodland Beach on Georgian Bay. www.biancalakoseljac.ca

JOHN LONGHURST is a religion reporter and columnist at the *Winnipeg Free Press* and a freelance writer. He is a member of River East Church, a Mennonite Brethren congregation, and a 1979 graduate of Mennonite Brethren Bible College—Rudy Wiebe was the speaker at his graduation ceremony.

GEORGE MELNYK is Professor Emeritus of Communication, Media and Film at the University of Calgary. He is the author of the two-volume *Literary History of Alberta* and the co-editor of two volumes of critical essays on Alberta writing: *Wild Words: Essays on Alberta Literature* (2009) and *Writing Alberta: Building on a Literary Identity* (2017). He has been involved in Alberta's literary scene since the 1970s, including the founding of *NeWest Review* and NeWest Press. He has authored or edited over thirty books on Canadian topics. His latest book is a literary memoir titled *Breaking Words: A Literary Confession* (Bayeux Arts 2021). www.georgemelnyk.com

SCOT MORISON has a BSc in zoology from the University of Alberta (1980) and an MFA in creative writing from the University of British Columbia (1988). He has written one novel, *Noble Sanctuary* (Doubleday Canada), and his short stories have been published in literary magazines and produced for radio. He has also written non-fiction for magazines. For the past 25 years, he has mainly told stories for TV and film, both drama and documentary. He has taught creative writing and screenwriting at MacEwan University, the Banff Centre and the Cinema Production Centre, in Ramallah, Palestine. He lives in Edmonton with his wife Karen Hamdon and their family.

MAUREEN SCOTT HARRIS is a Toronto poet and essayist. Maureen has published three collections of poetry: *A Possible Landscape, Drowning Lessons* (awarded the 2005 Trillium Book Award for Poetry), and *Slow Curve Out,* as well as three chapbooks. Her poems are found in anthologies and journals in Canada, the US, England, and Australia. Her essays have won awards in Canada, the US and Australia.

OLGA STEIN holds a PhD in English, and is a university and college instructor. She has taught writing, communications, modern and contemporary Canadian and American literature, as well as sociology. Her research focuses on the sociology of literary prizes. Her dissertation is titled *The Scotiabank Giller Prize: How Canadian.* Before embarking on a PhD, Stein served as the chief editor of the literary review magazine, *Books in Canada,* and from 2001 to 2008 managed the Amazon.com/Books in Canada First Novel Award. Stein herself contributed some 150 reviews, 60 editorials, and numerous author interviews to *Books in Canada* (the online version is available at http://www.booksincanada.com/). Stein is working on her next large project, tentatively titled, *Worldly Fiction: Literary Transnationalism in Canada*. She is interested in World Literature, and authors who address the concerns that are now central to this literary category: the plight of migrants, exiles, and the displaced. More specifically, she is interested in literary dissidents, and the voices of dissent—those who challenge the current political, social, and economic status quo.

PAUL TIESSEN, Professor Emeritus of English and Film Studies at Wilfrid Laurier University, has published extensively on the work of Rudy Wiebe. With Hildi Froese Tiessen he has published on "Mennonite" art and literature, including editions of L.M. Montgomery's letters to Mennonite writer Ephraim Weber (U Toronto P) and of artist Woldemar Neufeld's Canadian landscapes (Wilfrid Laurier UP). He has published essays on Miriam Toews and Sandra Birdsell, and on the relationship between Marshall McLuhan and Wilfred Watson. With a team of international colleagues, he co-edited a trilogy of novels by Malcolm Lowry (U Ottawa P, 2013–15). He has book-length manuscripts underway on Wiebe and on Lowry.

MIRIAM TOEWS is the author of eight bestselling novels: *Fight Night, Women Talking, All My Puny Sorrows, Summer of My Amazing Luck, A Boy of Good Breeding, A*

Complicated Kindness, *The Flying Troutmans*, and *Irma Voth*, and one work of non-fiction, *Swing Low: A Life*. She is a winner of the Governor General's Award for Fiction, the Libris Award for Fiction Book of the Year, the Rogers Writers' Trust Fiction Prize, and the Writers' Trust Marian Engel/Timothy Findley Award. When asked why she writes fiction, she has been quoted as saying that, "In her twenties, when she went to journalism school to learn how to make radio documentaries, she ... found that she wished she could embellish, add thunder and lightning where there had been only a gentle rain, and that is why she writes fiction." Her fiction has often dealt with the religious hypocrisy and patriarchal authority that she feels to be part of her heritage. She lives in Toronto.

UROŠ TOMIĆ holds a PhD in Literary and Cultural Studies, and his academic focus is on contemporary Anglophone fiction, genre fiction (especially crime) and literature-to-film adaptation. He has taught at universities and colleges internationally, and has published papers on Joyce Carol Oates, Margaret Atwood, Tennessee Williams, and Angela Carter among others. Having grown up bilingual, Uroš has worked as a literary and academic translator, with over 30 translated titles into both English and Serbian. He is a published author of fiction in English, including the novel *The Birdman Cycle* and numerous short stories and poetry. He is also a professional musician, and his other interests include theatre (especially anthropological and alternative theatre), photography, and filmmaking. He lives in Belgrade, Serbia, where he teaches Anglophone Literature and Academic Writing.

Acknowledgements

Margaret Atwood's cartoon, "Teaching Rudy to Dance ... all true events" was first published in *Rudy Wiebe: A Tribute*. Ed. Hildi Froese Tiessen. Kitchener, ON: Sand Hills Books, 2002.

Hugh Cook's "Interview: A Conversation With Rudy Wiebe" is excerpted from Hugh Cook's interview first published in *Image Journal*, Issue 90. (2016). https:// imagejournal.org/issue/issue-90/.

Hugh Cook's "Salted With Fire" is a book review of Wiebe's novel, *Come Back*. The review was first published in *Christian Courier*, (Jan. 7, 2016). https://www .christiancourier.ca/salted-with-fire/.

Hildi Froese Tiessen's essay "Between Memory and Longing: Rudy Wiebe's *Sweeter Than All the World*" was first published in *Mennonite Quarterly Review* 77:4 (Oct. 2003), 619–36.

Milena Kaličanin's "Fact vs. Fiction in Rudy Wiebe's *Where is the Voice Coming From*" was first published in *Springer Nature, Neohelicon*: Volume 44, Issue 1, June, 2017. 169–176.

Myrna Kostash's "A White Man's View of Big Bear" is a revised and updated version of Kostash's book review of Rudy Wiebe's novel, *The Temptations of Big Bear,* first published in *Saturday Night Magazine,* February, 1974.

Bianca Lakoseljac's essay, "Rudy Wiebe's 'Unearthing' of Big Bear: a Plains Cree Hero of Canada's Past" is a revised and updated version of the essay which was presented to York University toward the completion of the Master of Arts degree in English Literature, 1997. The title of the original essay was, "Rudy Wiebe's Portrayal of Big Bear in His Novel, *The Temptations of Big Bear*." The essay has been revised and updated using the Indigenous Peoples Terminology Guidelines from Indigenous Corporate Training Inc. https://www.ictinc.ca/blog/indigenous -peoples-terminology-guidelines-for-usage and https:// www.ictinc.ca/ Terms for Indigenous Peoples have evolved over time and continue to evolve.

Bianca Lakoseljac's poem, "Sound of Silence," was published in a poetry collection, *Memoirs of a Praying Mantis*. Turtle Moons Press, 2009.

John Longhurst's "Peace of Mind" is a slightly revised and updated version of the article published in *Winnipeg Free Press*, (Mar. 30, 2019) https://www.winnipegfreepress.com /arts-and-life/life/faith/peace-of-mind-507872951.html.

George Melnyk's "Literary Genealogy: Exploring the Legacy of F.M. Salter" was first published in *Alberta Views*, April 1, 1998.

Scot Morison's "The 'Rudy Wiebe Room'"—an earlier version was first published as, "The Annotated Rudy Wiebe," *New Trail*, (Autumn 2016) University of Alberta's alumni magazine. https://albertamagazines.com/wp -content/uploads/2019/07/The-Annotated-Rudy-Wiebe.pdf

Maureen Scott Harris' "A Gift of Understanding" is a book review of *Stolen Life: The Journey of a Cree Woman* (1998). The book is Yvonne Johnson's biography co-written by Rudy Wiebe and Yvonne Johnson. The review was first published in *Books in Canada*, Vol. 27, No.6, (Sep. 1998). 6.

http://www.booksincanada.com/article_view.asp
?id =1067.

Olga Stein's essay, "The 'Wistful, Windy Madness of
a Gift': Rudy Wiebe's Books for Young Readers" written
for *Rudy Wiebe: Essays on His Works* contains Stein's book
review of Rudy Wiebe's book for young adults, *Hidden
Buffalo*. The review first appeared in Books in Canada, in
2006. http://www.booksincanada.com/article_view
.asp?id=3683

Paul Tiessen's "Memoir and the Re-reading of Fiction:
Rudy Wiebe's *of this earth* and *Peace Shall Destroy Many*"
was first published in *Text Matters: A Journal of Literature,
Theory, and Culture* 1 (2011): 201–15.

Miriam Toews' essay "Peace Shall Destroy Many"
was first published in *Granta Magazine* 137. Nov. 23,
2016. https://granta.com/peace-shall-destroy-many/

* * *

NOTE FROM THE EDITOR: Bianca Lakoseljac—in collabora-
tion with and/or the approval from the respective auth-
ors—provided an introduction and/or an introductory
commentary to the following pieces: Margaret Atwood's
Teaching Rudy to Dance ... all true events; Scot Morison's
The 'Rudy Wiebe Room'; Hugh Cook's *Interview: A
Conversation With Rudy Wiebe*; Hugh Cook's *Salted
With Fire*; Myrna Kostash's *A White Man's View of Big
Bear*; Maureen Scott Harris' *A Gift of Understanding*;
and John Longhurst's *Peace of Mind*.

* * *

Photographs:

Special acknowledgement to photographer John Ulan, http://ulanphoto.com for providing a photo of Rudy Wiebe for the front cover; a photo of Wiebe included in Morison's article, "The 'Rudy Wiebe's Room'" and a photo of Wiebe with Margaret Atwood, also included in the same article.

Acknowledgement to photographer Dave Rogalsky for a photo of Hildi Froese Tiessen and Rudy Wiebe. The photo was originally published in the Feb. 6, 2012 issue of *Canadian Mennonite*.

Special thanks to Hildi Froese Tiessen for providing the nine photographs for her essay, "Between Memory and Longing: Rudy Wiebe's *Sweeter Than All the World*." The photos were originally published in the same essay in *Mennonite Quarterly Review* 77:4 (Oct. 2003), 619–36.

Special thanks:

I wish to offer my gratitude to all the distinguished authors who contributed their works to this worthy project in honour of Rudy Wiebe: Margaret Atwood, Miriam Toews, Hildi Froese Tiessen, Milena Kaličanin, George Melnyk, Maureen Scott Harris, Myrna Kostash, Paul Tiessen, Scot Morison, John Longhurst, and Hugh Cook; special thanks to those who wrote original pieces for this volume: Olga Stein, George Melnyk, Katherine Govier, and Uroš Tomić. I am grateful to Aritha van Herk for agreeing to an interview which provides a window into her work with Rudy Wiebe who was her mentor and later her colleague and co-author on a number of publications. My deep appreciation to Rudy Wiebe for agreeing to an interview which offers valuable insight into his writing and his life as an academic, a respected professor and mentor, and a distinguished author whom, through our correspondence during the difficult time of the pandemic crisis, I feel privileged to have had the opportunity to get to know as infinitely patient, caring, and kind. I am thankful to my family for their love and unwavering support: my granddaughter Sierra, grandson Austin, daughter Michelle, son Adrian, husband Mirko, and my family in Serbia: Planinčić, Ivanović, and Korać. Many thanks to Lindsay Brown (who edited my first novel, *Summer of the Dancing Bear*) for helping to put me in touch with Aritha van Herk. I am indebted to fellow-authors, colleagues and friends who read excerpts and offered valuable feedback, especially Hildi Froese Tiessen. My gratitude to my publishers, Michael Mirolla, Connie McParland, Anna van Valkenburg, and all at Guernica Editions—a staunch proponent of multicultural voices for over four decades.

About the Editor

· ·

Bianca Lakoseljac (née Branislavka Planinčić) is an award-winning author of two novels, *Stone Woman* and *Summer of the Dancing Bear*; a collection of stories, *Bridge in the Rain*; and a collection of poetry, *Memoirs of a Praying Mantis*. She holds an MA and an Honours BA in English Literature from York University, and has taught communications at Humber College and Toronto Metropolitan University. She is the recipient of the Matthew Ahern Memorial Prize from York University for essay writing, and the Book Excellence Award for fiction. While serving as president of the Canadian Authors Association, Toronto, she coordinated an anthology, *Gathered Streams*, featuring the branch members. She was the Open Book Toronto Writer in Residence; a defender for Georgian Bay Reads; and has judged various national literary contests such as the National Capital Writing Contest and the Dr. Drummond Poetry Contest. She has also served on the awards panels for the League of Canadian Poets and the Writers Union of Canada. Her poems, essays, and stories have been anthologized nationally and internationally, including in *Canadian Woman Studies*, Inanna Publications, York U; *50 + Poems for Gordon Lightfoot*, the Stephen Leacock Museum; *Migrating Memories: Central Europe in Canada*, the Central European Association for Canadian Studies;

War of 1812 Poetry and Prose: an Unfinished War, Black
Moss Press; and *Musings,* The Heliconian Club: Women
Living in the Arts. She has served as a board member at
The Writers Union of Canada, the Book and Periodical
Council, the League of Canadian Poets, among other
writers' associations, and is also a member of PEN
Canada. Bianca lives with her family in Woodland
Beach on Georgian Bay where she continues to write,
tend to her flower beds, herbs, and the organic vegetable
patch, and is inspired by the majestic pine trees and the
ever-changing cobblestone beach at the edge of her back-
yard bordering the lake. She adores her grandchildren
and loves cooking nutritious and she hopes delicious
dinners for her family and friends. She admires the rug-
ged beauty of the region and the spectacular sunsets of
Georgian Bay. www.biancalakoseljac.ca

Printed by Imprimerie Gauvin
Gatineau, Québec